Housing Finance in the UK

Housing Finance in the UK

An Introduction

Second Edition

Kenneth Gibb
Moira Munro
Madhu Satsangi

First edition 1991
Second edition 1999

Published by
MACMILLAN PRESS LTD
Houndmills, Basingstoke, Hampshire RG21 6XS
and London
Companies and representatives
throughout the world

ISBN 0–333–66436–1

A catalogue record for this book is available
from the British Library.

This book is printed on paper suitable for recycling and
made from fully managed and sustained forest sources.

10   9   8   7   6   5   4   3   2
08   07   06   05   04   03   02   01

Copy-edited and typeset by Povey–Edmondson
Tavistock and Rochdale, England

Printed in Malaysia

Contents

List of Tables

List of Figures

Preface to the Second Edition

Since the first edition of *Housing Finance in the UK* appeared in 1991, much has changed in the UK housing system, and there has been much improvement in our understanding of how it operates. The evidence of the house condition surveys of 1991 and 1996 attests to gradual improvements in housing and living standards for the majority of the population. And people's housing aspirations, if one accepts the results of countless satisfaction surveys as testimony, are more likely to be met in Britain now than in any other era. Yet even the most cursory research reveals that housing problems in this corner of the advanced industrial world have not been solved. Homelessness, rooflessness and squalor are not that far away, even from the leafier suburbs of our biggest cities. And access to the good things that an advancing society can bring – material goods or cultural participation – is still fundamentally conditioned by where one lives. So, housing policy still matters. And understanding housing policy relies upon understanding the financial means by which policy is implemented, and the economic arguments why some policies might work, and some are bound for failure.

This is part of the rationale for the second edition, but only part. In the first edition, we alluded to information gaps or instances of poor data. Thanks to the efforts of scholars, students, government, practitioners and ordinary citizens, many of these have been filled. With the burgeoning of the global telephone exchange that is the Internet, it is ever easier to access ever more facts and figures. But we need to make sense of these data, to be able to put them into an organised framework of understanding housing finance and policy. We hope that the revised work makes a modest contribution to meeting that aim. Our work is as up to date as it is possible to be. But, inevitably, policy change and the passage of time bring new figures to supplement or supplant our data. Our aim is to provide keys to understanding that can withstand likely change.

xii   *Preface to the Second Edition*

This work has been made easier by the efforts of many people. In particular, we acknowledge Steve Wilcox for his continuing data collation and analysis. Our colleagues Peter Kemp, Duncan Maclennan, Mark Stephens, Glen Bramley and Hal Pawson gave advice and encouragement and Jeane Jenkins, Heather Cruickshank and Jenny Ferguson made sense and order of our type and handwritten script. Errors of interpretation remain our responsibility.

KENNETH GIBB
MOIRA MUNRO
MADHU SATSANGI

1 Introducing Housing Finance

INTRODUCTION

This book analyses the contemporary housing finance system in the UK. Housing finance can seem complicated and difficult – the purpose of this chapter is to explain both why it is somewhat complex and also why it is worth persevering to understand the system. This chapter considers:

- Why does the housing finance system exist?
- Why is housing finance important?
- What are the main institutions involved in operating the system?
- What are the main problems for housing finance policy in the UK?

Some of these issues are dealt with in more detail later in the book, but this chapter is intended to give readers an understanding of the basic framework and principles of the system.

WHY DOES THE UK HOUSING FINANCE SYSTEM EXIST?

Housing is one of the basic necessities of life. It provides safety, security, a store for possessions, protection against the elements and a locus for family life. A central problem in the provision of housing is that, in all except the most primitive societies, housing embodies a considerable amount of capital and labour. To put it plainly, housing is relatively expensive.

Think about building a house from scratch. You would have to:

- Buy some land – and land can be very expensive, particularly in the more populated parts of the country.
- Buy all the materials to build the house – bricks, timber, windows, doors, wiring, plumbing, bathroom and kitchen fittings and so on.

1

- Pay for installation of and connections to the main infrastructure: roads, electricity and gas; clean water and sewers.

You would then have, in essence, the raw materials needed to construct a house. However, the construction process is in itself a relatively complex and skilled one. The various materials have to be bought on to the site in the right order so that the appropriate items are available when needed, but also so that valuable materials or fittings are not left unused on site, where they may be left at risk of spoiling or being stolen. There is a broad range of skills required in constructing a house, starting with laying out and constructing the foundations, then on through the whole range of bricklaying, joinery, plastering, plumbing and electrical work needed to construct the exterior and interior of the house, right up to completing the roof.

Few people have the appropriate range and depth of skills themselves, and at the very least most people undertaking a 'self-building' project need to arrange for some professional or tradespeople to undertake parts of the work on their behalf. It is clear that this is a significant organisational task, which helps explain why most people prefer to buy a ready-made house (from a developer or builder). However, it should be clear that this will generally add to the cost of buying a house, as the price paid has to cover the time that *someone else* has spent organising the construction process and also, to give some profit to the company undertaking the work. Because of the exercise of obtaining the materials and the complexity of the construction process, it is apparent that it is always going to be very difficult for people to have enough money saved to buy a house outright. The first *key purpose* of the housing finance system is *to make housing affordable by creating ways of spreading payments over a long period.*

What Would Happen Without a Housing Finance System?

The simple answer is that without a formal housing finance system people would have to rely on their own resources. There are two main ways that this might work:

(i)   Households could simply have to save enough money to buy a house. House prices are determined in part by ability to pay, so it is likely that house prices would be lower than now if there were no housing finance system. But it is still likely that housing would cost more than annual earnings. Typically, then, it would take a long time to save up enough money to buy a house. In the meantime, households would have to live somewhere, perhaps staying with parents (assuming that the older generation had managed to gain access to housing), and incurring costs and discomforts in doing so. Alternatively, housing provision can become a collective effort, within either families or communities, where labour and materials are donated to households, in the expectation that they will reciprocate for other households at other times.

(ii) Households might simply seek cheaper forms of housing, in either the short or the long term. In many poorer parts of the world a household will initially buy a very basic dwelling, or just a plot of land, and, over time – as materials can be bought – build, enlarge and improve their house. This is an obvious way of matching housing expenditure to the flow of income. Squatter settlements throughout the world show that the poorest households often have recourse to building rudimentary accommodation from cheap or discarded materials.

In Britain, though informal provision of housing is not widespread, there are a number of current and recent examples. In the 1930s, for instance, developments on the edge of some cities arose from self-building activities; sometimes starting with old railway carriages or 'huts', which over time have been improved and extended into fully serviced and 'normal' houses. Further examples of alternative housing solutions include caravans (whether fixed, as in many rural areas, or as used by travelling people), houseboats, and the tents and vans of new-age travellers. (See Ravetz and Turkington, 1995, for a discussion of such types of housing alternatives.) However, these are minority housing solutions in Britain, as in the rest of the developed world, largely because the development of a general housing finance system has enabled housing to become a commercially produced and traded commodity.

Financing Buying a House

A widespread mechanism to bridge the gap between current income and the cost of housing is through the use of a lending system. The basic elements of such a system are:

- An institution (bank or building society) lends the household the cost of buying a house.
- The household repays that loan over a long period (20 or 25 years) with interest.
- The institution makes a profit on the loan and has the added security of knowing that, if repayments cease, they can get their original loan back by selling the house.

Chapter 6 describes how these mechanisms operate in Britain in more detail. In general, they transfer savings from institutions or households to other households wishing to buy a house. The money for the loan is raised from savers in the bank or building society, who keep their money in such an institution so as to earn interest on it. The institutions make a profit by charging borrowers more (a higher rate of interest) than they pay to savers. The existence of lending institutions makes the transfer of savings much easier, because it avoids any need to make individual deals, which would require an exact match between individual desires to lend or borrow. Indeed, financial institutions make it possible to use money from savers, who only keep their money in the institution for a very short time – certainly, savings are typically promised to institutions for a shorter time period than the period committed to a mortgage loan.

The Financial Principles of Renting

The cost of renting is likely to be at least as great as owning. This is easily seen if we consider the economics of landlordism. From the landlord's point of view, the economics are simple. The money from rent must cover four major elements:

(i) *The capital cost of the dwelling*   This would be loan repayments were the capital to be borrowed, or the 'opportunity cost' were it to be bought outright, that is, the amount the capital would be earning were it invested elsewhere.
(ii) *Maintenance*   Because it lasts a long time, housing needs a certain amount of ongoing expenditure to maintain the condition of the dwelling and repair any faults that develop.
(iii) *Costs incurred in running the business*   These cover the management costs of finding tenants, collecting rents and so on, as

well as allowances for periods when the house is not let, bad debts, and so on.

(iv) *Profit* The landlord needs to be rewarded for the risks incurred in running the business – normally the rate of return should be at least as good as that that would be available in alternative business opportunities.

It is clear, therefore, that rents have to cover the cost of the loan (or equivalent) plus additional items. Renting a house therefore seems to be more expensive than buying a similar house. How can we explain the fact that renting is generally seen as more appropriate than buying for people on lower incomes?

- Access to loan finance tends to require a long-term stable income. Lower incomes are particularly likely to be unstable.
- People on lower or unstable incomes are likely to have to pay more to borrow than those assessed to be of lower risk – which would include larger organisations with a large rented property portfolio.
- Renting tends to be on a shorter-term basis – so choices can be made that are more closely matched to changing incomes.
- Renting tends to be associated with fewer legal costs.
- Depending on the legal rules and regulations, it can also be possible to rent smaller amounts of housing than it is possible to buy (for example, a room or a part of a house), making renting a cheaper long-term option.

However, the key point remains that someone who is not able to afford to *buy* a house (when long-term loans are available) is not likely to be able to *rent* that house without other mechanisms to reduce the cost. The second key purpose of the housing finance system is thus to make housing affordable by reducing the absolute cost of housing. This is the reason that subsidies are introduced; subsidies are financial mechanisms that reduce the price the consumer has to pay.

How Do Housing Subsidies Work?

In Britain, as in many other countries, the public sector has come to play a major role in rented housing. Social rented organisations can provide cheaper housing than can private landlords, at least because they need not make any profit from rents charged. An additional, important way of reducing the cost of renting is to allow rents to reflect *historic costs* rather than current capital values. That is, unlike a private investor, a social landlord does not necessarily have to make a return reflecting the opportunity cost of the whole current asset value of housing.

Instead, rents can be set to cover *actual* outgoings – that is, repaying the historic portfolio of debt plus current management and maintenance costs. However, as Chapters 3 and 4 will show, there are additional, subsidising measures that have enabled the social rented sector in Britain to charge lower than market rents. The complex structures and controls developed to support social rented housing are an important element of the contemporary system of housing finance. In order to understand the ways in which subsidies can be given, it is first important to understand the fundamental difference between capital and revenue costs, either of which can be subsidised.

(i)   *Capital subsidy*   A grant can be given towards the initial cost of building or buying housing, thus reducing its subsequent loan costs and the rents required. This is a once-off payment, made when the house is initially built or made available to rent.
(ii) *Revenue subsidy*   An ongoing grant can be given to the landlord to cover part of the costs of being a landlord – allowing a lower rent to be charged.

There are examples of both these types of basic subsidy in the British housing finance. It is also worth noting that it is not only renters who receive subsidies. As Chapter 6 will show, owner-occupiers also receive subsidies.

WHY IS HOUSING FINANCE IMPORTANT?

The previous section has provided part of the answer. The housing finance system is the key mechanism in making housing affordable by:

- spreading payments over a long period, or
- reducing the absolute size of housing payments, by subsidising housing costs.

However, housing policy in general, including the operation and design of the housing finance system in particular, has a wide range of other effects. Three are particularly important:

(i)   Housing policy can be conceived of as part of a broader social policy agenda. Housing policy can make an important contribution to goals concerned with the redistribution of wealth and advantage, or the improvement of living conditions for disadvantaged groups of people. The interaction of housing policy with other aspects of the welfare state, such as education, income support, health and community care policies can be such as to exacerbate and compound disadvantage. In particular, housing policy can create concentrations of disadvantaged people within certain areas. It can also make it hard for people to effect a material change in their living conditions. A key example is the interaction between housing costs, Housing Benefit and other benefits, which can create 'poverty traps' or 'unemployment traps'. These make it difficult for people to escape from dependency on benefits (they are discussed in more detail in Chapter 8). Alternatively, housing policy can play a constructive role in creating improvements for disadvantaged people and communities. Housing often plays a critical role in broader programmes of urban regeneration.

(ii) As the recession in the housing market of the late 1980s and early 1990s made very clear, the housing market is intimately linked to the overall performance and health of the economy. As house prices fell, many owner-occupiers, traditionally viewed as a relatively advantaged group, found themselves trapped in houses they were unable to sell. Others suffered from negative equity (which is where the outstanding loan taken to buy the house is greater than its current value). Problems in the housing market were argued to be an important causal factor in the fragility of consumer confidence which underpinned the long recession of the late 1980s and early 1990s. Even the lack of expenditure prompted by trading in the housing market (including all the costs of redecorating and refurnishing associated with moving house) contributes to low aggregate consumer demand. Additionally, as the majority of households in the UK are now owner-occupiers the linkages between the financial markets and the housing sector have become important and more politically sensitive. It became impossible for Chancellors of the Exchequer to use interest rates as a neutral instrument of macroeconomic management, without taking account of the fact that any increase in interest rates has an immediately detrimental effect on the Budgets of millions of home buyers. This may have contributed to the decision to devolve interest-rate-setting powers to the Bank of England – helping to depoliticise the decision.

(iii) Housing finance is a significant element of public expenditure. Direct and indirect expenditures on housing subsidies have been under constant scrutiny as part of the general desire to control public expenditure, enabling lower tax burdens. The overall constraint on public expenditure acts as a significant barrier to increasing public investment in housing.

THE MANAGEMENT OF THE HOUSING FINANCE SYSTEM: MAIN INSTITUTIONS

The greater part by far of the activity and relationships in the housing system are conducted in the *private* sector; choices are made by individual consumers, acting as tenants, buyers, sellers or landlords. Choices are mediated by financial institutions seeking to profit from their lending activities. Developers and construction firms operate to make a profit from building and selling new houses. All these individual decisions can be influenced by financial incentives. Subsidies and taxes on any element of these activities will change prices and profits and therefore the choices made. Much of the detail of the housing finance system represents the use of indirect incentives that are designed to alter the behaviour of producers and consumers by influencing the financial consequences of particular choices. Demand for housing clearly comes from the many individual households who are seeking a place to live. It is useful to list, briefly, the institutions that are important in providing housing for households (that is, the housing suppliers).

Housing Providers

Houses to buy

- *New-build houses* in Britain are typically built by private companies – developers and builders. They build *speculatively* – that is, they evaluate local markets and build what they hope will sell.
- *Second-hand houses* are largely transacted by individuals seeking to move and trade in the market. The main *institutional* involvement in this process is with the process of buying and selling; estate agents, surveyors, solicitors and lending institutions are deeply involved in turnover in the private market.

Houses to Rent

Most new-build housing for the rented sector is also constructed by private sector companies – though often working to specific standards for the public rented sector. The new and second-hand rented stock is accessed by tenants by approaching landlords. In the social rented sector access is determined by landlords operating criteria of *need*. In the private sector, access is determined by ability to pay.

There are three main types of landlord in Britain:

- *Local authorities* The combined effect of the right to buy and low levels of new construction have greatly reduced the scale of local authority housing. This reduction is continued through the effects of transfers of local-authority stock to other 'registered social landlords' – chiefly housing associations.
- *Housing associations* Traditionally considered to be the 'third arm' of British housing – sited somewhere between the private and public sectors – housing associations have been relatively favoured in recent years, partly because they have been able to raise private money to supplement public sector grants, unlike local authorities.
- *Private landlords* There has been a long-term decline in private renting, caused in part by the relatively unfavourable financial regime. It is now really a 'residual' tenure – few people look to it to provide a long-term housing solution.

Providers of social rented housing – local authorities and housing associations – rely on public sector money to provide housing, as their key aim is to provide housing for people in need of housing but on lower incomes. The detail of the financial mechanisms created by the government, therefore, has a profound influence on the activities of these landlords. It affects the scale and quality of developments, the level of rents charged, and the quality of management service that can be offered.

The financial system is of additional importance because it provides the framework within which housing agencies may seek to pursue goals that differ from those of central government. The detail of the financial regime sets the context in which competing policy agendas can be pursued, and it also defines the degree of discretion that can be exercised by individual housing providers. Because there is a potential divergence in the goals of various agencies, the consequences of changes in the financial regime are not always easy to predict in detail. Indeed, the 1980s were characterised by a strong central government seeking to contain the extent to which local government could act independently. The central government inevitably came into conflict with local governments, which were keen to preserve autonomy and exploit any loopholes in the financial regime to pursue their own ends. Similarly, the diverse nature of housing associations and their committees can produce varying responses to financial change within the sector.

Administering the Housing Finance System

As will be clear, central government plays a crucial role in the housing system. It sets the overall public expenditure limits, and the distribution of that expenditure between different programmes, and also creates the general rules under which households gain access to or are eligible for different housing finance measures (both taxes and subsidies). Further, of course, central government has responsibility for the legal context in which the limits and scope of action for other agents are decided.

It must also be remembered that government is not necessarily monolithic in its objectives. What we see as policy outcomes really result from the interaction between different departments in the government. It is important to note that the Treasury is responsible for exercising financial control, while spending departments (that is, all the others) are likely to be more enthusiastic about developing new programmes and policies that involve additional expenditure.

England and Wales

The key spending department for housing policy is the Department of the Environment, Transport and the Regions (DETR), which has responsibility for housing policy and relationships with local authorities. It is also central in the statutory land-use planning process, arbitrating finally over the release of land and judging any appeals. The Welsh Office takes these responsibilities in Wales. The DETR has regional offices throughout England, which are responsible for functions and implementation of policies devolved from central government. They also liaise with local authorities in their region. The Housing Corporation is the non-departmental public body (NDPB) which oversees the registration and operation of housing associations in England. Wales had a separate body – Tai Cymru – performing the functions of the Housing Corporation in Wales; after January 1999 however, it will not exist, its functions being administered by the Welsh Office.

Scotland

Scotland has her own history, her own legal system and her own administration. The Scottish Office is the government department responsible for overseeing the country, and the Scottish Office Development Department has responsibility for housing policy and relationships with local authorities. While Westminster has occasionally passed legislation to cover the whole of Britain, Scotland's housing policy has frequently differed from those in the other countries in important respects (Currie and Murie, 1996). As a result, Scotland's housing finance framework is significantly different from that of England, Wales and Northern Ireland. Following the referendum of September 1997, Scotland will have a parliament based in Edinburgh by the turn of the century. This parliament will develop and scrutinise housing policy, and it may well be that Scotland diverges further from the rest of Britain (see Goodlad, 1997, for further discussion).

One of the important institutional differences between Scotland and the rest of Britain is the existence of Scottish Homes. Scottish Homes has the functions of the Housing Corporation in Scotland, and also has the additional task of managing the remainder of the 74 000 units of stock that were inherited from the Scottish Special

Housing Association (SSHA, an organisation directly concerned with producing housing needed to support economic development throughout Scotland). One of Scottish Homes' objectives is to divest itself of this stock over time, encouraging other landlords, particularly housing associations, to take over management and ownership, and selling houses to individual tenants.

Northern Ireland

The distinct Department of the Environment in Northern Ireland is similar to the Scottish Office in the extent of its powers and the degree of its autonomy. The central agency for managing and producing social-rented housing in Northern Ireland is the Northern Ireland Housing Executive (NIHE). This body is appointed by the Secretary of State and was devised as a mechanism to avoid the sectarian conflicts that arose over housing development and management in this divided province in the 1970s.

HOW IS THE HOUSING FINANCE SYSTEM ANALYSED?

It can be argued that housing studies as a discipline has not been strongly theoretical in its approach. This book is no exception, in that it does not adhere strictly to a single theoretical framework. However, as the authors are economists, the emphasis tends to fall most heavily in that mode of analysis. It is possible to distinguish three more or less distinct traditions within the housing policy literature, as follows:

(i)   Political analyses focus on the act of policy formation and implementation and the way different actors shape processes and outcomes. This tradition has been most evident in the analysis of public expenditure (see Mullard, 1993) and the analysis of the relationship between central and local government, although much of the more detailed research into policy developments draws on the policy implementation literature.

(ii) Social administration and social policy frameworks have perhaps dominated housing analysis in Britain. These focus on the effects of housing policy in the context of other elements of the welfare state (see Clapham *et al.*, 1990). This has been an influential tradition in shaping the debates and framing the research issues that have exercised British housing analysis, and there is no doubt that much of the analysis in this book owes a great deal to it.

(iii) The economic analysis of housing has been less widely used in the UK, but it has much to offer, particularly in relation to analysis of financial mechanisms. The traditional approach of economics is to analyse outcomes that either do or would be expected to occur in a 'free market' and contrast the outcomes that occur when various different 'interventions' in that market occur. The economic approach is discussed in more detail in Chapter 2.

The British housing system is deeply divided by *tenure*, and most available research and policy analysis reflects that division, either by focusing on just one tenure or by dividing analysis into separate tenures. This book is no exception, in that most of the chapters focus on issues in just one tenure. Some writers have argued that this is a weakness in the analysis of housing policy – that too much importance is attached to tenure ('tenure fetishism'), in a way that can disguise the more fundamental processes underpinning outcomes in the housing system (Kemeny, 1982). The separation of the tenures remains a useful device for simplifying and clarifying aspects of the mechanisms of the housing finance system. But what should be remembered, and what should become clear at various points in the book, is that it can be misleading to focus too much on tenure *per se*, as the essential features are neither *inevitable* nor *immutable*. Tenure is important in the housing system to the extent that it encapsulates the bundle of rights and responsibilities that are currently associated with accessing housing by that particular route. To summarise, tenure is associated with the following:

- *Access to housing* Owner-occupiers and private renters have their housing consumption rationed by their ability to pay; access to social renting is determined in accordance with need as measured by different allocations schemes.
- *Financial arrangements* The subsidy mechanisms that alter the costs of housing to the consumer are fundamentally designed along tenure lines. There are even distinctions *within* tenures (so that owners with a mortgage can access different subsidies to

outright owners, and housing association properties are financed
differently from those of local authorities). Further, access to
individual, means-tested support with housing costs (through the
Housing Benefit or income support systems) is subject to
different rules depending on the occupant's tenure.

• *Individual rights and responsibilities*   The legal framework determines the rights and responsibilities of individual occupants, as
owners or tenants of property. Again, there are wide-ranging
differences of detail within tenures (for example, between lease-
holders and freeholders, or between tenants depending on their
tenancy agreement). These conditions can make a considerable
difference to outcomes for individual occupants – for instance,
repair costs tend to fall on owners and not tenants, but owners
typically enjoy greater freedom to alter and adapt their house and
benefit from any capital gains in an owned house.

Clearly, almost all of these elements can be amended by legislative
or other administrative changes. For example, in 1980 tenants
acquired a new right – to buy their rented local authority house.
In the light of this flexibility, it should not be assumed that, for
instance, owner-occupation is always a 'better' or more advantageous tenure – this judgement depends on the balance of advantages that are available at a particular point in time. But equally,
given the extent to which fundamental aspects of housing consumption are determined by tenure, it remains a convenient short-
hand device to structure the description and analysis of the housing
finance system.

Changing the tenure structure became an important political goal
in the 1980s, and policies were pursued to increase privatisation in
the housing system and to increase owner-occupation in particular.
This policy resulted in a considerable change in the tenure structure
over this decade. Table 1.1 shows the tenure structure in the UK
and Table 1.2 how it has changed from the early 1980s in Great
Britain.

The key findings to notice from the tables are:

• Owner-occupation is by far the largest tenure. Although there are
significant differences in the proportion by country (Scotland
having the lowest level), overall about two-thirds of Britain's
households are owner-occupiers.

Table 1.1   Tenure structure within the UK, 1996

	England	Wales	Scotland	N. Ireland
Owner-occupation	67.6	71.3	57.9	69.5
Private renting	10.3	8.5	6.9	3.8
Housing association	4.3	3.6	4.0	2.4
Local authority/new town	17.5	16.6	31.1[b]	24.3[c]
All dwellings[a] = 100 per cent (000's)	20 514	1237	2232	608

Notes
[a] Including vacant dwellings; these are excluded from percentage figures.
[b] Includes Scottish Homes' stock.
[c] Northern Ireland Housing Executive stock.
Source: Wilcox (1997a, tables 16b, 16d); Department of the Environment (Northern Ireland) (1998).

Table 1.2   Changing tenure structure in Great Britain, 1981 to 1995–6 (percentages)

	1981	1995–6
Owner-occupation	56.4	66.7
Private renting	11.1	10.0
Housing association	2.2	4.3
Local authority	30.3	18.9

Source: Wilcox (1997a, tables 16b, 16d).

• Owner-occupation has grown significantly through the 1980s and early 1990s.
• The local authority rented sector, by contrast, declined significantly to under 20 per cent of households by 1995.
• Housing association renting is a small tenure (under 5 per cent) but doubled through the 1980s and 1990s.
• Private renting remains a relatively small tenure (at 10 per cent) and it is largely static in size.

These dramatic changes in the tenure structure have been created through a range of interlocking policies:

• *Privatisation*, especially through the right to buy, caused a significant shift of ex-local authority stock into owner-occupation.

- *Demunicipalisation*, through other privatisation mechanisms, such as encouraging the sale of all or part of local authority housing stock, has also shifted public sector housing to other tenures – most commonly the housing association sector.
- *Direct public investment in the housing association sector* has been increased while that in local authorities was reduced.
- Many *indirect inducements* existed for people to become home owners – both in the comparison of available housing opportunities and in the expectations of money gains to be made from owner-occupation.

Such major changes have not been neutral in effect. A particular concern has been raised about the extent to which local authority housing is now or is becoming 'residualised' – that is, housing that is really a welfare service only accessed by the most disadvantaged who have no other options (see Cole and Furbey, 1994). One might argue that the sector is still sufficiently large to ensure that there is some social mix in the characteristics of those in local authority housing, but all the statistical analysis shows that the difference in the characteristics between those in social renting and those in other tenures is becoming much more sharp. The social rented tenures are increasingly dominated by relatively disadvantaged households – the long-term unemployed, the long-term sick, and single-parent households.

HOUSING NEEDS IN BRITAIN

Housing policy in Britain, of which housing finance is such a significant part, has had fairly constant goals over the longer term – encapsulated in 1988 as 'providing a decent home for every family at a price within their means' (Hills, 1991). This chapter will not attempt a full evaluation of the extent to which this goal has been met. Instead, it will highlight a few aspects of the contemporary housing scene in Britain that demonstrate that there are still significant challenges facing the housing system.

Unmet Housing Needs

In Britain, there is a crude surplus of houses over households. There must always be some vacancies to allow turnover in the system (some houses will inevitably be empty while waiting for a new tenant or as owners move between houses). The total crude surplus fell through the 1980s to 822 000 in 1991 (about 3.5 per cent of dwellings), which is probably not much more than the minimum level of vacancies required to enable turnover. However, this crude calculation cannot be taken to suggest that the housing problem is 'solved' in any sense. Because of the immobility and longevity of the housing stock, severe imbalances and mismatches can arise between what housing is available and where, and in what type of houses people want to live. Further, problems of the condition of some of the stock mean that not all houses that exist should really be considered to be habitable.

The most dramatic indicator of the failure to meet housing needs is in the continued presence of homelessness. The published statistics measure those who are accepted as homeless under the legislation. This is inevitably an underestimate of true homelessness for two reasons:

- The measure excludes those who are not accepted as homeless, either because they are judged to have made themselves homeless intentionally or because they are not considered as 'vulnerable' under the legislation.
- The count excludes those who do not seek help, either because they believe that they will not be eligible, or because they are not aware of the available help. As Figure 1.1 shows, the trend was upwards throughout the 1980s, showing only a minor decline at the end of the period. In Britain as a whole there were over 130 000 households accepted as homeless in 1996.

As well as policies designed to increase the general availability of affordable housing, there have been various specific measures to tackle the problems of those who have fallen through the net and become homeless. The continuing presence of people sleeping rough on the streets of our towns and cities shows that these policies are not wholly successful, and reveals the continuing severity of the real problems that some face in accessing any sort of accommodation.

Unmet Housing Aspirations

There are no grounds for complacency in the study of British housing policy. Although there have been dramatic improvements

Figure 1.1   Households accepted as homeless in Great Britain, 1980 to 1996

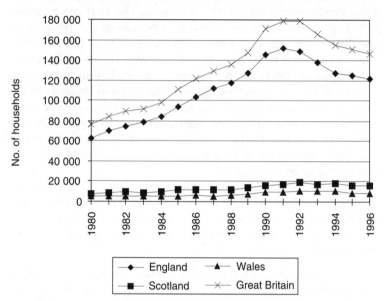

in the living conditions of the great majority of the population over the last century, some severe and intractable problems remain. This is partly because expectations change as general standards of living rise; a house considered to be an acceptable today is very different from one of a hundred years ago. But, despite the technological advances of the twentieth century, the housing system is still not able to provide a decent house for every household. There are many households living in houses that are damp, or in need of repair, or in neighbourhoods in which crime and vandalism are rife, or which have such a poor reputation that residents are stigmatised by their address. There is considerable and on-going debate about the quality of housing. Increasingly it is recognised that the concept of adequate housing must involve more than just physical condi-tion, and must encompass the broader elements of neighbourhood context, feelings of safety and control, and management quality.

While poor living conditions have been associated with the rented sector and large local authority estates in particular, it should not be assumed that the owner-occupied sector is occupied exclusively by affluent households. There are significant problems of poor conditions in this sector also as recent house condition surveys have dramatically revealed (full data on housing conditions are available in the house condition surveys of 1996, – see Department of the Environment, Transport and the Regions, 1998; Scottish Homes, 1997; Northern Ireland Housing Executive, 1998). Responses to these problems tend to be tenure-specific but arguably insufficient in total. The legacy of poor housing conditions continues to make demands on the public purse, particularly to respond to the damaging segregation of the poorest communities, who have become concentrated on the poorest-quality estates. It can be seen that housing is a significant contributory factor to the wider problems of social exclusion that are a primary focus of public policy towards area regeneration.

CONCLUSIONS: HOUSING FINANCE AND HOUSING POLICY

This chapter has sought to provide a context for the more detailed material in the following chapters. It has explained:

- why housing finance is necessary;
- why housing finance is an essential component of broader housing policy.

Because the housing finance system *is* so central to the operation of housing policy, many of the key challenges facing the housing system are also direct challenges to the housing finance system. Other mechanisms are also important in improving housing conditions for households in Britain – for instance in developing good management techniques and providing guidelines and regulation to improve housing quality. However, the scope for action, not least because most action has cost implications, is bound up intimately with the housing finance system. Chapter 10 returns to consider the major challenges facing the housing sector in the future and the potential capacity of the housing finance sector to meet those challenges.

FURTHER READING

In this chapter we have briefly introduced many fundamental issues in housing policy and housing analysis that are covered more fully later in the book. There are many sources now providing up-to-date data on the housing system; readers might start with either Newton (1994) or Wilcox (1997a) (which is updated on a regular basis). The annual *Survey of English Housing* also contains much useful data and analysis, as do the House Condition Surveys of 1996. Scotland will have comparable data during 1999 and thereafter from the rolling *Scottish Household Survey*. Discussions of the institutional arrangements for the formation and implementation of housing policy can be found in any basic textbook on housing policy. Recommended are Malpass and Murie (1999), which gives a good account both of current structures and the historical development of housing policy, Balchin (1996) or Balchin and Rhoden (1998). Currie and Murie (1996) analyse policy concerns in Scotland. The Council of Mortgage Lenders publishes a quarterly journal, *Housing Finance*, which contains much useful data about the private housing market and some commentary, largely but not exclusively from the lenders' perspective. An economic approach to the analysis of housing policy can be found in Barr (1993).

QUESTIONS FOR DISCUSSION

1. What do you understand by housing 'tenure'? What are the main advantages and disadvantages of the main tenures in Britain?
2. Imagine that government in Britain had never become involved in providing or subsidising housing. What would the housing stock be like? How would people gain access to housing?

2 The Economics of Housing Markets

INTRODUCTION

This chapter introduces the economics of the housing market. It is important to look at the underlying principles of the housing market, because economic analysis can inform important housing policy debates, not least about how markets may respond to new policy initiatives. For instance, the financial deregulation of mortgage markets has transformed the way economists, government and policy analysts think about the importance of housing in the macroeconomy. Similarly, changes in taxation, in incomes and in economic growth, and the introduction of new subsidies, all influence the housing market through the interaction of demand and supply.

The key topics examined in this chapter are:

- the basic way markets work;
- the main factors that determine demand for and supply of housing;
- the ways market analysis can be applied to answer policy questions.

It is worth detailing a little more of the economic approach to the analysis of housing systems in general (and not just home ownership), as it underpins much of the analysis in the book and will be relatively unfamiliar to some readers (inevitably the treatment of these issues has to be quite brief and at an introductory level; more detailed material on the various topics covered is suggested at the end of the chapter under 'Further Reading'). It should be recognised that some terms used in economic analysis potentially carry a heavy ideological weight. A naïve interpretation might automatically categorise 'free markets' as a 'good' and 'intervention' in the market a 'bad' thing. However, more subtle analysis starts from the premise that a perfect market is a theoretical construct never attained in practice, principally because the conditions required are an ideal conception of how markets can work. For instance, the conditions require a very large number of small producers who produce a homogeneous product and sell to consumers with perfect information, with free entry and exit from the market for all. All markets deviate to some degree from this ideal conception, so the starting point of analysis is not that state action is always better or worse than allowing the market to operate unchecked. Instead, the salient questions concern under what market conditions state action is helpful and which state actions are effective in producing better outcomes than free markets.

In order to judge such questions, clear criteria are needed. First, 'better' can potentially be interpreted in a number of ways (such as whether the objectives of the policy-maker are achieved or whether outcomes are better for most people, or whether outcomes are better for the poorest people, for instance). Such evaluation can be formally structured around the twin principles of equity and efficiency.

Efficiency in the economic sense is about making the best possible use of society's resources, capturing as closely as possible the benefits that are attainable from the ideal or perfect market. The main benefits of a perfect market are that competition between producers assures the attainment of the lowest cost production cost and lowest price for the consumer, and that the consumer is sovereign. 'Consumer sovereignty' means that consumer choices and preferences ultimately determine what producers will make. However, as indicated above, no market fully meets all the conditions required to be 'perfect', so that analysis of real-world markets must deal with the fact that they are all *imperfect* in various respects. Even so, policies can be implemented in imperfect markets that make them behave more like perfect markets – so that the benefits of low-cost production and consumer sovereignty are reproduced. The main available correction measures are taxation, subsidisation, and regulation. Market failure arises in many specific situations:

- Imperfect competition exists where, for instance, producer power is not shared equally among many producers, but is concentrated in a few hands or even in just one (monopoly) supplier. When this happens there will not be enough competition to ensure low prices or to ensure that production responds to consumers' wishes. In housing markets it is clear that such problems might be relevant in the construction sector and in the rented market.

- Externalities exist where the private costs or benefits of an action diverge from a wider (social) measure of costs and benefits. For instance, a polluting industry imposes the cost of a poor environment, which is borne by the wider body of society – in such cases one agent's action imposes a cost or confers a benefit on others. Externalities are particularly relevant for housing policy when analysing renovation and area regeneration activities, where action (or inaction) in one part of an area or by one set of owners will affect the scope for change by others.
- Imperfect information is found with complex commodities (such as housing), consumers having to make choices before all the relevant details can be known. The process of acquiring the relevant information can be lengthy and costly. This is most clearly apparent when people are choosing houses to buy. Despite the range of 'exchange professionals' (building societies, surveyors, estate agents, and so on), it is ultimately impossible to know what living in the house will be like (for example, whether you will like the neighbours). Imperfect information is also relevant to capital markets for mortgages, where lenders may discriminate against certain borrowers or be very conservative in their lending policies because they do not possess sufficient information about the future riskiness of particular borrowers to make wholly fair lending decisions.

It can be argued on economic grounds that, while the housing market does indeed exhibit these problems, they have not been the main reason for the growth and complexity of housing policy in the UK. Perhaps the main exception to this is in relation to the earliest interventions in the housing system, which were motivated by concerns about public health. (Accounts of the history of housing policy and the rationale for early interventions can be found in Grant, 1997; Holmans, 1987; Harloe, 1995.) Public health threats are a classic negative externality, which arose because slum housing was seen as the source of communicable and contagious diseases which could potentially affect and infect a wider (middle-class) population. However, apart from this, the main impetus behind housing policy has been to tackle considerations of equity. Equity can be considered as having two dimensions, as follows:

- Horizontal equity is about treating people in similar situations in a similar way.
- Vertical equity is about different treatment for different people and reflects a desire to countermand the inequality of the income distribution by reducing the inequality in outcomes.

We have argued that the main goal of the housing finance system can be summarised as having been to produce (adequate) affordable housing. This is obviously an 'equity' motive, as the (implicit) reasoning is that without these measures people would *not* be able to afford the housing we consider they 'need', or that society would deem to be adequate and acceptable.

For an economist this raises the question of redistributing income. If poor people cannot afford (demand) adequate housing, why not simply raise their income by taxing the rich and providing poorer households with enough income to afford (demand) what they 'need'? Economic analysis of social policy has two answers to this question:

(i)   Housing is a 'merit good'; that is, as a society we take the view that we want to ensure that people are able to attain a minimum acceptable standard of housing. Just as policy towards education and health has been about ensuring that they are accessed according to need and not income, so the development of council housing in particular can be interpreted as a direct attempt to provide a parallel baseline level of housing provision for people deemed to be in need. Other examples are found in long-standing housing policy measures to clear slums and to ensure the provision of basic amenities (clean water, inside WC, and so on) to all households.

(ii) Direct provision of what we deem people to need is generally cheaper than a wholesale income redistribution. Any general increase in income for the poor (such as that given through the benefit system) is inevitably spent across the whole range of consumption goods and *not* just on the particular 'merit good' whose consumption we desire to increase. That is, we cannot assume that extra income is spent in the 'right' way, on the 'right' things.

These two factors mean that it may not always be sufficient simply to redistribute incomes to achieve certain desired policy goals. Two important points should be made, once we have accepted that society takes a view about what housing is needed by households:

- Direct provision is not the only way of achieving these aims. The provision of council housing is only one of a range of possible ways of meeting needs.
- 'State' failure can be as important as 'market' failure. That is, it cannot be assumed that, just because the government has good intentions, it necessarily attains its goals or that it always acts in the most cost effective or efficient manner. The depressed and disadvantaged nature of some council housing estates is clear testament to the potential shortcomings of public sector action.

Issues concerning the best and most efficient ways of responding to housing needs are at the heart of current debates in housing policy as well as across other parts of the welfare state.

THE MARKET FOR OWNER-OCCUPATION

What is it that makes owner-occupied housing so different from other commodities? Economists have pointed to a number of distinguishing characteristics possessed by housing. Other goods have some of these characteristics but no other commodities possess *all* of them:

- First, housing is *durable*. It generally lasts a long time, and, indeed, in Britain a significant proportion of housing still occupied was built before the Second World War, and even before the First.
- Second, housing, as an asset, has a *large supply price* relative to average earnings. This means that most people have to use a mortgage loan secured on the property in order to purchase it. So, the mortgage market and its sources of funding, are critically important to the nature and the performance of the housing market.
- Third, housing is a complex commodity. Textbook analysis usually considers markets for homogeneous (that is, identical)

products. However, housing is fundamentally a *heterogeneous* product where, literally, no two houses are identical. Each house will be of a particular type (detached, terraced, and so on). In addition, it has its own building materials, finishing and so on, it will be in good or bad condition, and its value or amenity will be influenced by the location of its site relative to workplaces, services, and the quality of the neighbourhood. All of these attributes can be considered as contributing to the unique value of each individual dwelling.

- Fourth, housing is *spatially fixed*, making accessibility and neighbourhood attributes important dimensions of a dwelling, along with the effects of externalities.

- Finally, in all developed economies, large-scale *government intervention* in the housing market, including the owner-occupied market, is the norm.

To the economist, the housing market is represented as an interplay of demand and supply. When demand is equal to supply and both are stable, the market is said to be in *equilibrium*. In other words, there is no tendency for prices to change. If the market gets out of equilibrium, the forces of demand and supply will adjust to a new equilibrium. Thus, if the demand for owner-occupied housing increases, for instance because renting becomes more expensive or more scarce, this will lead to an increase in the price of owner-occupied housing. The final equilibrium price after this demand-side change will depend on the way suppliers react to the new price. They may increase supply in an attempt to capture higher profits, but in so doing they will bid down prices, to some extent. Depending on the competitiveness of the market, the process of adjustment, and hence the period of disequilibrium, may be shorter or longer. Empirical evidence over recent years indicates considerable instability in the UK housing market (Maclennan, 1994; Meen, 1996). The UK housing market has experienced three violent swings in activity and house prices since 1970, the longest and deepest recession of them occurring between 1989 and 1996 when house prices actually fell, the volume of activity halved compared with the cyclical peak in 1988 and many thousands of households lost their homes when they could no longer repay their mortgages (see Chapter 6). This cyclical or volatile tendency suggests that *either* adjustment takes a long time to resolve itself *or* that the market is being buffeted in different directions by a large number of changes on the demand and supply sides) It is likely that the supply side is generally relatively slow to respond to price changes or demand changes. This can be seen when we consider that new construction is relatively slow; it takes time to find sites, win planning permission and then build houses to meet demand. Further, the greatest part of supply already exists and cannot be significantly altered. Technically, housing supply is said to be inelastic in the short run because it is unresponsive even in the face of significant price change. Elasticity is a summary measure of the responsiveness of demand or supply to changes in economic variables such as house price, income or interest rates; the most important kinds are:

(i)   (*Own*) *price elasticity of* demand for housing which measures the responsiveness of housing demand to a marginal change in its price. It is negative because demand typically rises as price falls. Empirical estimates show that demand for housing is price-inelastic, that is, a price increase leads to a less than proportionate reduction in the demand for housing.

(ii) The *income elasticity* of demand for housing measures the responsiveness of housing demand to changing household incomes. Higher incomes allow households to spend more on everything, especially luxuries. Shelter is clearly a necessity, but penthouse flats and double garages might be expected to accommodate the demands of higher-income groups. Empirical evidence suggests that the income elasticity of demand for housing is around one. In other words, if a household's income were to rise by 10 per cent, then their demand for housing would also rise by the same proportion (housing demand is income-elastic).

(iii) The *price elasticity of supply* refers to the responsiveness of housing supply with respect to changes in house prices. It is generally considered that the (new build) supply of housing in Britain is rather insensitive to house price change, and is relatively inelastic. A typical estimate for the UK price elasticity of supply of new construction is between 0.5 and 1, that is, a 1 per cent increase in house prices will eventually bring forth a 0.5 to 1 per cent increase in new construction. This is very important, if it is true. It suggests that the British market will convert increases in demand into higher prices for housing, rather than more housing produced by builders, even over a relatively long period of time. This is a recipe for both instability and a general trend of increasing real house prices.

DETERMINANTS OF DEMAND

Elasticity measures are summary indicators of the way that the housing market can be expected to react when underlying conditions change. It is also useful to look in more detail at the various factors that influence the demand for owner-occupied housing. Economists call the relationship between demand and its determinants a *demand function*. The key determinants of housing demand include:

- the price of owner-occupied housing;
- disposable household income;
- credit/mortgage availability;
- the interest rate on mortgage repayments;
- household formation and other relevant demographic factors such as household composition, age, and so on.
- location relative to work/travel to work costs;
- the price of close substitutes (such as private or public renting);
- tastes and preferences for different forms of housing, location, and so on.

It is worth discussing in more depth three of the most important factors influencing housing demand: the price of owner-occupied housing, the cost and availability of mortgage credit and the influence of demographics trends and changes.

Price and the User Cost of Housing

Price is usually a straightforward market feature to identify. But for housing it is complicated. This is because housing is important to consumers in two distinct ways:

- it provides comfort, shelter, warmth, privacy and so on, (that is, it is a consumption good), and
- it can provide a real capital return (or loss) to the owner (it is also an investment good).

Rather than use the market value of the property (its selling price), economists consider a better measure of price to be one that

- reflects the capital gains that can be made in housing;
- reflects the true cost of holding one's investment in housing rather than something else.

This is known as the '*user cost of capital*' approach. Economists refer to the opportunity cost of capital, which is an alternative way of thinking about the meaning of 'cost'. It is measured as the best alternative use of one's funds. Thus, the opportunity cost of tying funds up in housing is the return that could have been earned had one invested in the next best form of investment of similar risk and liquidity (for instance stocks and shares or a savings account). Thus the user cost concept reflects the opportunity cost inherent to investing in the housing market.

Thinking about housing as an asset helps us to explain some of the seemingly odd things that happen in the housing market. For instance, if prices are rising, one would expect the demand for most goods to fall. The experience of the housing market is exactly the opposite, however, because investors are interested in capital gains to come in the future. In other words, the user cost can be falling (even if prices are rising) because of large, real expected capital gains, making owner-occupation an increasingly attractive buy. The same can happen when high general inflation rates and house price inflation rates coincide (housing can become a safe store of value and a hedge against inflation).

Mortgage Credit

Mortgage availability is partially affected by a household's long-term income prospects and the lending institution's evaluation of the creditworthiness of the applicant. Credit rationing, based on queuing, however, is largely a thing of the past (see Chapter 6). Today, rationing is achieved through the price mechanism by changing mortgage interest rates (and required deposits). Interest rates are a critical influence on the demand for home ownership. Also, lenders select their borrowers cautiously, partly because they have to protect their investors (those with savings in the institution). Lenders can never be certain what will happen to borrowers' capacity to repay their mortgages, but they have found the best way of reducing uncertainty is to look at the occupation and income of the borrower.

Demographic Factors

Demographic trends are a major influence on housing demand. (The main driving force for the aggregate demand for housing through time is the number of new households that are formed) The rate of household formation increases when there are more:

- couples separating;
- couples divorcing;
- young single people wishing to leave parental homes and live independently;
- single-parent families;
- older people, living longer and living alone.

It is household formation rather than population change that is important, because, over recent years, the population has been static but the demand for housing has continued to increase as the average size of households has fallen) At present the growth in the number of smaller households, both young and old, is changing the structure of housing demand towards the need for more specialised housing. (Furthermore, below the national level, in urban and metropolitan housing markets, there can be important shifts in demand brought on by migration in and out of areas, reflecting processes of economic restructuring and changing employment opportunities) The increase in demand for housing can be expected to be much greater in some (economically prosperous) parts of the country than in others.

SUPPLY DETERMINANTS

The supply of housing is affected by a different range of factors. There are three major elements of the supply of housing currently available:

- new construction;
- second-hand properties available to buy;
- sales by private or public landlords to sitting tenants.

These factors determine the *quantity* of supply; the *quality* can be changed by investment in the housing stock, including improvements to existing stock and the conversion of existing stock into new uses. We have argued that housing supply is relatively unresponsive to increases in the general level of house prices.

We can say that the housing market is demand-led. Builders and developers respond to profit signals in the form of high prices. But even with large and well-located land banks (supplies of building land owned by the developer), there are considerable lags (up to two years) in constructing new developments (see Chapter 1). The developer, at an earlier stage, has to deal with the various nuances of the planning system to gain approval to buy the land and to develop it for residential investment (if land banks are not available to the builder). Builders can face many difficulties: from green belt resistance; negotiating shared infrastructure costs or dealing with other requests for planning gain; and predicting the volatility of a market where prices and profits can collapse very quickly. House-building in the private sector in the UK is speculative and inherently risky. In other words, developers build to meet the general level of demand rather than in contract with a specific client, as is the case in most of the rest of Europe.

Construction is an industry where the effect of new technologies has not been as radical as in other production processes (see Ball, 1988). In Britain, compared with the rest of Europe, construction labour costs are relatively low. The industry appears to be resistant to mass production techniques and other attempts to increase productivity. This is not just because the process of construction is quite inflexible but also because of the speculative nature of building in this country. The large-scale capital equipment required on site would be very expensive to maintain during downturns in the market. It would require an extremely high level of specification to match the individual needs of each type of unit. So, plant hire and leasing are widespread. For these reasons, mass production techniques have not yet superseded the adaptable skills of joiners, bricklayers, plumbers and the like. Barlow and Duncan (1994) argue that housebuilding in Britain is fundamentally speculative – builders make most of their profit from speculative land development gains, rather than from producing better houses. Furthermore, they argue, the planning system encourages this behaviour. As a result, the UK building industry is geared to simplification, standardisation and cost reduction in building. This is in complete contrast to Sweden, for example, where innovation and higher productivity are facilitated by an industry where the profits come from the actual housebuilding process.

Building for the public sector is usually subject to competitive tender among private firms. Building firms are therefore vulnerable to changing public policy as well as to changing economic circumstances. Building is inevitably risky, because building a house ties up capital that cannot be realised until the sale of the completed dwelling, which may take eighteen months or more. With the increased emphasis on private sector provision since the early 1980s, public sector construction has been reduced, so the building industry has faced particularly turbulent times. (In the past, conversely, public sector work has frequently played an offsetting role often called a counter-cyclical one in providing work for the building industry when private sector activity has declined.) Figure 2.1 shows the changing balance of public and private sector

Figure 2.1   Housing completions in the UK, 1980 to 1996

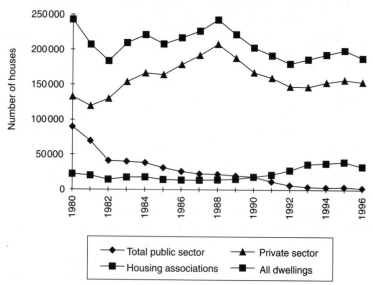

Source: Wilcox (1997); Northern Ireland Housing Executive (1998, personal communication).

building over the recent years; the decline in public sector building is clearly visible.(There were widespread bankruptcies in the unstable housing market of the late 1980s and early 1990s, particularly in smaller and medium-sized firms, reinforcing a trend towards the increasing concentration of activities into large building firms.) Those in the industry describe the competition as 'cut-throat', resulting in low prices for the consumers and low profits for the builders, to the extent that it is believed that the business is now suitable only for those able to produce a relatively high volume of output (Gibb *et al.*, 1995).

THE OPERATION OF THE HOUSING MARKET

In this section, an example is given of how economic analysis can help analyse housing policy change. It is important to understand the way demand and supply react to external changes if house prices are to be predicted. The example developed here is the hypothetical impact of the immediate abolition of mortgage interest tax relief (as opposed to the gradual reduction witnessed in the 1990s). This example shows, among other things, how important is the role of government in the housing market, and the repercussions that policy changes can have on owner-occupied households.

The Abolition of Mortgage Interest Tax Relief (MITR)

Mortgage payers have a reduction in their interest payments on the first £30 000 of their mortgage. Until 1993–4, this was set at the basic rate of income tax (25 per cent) before being reduced to 20, 15 and 10 per cent in successive tax years, (this last change being implemented in April 1998). It appears that the government intends to abolish the tax relief in the medium term. MITR cost £3.5 billion in 1994–5. In addition to its expense, it was often argued that MITR was not a good use of public money as it failed to help lower-income and first-time buyers. It is this aspect of the subsidy that we consider here.

If a specific subsidy reduces the costs of being a home owner relative to other goods and services (including other housing options) then home ownership becomes relatively cheaper, and demand for it will increase. Housing has an unresponsive supply. So, the higher demand created by the introduction of tax relief will result mainly in higher prices rather than lower costs for owners. The market value of owner-occupied properties will thus be higher than would have been the case in the absence of the tax relief. This means that new entrants to the market will require larger mortgages, larger deposits and will then face higher mortgage repayments than had the subsidy not been introduced. This process is called *capitalisation* of the subsidy, since the subsidy is now reflected in the higher capital value of the asset and does *not* reduce owners' costs. Existing owners of property do benefit from a windfall gain when the subsidy is introduced, as they benefit from the increase in asset values without having to pay extra.

Pearce and Wilcox (1991) attempt to estimate the wider effects of abolishing MITR, including its effects on house prices. They model the case in which, from 1991 onwards, MITR was abolished over a period of five years. They then look at the knock-on effects of removing the subsidy for other parts of the economy. They do this by generating results using the Treasury model of the UK economy.

What are the Results?

In 1990–1 (the year of the study) MITR cost £7.8 billion. If the subsidy was abolished, this would reduce house prices, increase net mortgage payments (as the tax relief is no longer available) and reduce the wealth effects of housing, leading to reductions in wider consumer spending. In short, the effects are deflationary for the economy as a whole. However, the fiscal saving on MITR would allow government to cut tax rates, increase public expenditure or reduce interest rates – or some combination of the three. This is expansionary, and helps to offset the deflationary housing sector consequences of abolition. Of course, reducing interest rates would additionally help the housing market. Pearce and Wilcox's exact results may be open to challenge, but their discussion highlights the possibility of widespread repercussions throughout the economy resulting from the policy change. The housing market is so large that it has the potential to impact heavily on the rest of the economy (the subject of Chapter 6).

CONCLUSIONS

This chapter has looked at the economics of the housing market. Some time was spent introducing the forces that shape demand and supply in this unique market for a good that is both a consumption and an investment good. The chapter applied these principles to the housing market in practice, examining the impact of a particular policy change.

The reasons for government action in the housing market were outlined. For owner-occupiers, the impact of intervention has covered several broad areas. New construction is built to specific standards on land that is rigorously planned and zoned by local authorities. The tax system treats housing favourably even with reduced mortgage tax relief, and further subsidies are available to council tenants in the shape of large discounts to entice them into home ownership. What are the effects of these policies? Well, for one, home ownership has expanded rapidly. This might reflect constraints and not just preferences, for instance, the lack of rental alternatives at a reasonable price. But it has, at the same time, made the housing market much less stable. Maclennan (1994) has stressed the contradiction in the government pursuing supply-side labour market policies aimed at deregulation, non-unionisation and labour flexibility (the growth in non-traditional employment contracts), while, at the same time, pursuing a housing policy based on mortgage debt that is long-term and high-geared (that is, with a high debt-to-income ratio) where mortgage rates are variable and fluctuate with general changes in interest rates. Chapter 6 continues this theme by analysing how the mortgage market works, and, from there, examines how the most recent boom and bust occurred in the national housing market. The central connectedness between the housing market and the economy has made it all the more important that these relationships are more clearly understood.

FURTHER READING

Further material on the determinants of the housing market can be found in housing economics textbooks (Robinson, 1981; Maclennan, 1982; Fallis, 1985), although these are now quite old; discussion of the policy impact on housing markets is set out in LeGrand *et al.* (1993), Maclennan and Gibb (1993) and Barr (1993). General introductions to economics all provide the basic demand and supply material. In particular, you might look at Stiglitz (1994), Begg *et al.* (1997) and Lipsey and Harbury (1992).

QUESTIONS FOR DISCUSSION

1. What makes housing different from other sorts of commodity sold on the market? What are the consequences of these differences?
2. What are price and income elasticities? Why is housing demand price and income elastic and housing supply price inelastic in the UK housing market?

3 Public Expenditure

INTRODUCTION

Important aspects of housing activity are financed by the public purse (including grants to housing associations, Housing Benefit for public and private tenants, and mortgage payments for owners receiving income support, for example). The intention of this chapter is to provide an understanding of the broader context in which decisions about the level of expenditure on housing (and other public services) are made. It will:

- examine the UK's system of controlling public spending;
- assess the system's strengths and weaknesses;
- explain the way local government spending is organised.

Decisions about public expenditure are central to all government activities. Put simply, there are two key functions that have to be undertaken:

- **Deciding on Spending**   This involves a range of complex decisions. Total spending will be decided in relation to what the country is believed to be 'able to afford'. Within that broad total is a myriad of less aggregated decisions – how much will be spent on particular policy areas (such as housing, health, education)? What are the priorities within each sector? How much will particular policies cost (for example, if some benefits are up-rated, or if higher education is expanded)? Some types of expenditure are very hard to predict and control – for instance, the cost of unemployment benefits depends on the number of people who become unemployed.
- **Deciding How to Raise the Necessary Money**   The main source is taxation, but government can raise less than total spending and borrow the balance, or it can raise more and repay existing debts. Again, within the overall total required there is a wide range of

options available. How much should come from individuals or the corporate sector? What will be the balance between taxes on spending and taxes on incomes? In making these choices it must be recognised that taxation regimes have consequences for economic activity, and the total amount of tax raised will also depend on the level of aggregate economic activity. The government may deliberately seek to provide particular incentives (for example, in encouraging people to switch from leaded to un-leaded fuel, or to reduce cigarette smoking), but will also need to take account of unintended incentives (for example, high income taxes may discourage people from working). The other ways of raising money are either to extend or increase charges (for example, prescription charges) or to sell assets (as in privatisa-tion). Assets can, of course, only be sold once.

These decisions have major implications politically, economically and in terms of the quality of life of the population. The basic problem that faces the government, each year, is to plan that year's spending and then to raise the appropriate amount of money in the annual Budget. The alterations implemented in tax regimes and expenditure plans announced in the Budget (which is presented to Parliament in March each year) are intended to attain this balance. Any shortfall in revenues over expenditure can be borrowed (the Public Sector Net Cash Requirement or PSNCR, formerly known as the Public Sector Borrowing Requirement or PSBR) by issuing government bonds or funded by increasing the money supply. This has costs for the economy in the longer term and is a politically contentious choice. Throughout the 1980s, the Thatcher govern-ments were committed to maintaining a balanced budget on grounds of 'prudent housekeeping'. In the mid-1980s budget sur-pluses were achieved (in part by means of the proceeds of privatisa-tion), which were used to redeem some of the national debt. In the early 1990s, this policy was abandoned by John Major's govern-ment which, faced with an economic recession and a forthcoming election increased public expenditure by borrowing. In the first years of the Labour government budget surpluses have arisen again and some national debt was repaid in early 1998 (in keeping with a stated policy of overall fiscal prudence).

This highlights the strongly *political* nature of public expenditure decisions. Public expenditure decisions are a product of a complex balancing act between the conflicting demands of taxpayers (who want low tax bills) and beneficiaries of public spending (who want good-quality (expensive) public services). Of course, these two groups overlap to a very large extent. However, there have been shifts in the broad consensus about where the balance should lie. Arguably, since the 1980s, most voters have increasingly favoured low taxation, requiring continued downward pressure on public expenditure. This can be seen as a reaction to the position reached in the 1970s, when public expenditure seemed to be to be growing out of control. The public sector was believed to be 'crowding out' private sector activity, and to have become inefficient and bureaucratic. The agenda vigorously pursued by Margaret Thatcher through the 1980s of 'rolling back the frontiers of the state', through the reduction of public spending, taxation and privatisation, captured popular imagination and support (Glennerster and Hills, 1998, provide a good overview of changing patterns of public spending in the post-war period).

Traditionally, Conservative governments have been believed to favour low tax/spend regimes, while Labour governments have been viewed as being supportive of higher public spending. Indeed, this belief is widely thought to have cost Labour the 1992 election. At that time, despite much apparent public concern about declining public services, at the ballot box, a majority voted against Labour proposals to spend (and tax) more. In 1997 Labour committed itself to maintaining the spending limits already set out by the previous Conservative government, and its large victory suggests that the low tax/low spend agenda remains the politically most popular. Despite some relaxation conditional on economic growth, there remains concern that some elements of spending are too low, leading to the situation of 'private affluence and public squalor', whereby people are forced to confront the implications of low public spending in dirty and inefficient trains and undergrounds, poorly maintained public spaces, and deteriorated and depressing school and hospital buildings. It is also worth noting that despite the election results successive British Social Attitudes Surveys have shown continued public support for increasing public spending on high-quality public services (Jowell *et al.*, 1997). This chapter will argue that there is still political commitment to continuing some of the main reforms of the 1980s, particularly in shifting the boundary of the public sector and in increased efficiency within it.

PUBLIC EXPENDITURE: DEFINITIONS, TRENDS AND PATTERNS

In order to monitor trends in public spending we need to have a consistent definition of what should be counted. This is not a simple question. There is no single 'right' answer as to what should be counted as public expenditure or indeed what really is the public sector. Broadly, public expenditure totals are intended to reflect the money spent by the government on the whole range of its activities. Expenditures are currently disaggregated in various ways:

(i)   first, according to the public body that makes the expenditure (for instance local government or central government);
(ii) second, by the function of the spending (such as on housing or education), and
(iii) third, by the government department that is responsible for the expenditure (for instance, housing expenditures are the responsibility of the Department of the Environment, Transport and the Regions in England and Wales, and the Scottish Office in Scotland).

Although there is some broad agreement as to what can be counted as public expenditure, changes in the precise definition of what is to be included in the total are very frequent. Likierman (1988) estimates that there were no fewer than 26 definitional changes between 1977 and 1983. Definitional changes are typically justified on technical grounds, such as improving the comparability or consistency of the measurements used. However, it must be recognised that there is a strong political element to many changes in definition (Thain and Wright, 1990). Governments aim to control public spending, but this is difficult in a context of upward pressure, and they are in danger of consistently missing the targets they set for themselves. The clear political attractions of definitional changes are:

- stated total public expenditure can be reduced by excluding or redefining some items;
- if definitions are changed it becomes more difficult for external commentators (or critics) to make direct comparisons between plans and outcomes, or plans from year to year.

The 'headline' target measure for public spending has been subject to various amendments, the majority of which have reduced the measured spending. In 1976 the key definition was 'total public expenditure' which included central and local government expenditure programmes, nationalised industry and public corporation capital spending, and gross debt interest payments. Debt interest has since been removed from the definition of 'General Government Expenditure' on the grounds that it is an item beyond the control of government. These changes are not trivial. For instance, the decision to exclude the interest payments on government debt effectively excluded an item of expenditure of the same order of magnitude as spending in the biggest departments (such as Defence). Allowing privatisation receipts to offset spending totals also significantly reduced the total throughout the 1980s.

A new 'Planning Total' was introduced in 1988. This was, in turn, superseded by the so-called 'New Control Total' in 1993. This is defined as General Government Expenditure, minus privatisation proceeds, debt interest and 'cyclical' social security expenditures. Cyclical social security expenditures are defined as Unemployment Benefit and Income Support to non-pensioners. The justification for excluding 'cyclical' social security expenditures was that these were argued to be determined in large part by the state of the economy. In particular, they become higher in times of economic downturn rather than because of government action. This definition results in a Control Total considerably less than general government expenditure (in 1993–4, for example, the New Control Total was just 85 per cent of General Government Expenditure).

In 1998 the Labour Government reformed the planning and control of expenditure for its Comprehensive Spending Review and for future control from 1999–2000 (Treasury, 1998a; Treasury, 1998b). The reformed system has four main features as follows:

- Overall spending by the public sector (a new measure, 'Total Managed Expenditure' or TME) would be guided by the *golden rule*: government pledged to borrow only to invest, rather than to fund current expenditure and the *sustainable investment rule*: holding net public debt as a proportion of national output at a 'stable and prudent level' (Treasury, 1998a, p. 3). So, capital and current expenditures would be planned and managed separately.

- Departmental expenditures would have limits (Departmental Expenditure Limits, or DEL) planned on a three year basis. There would be a small reserve, and inter-Departmental budgets such as Welfare to Work would have special control arangements. In its previous form, the annual Public Expenditure Survey would cease.
- Government recognised that some elements of expenditure – social security benefits being a key example – could not easily be subject to three-year limits. These elements would comprise a further new measure, 'Annually Managed Expenditure' or AME.
- AME would be subject to scrutiny as part of the annual Budget process and in setting DEL for a further three years in 2000.

These alternative measures are relevant for the headline *targets* that government sets and can be politically controversial, as they imply broad directions for government policy.

Here, we consider trends in the main published measures General Government Expenditure and the Total Managed Expenditure. On any definition, the amount of money involved in public expenditure is substantial. In 1997–8 General Government Expenditure was around £330 billion. This amount equals about £100 per week for every man, woman and child in the UK. A more conventional way of measuring the size of the public sector is to consider the proportion of total economic activity that is in the public sector. This is typically calculated by measuring total public expenditure as a proportion of *Gross Domestic Product* (GDP) – a summary measure of the total amount of economic activity in the economy. Figure 3.1 shows the trend in public spending as a proportion of GDP since 1979–80. It can be seen that the proportion reached a peak of over 47 per cent of GDP in the early 1980s and thereafter steady reductions were made. The lowest point, of under 38 per cent (after taking account of privatisation receipts), was reached in 1988–9. Since then the proportion has risen again, and the estimated out-turn for 1997–8 was 40 per cent. The target for expenditure as a proportion of GDP has shifted through time. When it was at its lowest level, it was hoped that it would be possible to stabilise expenditure at below 40 per cent of GDP, but subsequent years saw a retreat from that target. Projections in 1998 are again aiming below 40 per cent to the end of the century, with some modest increase thereafter.

Figure 3.1   General Government Expenditure as a percentage of GDP, 1979–80 to 2001–02

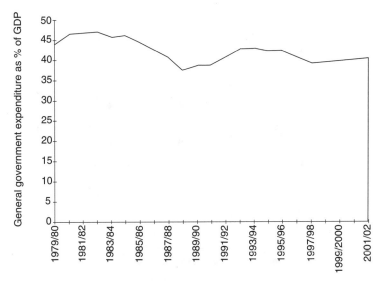

Note: Figures for 1997–98 are estimates of out-turn, for subsequent years planned out-turns.
Source: Treasury, 1998b, Table A6.

Total Managed Expenditure is a more restricted definition of spending. Figure 3.2 shows recent change in expenditure using this measure. Despite some decline in the rate of growth of nominal expenditure, it can be seen that overall real growth has continued. The majority of year-on-year real changes are positive). It is striking that growth has continued in spite of the government's strong rhetoric of public expenditure cuts and, indeed, the perception during its term of declining spending in many important areas of public service provision.

Analysis by Mullard (1993) showed that real levels of expenditure have risen almost every year since 1963–4, except during the mid-1980s. This is despite the strong commitment, especially over the last 10 to 15 years, to controlling expenditure. There are argued to be two main reasons for the strong upward pressure:

- First, there is pressure to continue existing programmes at least at the same level once started.

Figure 3.2   Real and nominal changes in Total Managed Expenditure, 1990–1 to 2001–02

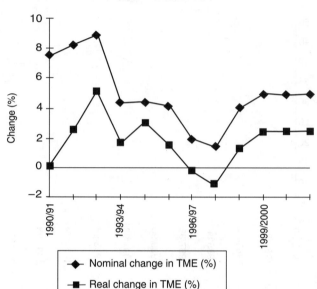

Note: Figures for 1997–98 are estimates of out-turn, for subsequent years planned out-turns.
Source: Treasury, 1998b, Table A6.

- Second, there is pressure to introduce *new* programmes, either because of particular governmental goals or because there are unanticipated circumstances that require government spending (such as wars).

What this implies is that any government wishing to pursue its own objectives and priorities will find it very difficult to contain the growth of total expenditure at the same time as maintaining existing services. It is also evident that *private* incomes and expenditures have also risen markedly. It is perhaps not surprising that parallel increase in quality and spending on public services should also be expected by people who enjoy improved general standards of living.

Of course, this is not to suggest either that government has no influence on its spending, nor that spending is not lower than it would have been had the policies of restraint not been followed in

Table 3.1   General Government Expenditure by function, 1996–7

	Share of expenditure on services (%)	Real growth 1980–1 to 1996–7
Law, order and protective services	6.0	85.5
Social security	35.6	81.2
Agriculture, fisheries and food	2.3	75.8
Health and personal social services	18.7	63.3
Education	13.5	29.7
National heritage	1.0	25.9
Overseas services and aid	1.2	17.6
Other environmental services	3.6	16.0
Transport	3.3	−5.9
Trade, industry and employment	3.4	−11.9
Defence	7.7	−17.4
Housing	**1.5**	**−67.9**
Miscellaneous expenditure	2.8	16.9
Total (= 100 per cent) (£ billion)	**267.5**	**33.8**

Source: Derived from Wilcox (1997a, table 14b).

the 1980s. The significance of government priorities is evident when examining where expenditure has increased and declined relatively more (see Table 3.1). Table 3.1 shows the breakdown of expenditure across various functions of government in 1996–7 and changes in spending since 1980–1. Table 3.1 shows that:

- Social security is by far the biggest single area of expenditure, accounting for over one-third of the total.
- Health and education are the next largest, with 18.7 per cent and 13.5 per cent of the total, respectively.
- Direct expenditure on housing is relatively small, at less than 2 per cent of the total, (excluding Housing Benefit and other social security costs).
- Investment in housing has suffered the largest real cuts.
- In contrast, large real growth in expenditure was experienced by law-and-order services and social security in particular.

Some types of expenditure are harder to control than others. For instance, it is hard to set cash limits on social security spending, as it is largely demand-led: expenditure depends on the number of people entitled to claim pensions, Unemployment Benefit, or other social security payments. The need for such expenditure varies across the economic cycle, being higher during recessions. It is always easier to cut capital expenditure – it is relatively easy simply not to start new capital projects, thereby saving projected expenditure. Capital expenditure on housing has been an obvious victim of this fact. Arguably, this is a short-sighted approach, as there is a continuing need for investment in the country's infrastructure, but there is no doubt that such cuts have frequently seemed politically expedient.

As indicated above, Labour's Comprehensive Spending Review (Treasury, 1998b) signalled a shift in the way in which public resources are allocated. It also allowed for some redirection of resources, with current expenditure predicted to have annual real growth of 2.25 per cent and public investment growing to 1.5 per cent of GDP in the 1999–2002 period. The principal targets for re-allocation for that plan period were as follows:

- education – an additional investment of £19 billion;
- the National Health Service – an additional provision of £20 billion;
- transport – an additional £1.7 billion;
- crime; and,
- regeneration of cities and housing – £3.6 billion of additional housing investment, and £800 million for the New Deal for Communities (see Chapter 9).

Government also indicated that it would inspect more closely programme outputs against these cash inputs. At the time of writing, it is not possible to evaluate the success or otherwise of the revised approach.

THE DEVELOPMENT OF PUBLIC EXPENDITURE PLANNING AND CONTROL SYSTEMS

Because of the scale and scope of public expenditure, its management is a major task. The way this is done has become increasingly sophisticated throughout the post-war period. The public expenditure survey (PES) system developed from a review of the planning and control systems conducted by Lord Plowden in 1961. Prior to this review, in the 1950s, departments sent estimates of likely spending to the Treasury, which then decided on the amount of revenue required from the Budget. This procedure was criticised because it took a very short-run (year-to-year) view of spending. It was blamed for a 'stop–go' pattern of expenditure on programmes, as from time to time budget shortfalls meant that capital projects had to be left unfinished. The system did not encourage any clear assessment of present or future priorities in public spending (Glennerster, 1997).

The 1961 Plowden review instituted basic and long-lasting principles for planning and controlling public expenditure. The most important considerations were to be prioritisation and affordability – expenditure programmes were to be planned with regard to prospective resources. A key innovation was that plans were to be presented for the following five years, with a clear statement of priorities allied to physical plans for spending under each heading. The two core principles of prioritisation and affordability have remained in place to date, although the details of the method of achieving these objectives has changed significantly since the initial Plowden reforms.

Initially, plans were made in volume terms. Volume plans are made in physical terms, such as the number of houses or schools to be built, or the number of people to be employed in the armed forces. Future trends were estimated on an assumption of constant prices. Any rise in the actual price of the elements was accommodated by an increase in out-turn expenditure.

This method of planning was suited to times of low inflation, but serious problems arose as general inflation increased rapidly in the late 1960s, and more especially in the early 1970s. Rapid price rises meant that out-turn expenditures were increasingly unrelated to the initial plans. The actual amount of public expenditure was expanding even faster than the rate of inflation. This was seen as unsustainable.

These problems, allied to pressures from the International Monetary Fund, caused the Labour government to impose cash limits on spending outcomes in 1976. These were intended to strengthen the control of public spending and also to aid the fight against inflation in response to the deep economic crisis of the time. Cash limiting was integrated with the volume planning that had preceded it. Physical plans were still made, the costs assessed, and the future flow of expenditure estimated by assuming that all costs would increase in line with a predicted general inflation rate. Cash limits were set to reflect this estimated future flow. Unfortunately, this did not provide a simple reconciliation of physical and cash planning, because all costs are not likely to increase in line with one single index (called the deflator). Specific inflation rates will be appropriate, depending on the particular activity. These differences result in some unplanned reallocation of resources between different functions with any fixed cash limit. Consider an example. Wages tend to increase faster than general price inflation. Some areas of public spending, such as education and health, are very labour-intensive. So, more of the cash allocated to them is taken by wages than in less labour-intensive areas like transport. When cash limits are imposed reflecting a general inflation rate, the more labour-intensive areas suffer more stringent real limits.

This problem is called differential inflation, and underpins continuing debates concerning the adequacy of expenditure in particular areas. Going back to the example, Table 3.1 showed that health expenditure has increased by nearly two-thirds in real terms since the early 1980s. But there remains an often-expressed fear that standards are falling and indeed that the NHS is in crisis. How can these apparently contradictory perceptions and facts be reconciled? Part of the explanation lies in the difficulty of defining an appropriate deflator, given that a great proportion of health spending is on wages, which have tended to rise faster than general prices. This adds to other important factors that have added to the cost of providing health care, such as the increasing demands of an ageing population and the greater cost of technological advances in health care and treatments.

The system that we now have is called *cash planning*. Initially it was introduced by the Conservative government in 1982. In this system, plans are made and limits set in cash terms, not in terms of planned programme outputs. There are potential drawbacks involved in cash planning. It is not possible to set cash limits on all types of expenditure, particularly that which is demand-led. This difficulty is overcome by allowing a certain discretionary flexibility in total spending through the provision of a relatively large unallocated 'contingency reserve', which can be used to meet unforeseen increases in spending requirements, so that the overall cash limit can be preserved (Thain and Wright, 1990).

In the years since the Plowden review, then, the basic principles of controlling and planning public expenditure have been implemented through three quite different types of planning system: first volume planning, then volume planning with cash limits and now cash planning with cash limits. The advantages of the present system, from the government's point of view, is that it gives the greatest potential for controlling the actual amount of money spent. However, it is less adequate in relation to the *planning* goals, because there is less emphasis on the explicit planning of the physical outputs that are to be produced by government expenditure. This is not to say that the physical outputs are forgotten, for plans are backed by the extensive documentation that is prepared by departments preparing their bids. Also, the intensive negotiation that ultimately results in an agreed budget is based on proposed programmes and activities and their estimated costs. These decisions are at the very heart of political debates. With cash planning, there is always a risk that planned programmes may have to be altered quickly and significantly if any unexpected increases in costs occur, in order to keep within the cash limit.

The Budget Timetable

As will be clear, there are many complex and conflicting demands that need to be resolved by the government. Traditionally, the process of setting a Budget and deciding on expenditure plans have revolved around two major separate events in the parliamentary timetable: public expenditure plans were announced in an Autumn Statement (in November), and then the March Budget concentrated on the revenue side, announcing tax changes for the following year. In November 1993, the first combined Budget announced both the expenditure plans and the proposed tax changes to be implemented in April 1994. There is a clear logic in having the two sets of decision closely tied together – revenue raising and expenditure are clearly two sides of the same coin.

In 1997 the incoming Labour government reverted to a two-stage process, with spending announced at the end of the year and the Budget held in March, though the Chancellor, Gordon Brown, presented an additional 'Green Budget' in November. This was intended to provoke discussion, like a more usual Green Paper. At the time of writing, it is not clear whether this new arrangement will become permanent.

A second major change was made to the process of decision-making within the government in 1993. The final decisions on public expenditure were to be made by the full cabinet. This replaced the 'bilateral' talks that had previously occurred between the Treasury and individual spending departments. The cabinet, with the Treasury playing a central role, therefore first decides how much total spending should be, taking into account the projections made in previous years and what conditions are expected in the macroeconomy (for example, growth rates, inflation rates, unemployment, and so on). The total spending limits that will be imposed tend to become public in early summer (May or June). Individual departments then make bids for the amount of money they wish to spend and the final allocation is agreed within the cabinet by autumn, to be finalised in time for the new financial year. The cabinet of course includes the minister from each of the major spending departments, who can each argue their case for their desired share of money. Some negotiating process is necessary, because it is virtually inevitable that the sum of the demands by the various departments will be more than the total expenditure limit agreed by the cabinet. The major criticisms of the 'bilateral' negotiating process were:

- First, that it was too adversarial, in that the final decision was reached by a series of arguments that became presented as a trial of strength between the Treasury and the relevant minister – a 'strong' minister was able to get a greater increase in funds. This is not wholly avoided by having the decision made by the whole cabinet, as ministers still have to argue their case.
- Second, it was argued that reaching agreement between the Treasury and each individual department was not the most rational way of reaching a considered judgement as to the best balance between the competing demands on the public purse.

Debate around Labour's Comprehensive Spending Review (Treasury, 1998b) points, at the time of writing, to a continuation of 'collegiate' decision-making. It is too early to say how economic change and the political tensions it causes may alter that.

There seems no doubt that the more centralised system can potentially provide better decision-making. It may also seem more democratic, because it is easier to tie spending to revenue, and to tie these to political priorities as thrashed out in the cabinet – like commitments to reduce public expenditure or cut taxes. But it is clear that the final decisions have ultimately to be presented to and passed by Parliament before they become enacted, in order to implement changes to the tax regime for the new financial year.

EVALUATION OF THE PES SYSTEM

The obvious yardstick by which to judge the PES planning process is to examine the extent to which it has succeeded in meeting its targets. Walshe (1987) estimates that over the first three planning cycles the slippage from cash targets was in the order of £3 or £4 billion, or between 2 and 3 per cent of the target. This is probably evidence that the system can achieve the central aim of limiting cash spending, not least because there are bound to some unavoidable changes in policy goals over the planning period. However, as shown above, despite the aim of reduction, overall public expenditure has continued to drift upwards (amounting to a 34 per cent real increase between 1979–80 and 1996–7). The continued rise lies partly in a mismatch between political rhetoric and the more pragmatic decisions that tend to be made in power.

The failure to stem real growth in spending is more striking when it is remembered that the PES system is only part of the **overall** control mechanism. Other very significant changes have been implemented post-1980 to reduce the scale and scope of the public sector. Privatisation is the most obvious example, having resulted in a steady conversion of what were previously public sector operations into independent, private sector companies (electricity, gas, British Telecom and water are among the best known of these). There are parallel shifts into the private sector through contracting out of particular activities within the public sector to private companies (such as refuse collection services or hospital cleaning and catering). In housing terms, the key example of shifting activities out of the public sector was seen in the Conservatives' proposals to subject the housing management services to compulsory competitive tender (CCT). (Following the 1997 election, Labour signalled that this policy will not be pursued.) The consequence of all these changes is clearly to reduce the scope of what is counted as 'public sector' activity. The initial impact of these moves is typically to save public expenditure, partly because of the benefit to the public purse in the form of the money received from the sale of the enterprise. The final financial gain or cost to the public purse of such changes depends on a complex balance of contributions to and costs imposed upon the public sector. A privatised, profit-making enterprise will pay taxes, but the public sector has lost any profits that might have been made within the public sector. That is, there may be a long-term cost.

There are three more fundamental criticisms that have been levelled at the current system of planning and controlling public expenditure. Very briefly, critics have argued that the system:

- does not measure and control the right things;
- does not treat capital expenditure in a sensible way;
- imposes unnecessary constraints on public sector activity.

These criticisms are considered in turn.

Does the System Focus on the Right Things?

There is no doubt that prudent financial management requires that proper account is taken of the financial costs of public sector activities. However, critics argue that a major weakness lies in its focus on *inputs* of cash, although what is really important are *outputs* from public spending. The 'volume' planning elements of the system at least provide information on 'intermediate outputs'. Volume indicators show the number of houses to be built or the number of new recruits needed in the army or whatever. However, these volumes are only intermediate to the final output, which may be to improve the housing conditions of the population or to make more effective the defence of the country. In the current system of cash-dominated planning, with a central focus on the overall spending limits, even the intermediate outputs play a less important role than cash spent. In any case, true final outputs are very hard (in some cases probably impossible) to measure. This is problematic, as it is these *final* outputs that are most closely related to the true aims of government policy. An understanding of the relationship between inputs of public expenditure and final outputs is clearly crucial in attempting to allocate resources efficiently and fairly. Otherwise, how can it be decided, for instance whether decreased costs in the health service arise from the same service being provided more efficiently rather than a decline in the standard of the service?

There have been various policy initiatives attempting to address this criticism. These initiatives can be considered as part of a general change, generally described as the 'new public management'. In this approach, markets and 'quasi-markets' (that is, systems and structures designed to replicate market mechanisms) are increasingly important in the management of public services, with a particular emphasis on establishing and maintaining efficiency in the delivery of services. This is an important rationale for the use of competitive tendering and market-testing of public sector activities. There are also increasing efforts made to evaluate the outcomes of policies and services, through performance indicators and other output measures. The Treasury recognises that the lack of evaluation of the benefits of expenditure is a major shortcoming with cash planning. Other evaluative techniques such as cost–benefit analysis and options appraisal are increasingly used to compare the costs and outcomes of alternative policies. However, such techniques are only partial solutions, for at least two reasons:

- First, there are profound technical difficulties in implementing such appraisal techniques, particularly with respect to measuring the less tangible costs or benefits, which may arise in any policy area. So, while it is relatively easy to count the cost, for instance, of new build housing and even to compare it with a rehabilitation alternative, it is harder to evaluate the differential benefits that may arise from enjoyment of an improved environment or reduced fear of crime. There is then, a danger that these techniques focus too narrowly on the quantifiable elements of the picture.
- The second problem is that the analyses tend to be narrowly focused within one policy area. It is also desirable, however to be able to compare across expenditure headings – to ask, for instance, what are the consequences of spending an extra amount on more police rather than spending the same additional amount on teachers? This information (the 'opportunity cost' of spending) is fundamental to making choices when dealing with the

allocation of scarce resources. The difficulty is that the great technical problems in undertaking analyses in single policy areas are compounded when trying to compare costs and benefits of quite different types of policy.

Cash planning focuses on the overall cost of programmes – it does not systematically compare spending on different functions. However, extensive documentation is required to accompany the formulation of plans and to detail proposed expenditure within every department. This enables a very detailed account to be given of how the agreed expenditure is to be distributed in the next year.

Is Capital Expenditure Correctly Treated?

Conventions of accounting in the public sector have been different from those of the private sector, and this is particularly notable in the case of spending on capital assets (that is, assets which are expected to last over a long period). In the PES system, the expenditure on capital is assumed to be incurred in one year. This may be sensible in relation to borrowing requirements and monetary targets, but it does not allow any account to be taken of the fact that the benefits from capital spending are generally enjoyed over a longer period of time. Nor, conversely, does it take account of the gradual 'using up' of capital assets (depreciation), which is potentially useful to give an indication of the rate at which existing capital goods are wearing out and hence the level of reinvestment that is needed. Thus, PES ultimately has not taken account of the benefits of capital or current expenditure in any truly meaningful sense. In housing this results in obvious short-sightedness. For instance, expenditure on new houses in the public sector is treated in just the same way as expenditure on temporary bed and breakfast accommodation.

The government has recognised the force of these arguments and is moving to a system of resource budgeting and accruals accounting, which is to be in place by 2000. This allows capital inputs to be counted across a longer period, rather than assuming that it all occurs in the first year. In June 1998 the government announced that it would in future separate capital and current expenditures. It also announced that it would set a target for steady growth in capital expenditure, even while maintaining overall expenditure constraints. This is potentially a valuable reform to capital expenditures, giving an increased accountability and visibility that might enable a clearer account to be taken of the extent to which such expenditure can have more widespread and long-lasting benefits than most current expenditure.

Should There be a New Definition of Public Expenditure?

The third major current criticism of the system of public spending is that the definition imposes unnecessary constraints on public sector activity. We saw earlier that there have been many detailed changes in expenditure definition for various purposes. While there are strong arguments *against* change, to the extent that it undermines clarity of control and hence accountability, there are strong public sector supporters of making a change that would allow some types of borrowing in the public sector *not* to count as direct public sector expenditure.

The measure – General Government Financial Deficit (GGFD) – has been proposed, as a better measure than General Government Expenditure. Although the arguments in support of this may seem rather obscure and difficult, some of them are strong. The key argument is that the GGE constrains public investment by counting all monies spent by local authorities, even where it is financed by private lending, and even though in the long term it is repaid in rent. The GGFD, in contrast, would not count money borrowed from the public expenditure by public corporations (including social landlords) as public expenditure.

At the time of writing, the argument in favour of reform seems to be gaining ground. The GGFD has the advantage of being the measure used across Europe. It is the target measure for convergence under the Maastricht treaty and is already reported in British documentation. It has potential attractions for the Labour government, which might allow some expansion in the scope and flexibility of the public sector, including local authorities. The new approach implied to public sector activities would allow the development of mechanisms by which public sector bodies could compete more directly and on more equal terms with private sector bodies (for example, through the development of housing companies, discussed more fully in Chapter 9). The change would also be very much in tune with other measures designed to increase private sector involvement in public projects (through mechanisms such as the Private Finance Initiative (PFI)). At present, the issue of whether this reform will occur is unresolved. However, pressures arising from narrow definitions of public spending may well have led to the invention of various solutions to avoid these constraints – such as the use of large scale voluntary transfers (LSVTs) to escape local authority borrowing rules (discussed in more detail in Chapter 9). Whether or not the change is implemented, it is arguably not sensible to allow major policy developments to be driven chiefly by artificial restrictions in the definition of capital expenditure.

SUB-NATIONAL ALLOCATIONS OF HOUSING EXPENDITURE

The *total* public housing expenditure having been decided on, the money must then be allocated across the UK. This decision takes account of assessed need among other factors.

What Is Housing Need?

Need is a complex concept, which can be defined in a number of ways. 'Need' implies some sort of commitment to public action. But there is scope for considerable disagreement over who and what may be considered to be legitimately 'in need' of public expenditure. Need is hard to measure; in housing terms, it is immediately possible to think of multiple dimensions of the concept:

- shortages, as expressed in homelessness or long waiting lists;
- mismatches, where people cannot get access to a house of a suitable type and size – as manifested, for example, in over-crowding, or the inability to find a suitable house to accommodate their disability;
- needs for expenditure based on house condition, for instance where dwellings fail the fitness standard, or else require investment to cure dampness or improve thermal efficiency, or to bring standards into line with more modern expectations.

All of these can legitimately be considered to be aspects of housing need. However, an expenditure distribution based on an attempt to meet these needs has to address two key questions: first, how can the extent of the need be measured in a consistent and reliable way and, second, how are the various needs to be prioritised?

In England, the solution adopted by both the DETR and the Housing Corporation is to construct an index of housing need; the GNI (General Needs Index) of the DETR and the HNI (Housing Needs Indicator) of the Housing Corporation. Although they are different in detail, each is compiled in broadly the same way:

- A set of needs measures is identified (for example, number of homeless people, outstanding repair costs).
- A measure is defined, usually based on nationally comparable figures (for example, census data, or the data that local authorities are obliged to return to the DETR).
- Each district or region calculates its own score on each of the dimensions of need.
- The total expenditure can then be divided according to an *a priori* division of the money; for example, if a certain proportion of the limit is to alleviate homelessness then this part of the total can be divided between areas in relation to their share of the homelessness indicators.
- Alternatively, each dimension can be given a weight and each area awarded a total score, by multiplying individual indicators by the weight and summing. Money can then be divided according to total scores.

At first sight, indices appear to provide a non-contentious way of allocating between different and competing needs. However, although the process of prioritisation is more transparent it is not value-free. It is, essentially, a political decision as to how the different elements of need should be measured and weighted. There is no objectively 'right' answer. It is, further, inevitable that when spending outcomes are sensitive to the details of the formula then it, too, will be politically contentious. A brief example will clarify these points.

Towards the end of the 1980s, an argument emerged that the biggest housing problem was access to owner-occupation. A booming housing market made it difficult for many to gain access to the sector. A measure was developed for the Housing Corporation reflecting the relative affordability of owner-occupation across the country. Use of this indicator was hugely controversial. Its major effect was to shift resources towards the south of the country where owner-occupation was very expensive and away from the north, whose need for expenditure had previously relied on the disproportionate presence of older dwellings in poor repair.

In Scotland and Wales, the respective Secretaries of State receive an allocation of funds from central government. They have freedom to allocate money between areas of expenditure and, subsequently, to allocate those totals across the countries to constituent local authorities. In Scotland, resources are allocated on the basis of judgement of need and the claims made by councils in their housing plans. The Scottish Parliament will be able to debate these issues and decide on the distribution of available resources, and it may be that a more transparent allocation process will result from such debate. We look at the issues further in Chapter 4.

LOCAL GOVERNMENT FINANCE

The contentious and often acrimonious world of central–local government relations is currently experiencing a relatively calm period following ten years of upheaval. The focal point of much of the conflict was related to the funding of local government. In fact, difficulties over the level of local government spending date back at least to the mid-1970s. In this section, the story of local government finance under the Conservative administrations of the 1980s and 1990s is briefly told. It is relevant to this book, first, because of questions concerning property taxation and, second, because local government finance continues to play a large role in the public spending system. Readers interested in a fuller account of local government operations and finance are recommended to Stewart and Stoker (1995).

Capital Funding

First, the way that local government funds capital spending is financed should be set out. As we saw in Chapter 1, capital spending relates to long-term purchases of assets that will last beyond the current financial year (often for decades). Funds are usually borrowed for such spending. Since the 1989 Local Government and Housing Act, local government has raised its capital funding from four sources (parallel definitions are presented for housing expenditure in Chapter 4) (Wilson and Game, 1994, pp. 137–8):

- borrowing up to a prescribed credit ceiling;
- capital receipts;
- capital grants from the centre;
- using current (revenue) income.

The government allows local authorities to borrow up to a certain limit (called the Basic Credit Approval in England and Net Capital Allocation in Scotland). It may also allow Supplementary Credit Approvals for certain approved activities. Further, councils can augment their capital expenditure from capital receipts, largely from housing or the sale of land and other assets. However, central government has generally (although not always) kept a tight control over the use of these receipts (since they count as public spending). Third, the use of capital grants from the centre, for instance in relation to urban regeneration programmes such as City Challenge, can also be used to fund capital projects, but again these are tightly controlled by Whitehall. The main additional local source of funding for local authorities is income from local taxes. As will be shown below, there is in practice little scope for most councils to use their local tax base in this way.

Revenue Funding

Local government traditionally relied on four sources of income to meet its running costs, namely:

- fees and charges to the user of some local services (museums, recreation, and so on);
- central government grants (which may be tied to specific activities or may allow local authorities to spend at their discretion);
- non-domestic local taxes levied on the business community;
- the local tax levied on the domestic sector and set by the council.

Because of the desire to control local government public spending, since 1979, the government has attempted in different ways to curb its perceived growth. This has been possible because central government has considerable control over local government in the unitary British state (or has had, prior to devolution).

The first Thatcher government approach to reforming local taxation was to attempt to control overall council budgets, by a mechanism known as rate-capping. When it failed to deliver lower spending levels, more radical surgery was attempted through the Paying for Local Government system in 1986 (Department of the Environment, 1986). The previous system, domestic rates, was largely discredited by the mid-1980s, and a replacement became an urgent priority for the Conservative government. The main problems with rates were as follows:

- It was politically difficult to revalue the tax on a regular basis, yet revaluation is a prerequisite of any property-based tax.
- The tax was historically based on annual rental values, with the private rented sector its chief reference point. However, with most properties in the country owner-occupied and less than 10 per cent renting in the market sector, this no longer made sense and caused confusion.
- Only half of registered voters were formally liable to pay rates (because it was a household tax). The spurious argument that this led to many people being able to vote for high spending without their being financially affected, was able to gain ground.
- A tax on property was argued by many to be unfair on those with few cash resources.

The new system made a number of key changes to local government finance:

- abolition of local business taxes replaced by a centrally levied 'unified' tax on businesses;
- a simplified grant system;
- the abolition of local rates (a property tax), and their replacement with the community charge, a poll tax (that is, per head of adult population);
- the decision to force all households to pay 20 per cent of their local community charge, even if qualifying for Income Support, so that low-income households no longer qualified for 100 per cent assistance.

The objective of the new system was to create strong, downward pressure on local government spending. How was this to be achieved? Basically, the system reduced the proportion of finance raised locally but left *all* additional spending over guidelines to come from the poll tax revenue. This is known as the *gearing effect* and works in the following way. If 20 per cent of revenue comes from the local source and overall spending has to rise by 1 per cent, this does not lead to a 1 per cent increase in the poll tax but to a 5 per cent increase. This is because one-fifth of the total revenue is poll tax and all other sources of income are effectively fixed. The 1 per cent rise in spending, therefore, must *all* come from poll tax revenue – leading to a 5 per cent rise. The smaller the local revenue proportion, the bigger the gearing effect. government calculated that large gearing ratios would deter local governments from higher spending. However, as it turned out, councils were able to exploit the unpopularity of the poll tax and to blame higher bills on government. But as we shall see, the gearing ratio in the 1990s has been increased even more, so that the successor, council tax, faces even higher gearing ratios.

The poll tax system worked in the following way. Central government decided how much grant each local authority should receive (based on population levels, calculations of need and an averaged standard amount of costed service – known as the Standard Spending Assessment). In addition to this, the centrally collected business tax was returned to local councils on a common per capita basis, effectively turning it into a per capita grant. What was left had to be raised from the poll tax, a flat-rate charge on all adults in the local authority.

After a long search for an alternative, the community charge (widely called the poll tax) was chosen as the successor tax embedded in the system already described. The government argued that it was simple to understand, was fair, represented the average cost of local government services, would allow voter-taxpayers to compare local authority 'prices' and would greatly enhance local accountability. The community charge was one of Britain's most spectacular political disasters (Glennerster, 1997). It is difficult not to use hyperbole in the context of £14 billion wasted on the tax, large-scale public unrest and civil disobedience, the reluctant raising of VAT to finance reductions in poll tax, and the resignation of the

Prime Minister. What went wrong? A number of factors played a part in the downfall of the community charge:

- It was not phased in but was introduced in one go, first in Scotland and then a year later in the rest of the UK, making it much harder to soften the blow of the new tax.
- Taxpayers had to be registered, but people, especially young people, are, unlike property, mobile, difficult to find or unwilling to be found.
- The tax was universally condemned as unfair (it was obviously regressive).
- Mass non-payment undermined the legitimacy of the tax.
- It did not reduce local government spending.

The Present System of Local Government Finance

Introduced as a hybrid and bolted onto the Paying for Local Government system, the council tax compromise was the Major government's solution to the problems it inherited in local government finance. The council tax is a crude property tax. Based on banded capital values, each property was valued in 1991 and located within one of eight wide bands for tax purposes. Although there was to be no general revaluation, the idea was that when an individual property was sold it would move into a new band on the bais of its selling price though this has not generally been done. The tax payments associated with each band are flat in the sense that they are not proportionate to the capital value of the property. Instead, properties in the lowest band (A) pay two-thirds of the reference band (D) and highest-value properties (in band H) pay twice that of band D. This means that properties that are valued at, for example, £25 000 (band A) pay a third of the tax paid by properties worth £500 000 (or £1 million) in band H. The new tax has not returned to 100 per cent rebates for those on low incomes but has a discount for single adult households. The fact that it has settled in relatively quietly suggests it has successfully averted the most contentious elements of previous systems. However, this peace may not last.

The council tax system sits within a tight set of central government controls. The gearing ratio is now in excess of 1:7 and there are capping controls on the band D level of council tax which Whitehall can impose on errant councils. There is clearly future scope for conflict in such a tight regime. From a broader perspective, there are a number of criticisms that can be made of the sustainability of the council tax system:

- There is no provision for general revaluation.
- The major changes to finance have taken place in isolation from proper debate about the role, functions and structure of local government, and its relationship with central government.
- For local democratic accountability, the proportion of locally raised revenue has to be increased.

CONCLUSIONS

This chapter has reviewed the control and management of public expenditure in the UK. It has defined public expenditure, and shown major trends in that over the past two decades. The chapter has also reviewed the means by which local government is financed. A major theme of the discussion has been that public expenditure is very much a political matter, with changing policy emphases having important legacies for the volume shape of public services paid for and received. The fact that expenditure decisions are political also implies that the system by which they are made is the product of incremental change rather than root-and-branch review, planning and implementation – which also helps to explain why it is complex, and may seem to have inconsistencies to some. The chapter has alluded to recent reforms to the management and control system which may serve to remove some of the perceived problems of the past. Our review of reform of local government finance must, lead us to a degree of caution – mistakes can happen, unforeseen problems may arise.

FURTHER READING

There are many excellent books available covering local government finance including Glennerster (1997) and Wilson and Game (1997). Two books particularly to be recommended dealing with the development of public spending across the whole range of public sector services are Mullard (1993) and Glennerster and Hills (1998). The annually updated publication by Steve Wilcox, *Housing Finance Review*, provides a comprehensive overview of general public spending and housing spending in detail. With respect to local government finance, you should also consult Department of the Environment (1986).

QUESTIONS FOR DISCUSSION

1. Housing investment is often linked to crime reductions, health improvement and unemployment reduction. How easy is it for government planning to take account of these links? Why?

2. What are the arguments in favour of and against raising local revenue for local services? Is the council tax a fair and efficient way of doing this?

4 Financing Local Authority Housing

INTRODUCTION

Although the local authority sector has been falling in size over the last twenty years, it remains the most significant provider of social rented housing. Its financial arrangements are still at the heart of the provision of rented homes at below market prices.

This chapter will:

- Introduce capital and current expenditure on local authority housing.
- Look at how local authorities' housing expenditures are controlled in England and Wales and Scotland.
- Describe the structure of the Housing Revenue Account.
- Look at how subsidies to council housing are determined.

HISTORICAL BACKGROUND

Local authorities began to provide housing in the aftermath of the First World War. It was clear that some action was required to provide some of the 'homes fit for heroes' that were in desperate shortage. There is no space here to provide a history of housing finance (which is covered admirably in Malpass, 1990, or Malpass and Murie, 1999). However, it is worth highlighting some of the main developments to give some background to the current situation.

The subsidy to post-World War I local authority housing was paid as an ongoing contribution to the repayment of the loan for the cost of building the property (that is, capital costs, see Chapter 1). The subsidies were of the form of receiving £x for y years and houses built under different Acts (such as the Housing Act (1923) and the Housing (Financial Provisions) Act (1924) – commonly known as the Chamberlain and Wheatley Acts respectively) were subject to slightly different rules concerning the amount of £x, the y years and the allowed total cost of building the house. The balance of landlords' costs (the part of the loan *not* covered by subsidy plus the costs of managing and maintaining the house – see Chapter 1) had to be covered by rent. There was no system of Housing Benefit (or its equivalent), and so local authorities had to be sure that they had sufficient demand from potential tenants who could afford the final rent of the houses they planned to build.

The subsidy system could be manipulated to produce houses that were relatively more or less expensive to rent (and therefore that would be affordable to different sections or classes in society). In general, the council housing built in the first decade after World War I was built to high standards and, though subsidised, was relatively high-rent. This housing was built for the relatively affluent, 'respectable' working classes and still constitutes some of the most desirable council housing in many parts of the country, being dominated by traditional houses in spacious 'garden city' type estates.

By contrast, the focus of housing policy in the 1930s shifted to clearing the slums. Housing for this much poorer group had to be cheaper for the tenants, and so was built to lower overall standards (the level of subsidies was generally *lower* rather than higher). These estates frequently became immediately stigmatised and that, allied to the relatively lower standards, left a legacy that was ultimately revealed in estates that were very unpopular and 'difficult to let'.

Housing built under each subsidy regime was initially kept separate financially. Expenditure on each vintage of development had to be covered by the particular subsidy received and the rents paid by occupants. However, inflation after 1945 made this system look unfair. As general prices became ever higher, inevitably the newest developments were the most expensive despite the fact that new building was *not* necessarily of better quality. From the mid-1930s, local authorities were first allowed and then under increasing pressure (from the mid-1950s) to 'pool rents' – that is, put the accounts of all their different housing developments together. This allowed rents in older properties to go up (to more than cover costs), so that rents in newer properties could be lower (thus tenants in newer houses were effectively cross-subsidised by tenants in the older properties).

Rent-pooling meant that rent structures could be developed in which quality was more closely reflected in the rents. However, this impacted badly on occupants of older, better-quality housing, who found themselves facing rapid rent increases. Local authorities had had, since 1930, the power to give rent rebates to those tenants they wished to support, but in 1972 this was superseded by a single, mandatory national system. This allowed consistent, means-tested contributions to be made towards the rents of poorer tenants.

Consolidating local authorities' housing accounts in this way also made the linking of specific subsidy amounts to different vintages of development more notional than real. Ultimately, this was abandoned (in the 1980 Act) in favour of a system whereby the government took a view as to the average rents that should be charged and gave a general subsidy to enable each authority to 'balance its books', assuming that other expenditure on the housing stock was also kept within the limits assumed by government.

It will be appreciated, even in this very brief overview, that finance for local authority housing is a complex and potentially contentious issue. Small changes in the financing rules can have major changes in the real outcomes (rents, standards of service) affecting tenants. Because of this, an understanding of the finance system for local authority requires a fairly detailed understanding of the structures and rules that govern the system.

THE CURRENT SYSTEM OF FUNDING LOCAL AUTHORITIES

The purpose of this chapter is to outline the present system of financing local authority housing. The current regime for capital and current spending was introduced in England and Wales from 1990–1, and was designed to restore effective control to the government over rents and expenditure in the social rented sector. The system also reflects the changing role intended for local authorities; the Conservative government wished to see local authorities becoming enablers rather than being major, mainstream providers of housing. The system in Scotland did not change at the same time, and at the time of writing there appears to be no immediate intention for similar changes to be implemented. The system of supporting local authority housing provision in Scotland has always been different in detail from the English system, in ways that meant that some of the worst problems that emerged in the English system through the 1980s did not occur in Scotland. In the chapter, the Scottish system is described separately. With the election of a Labour government in 1997, local authorities may hope to have some greater freedom in housing than over the past twenty years. It is, however, unlikely that they will quickly return to being major providers of new housing.

Capital and Current Expenditure

First, the important distinction between the two main elements of local authorities' housing finance activities, current spending and capital spending should be reiterated:

- Capital expenditure is for work that will last a long time, such as building houses or making major improvements to them that significantly enhance the quality of properties or their life expectancy.
- Current (or revenue) expenditure is the expenditure that is incurred by a local authority's day-to-day activities as landlord; in particular the costs of maintaining the stock, and all management functions, such as dealing with present and prospective tenants, rent-setting, rent collecting and arrears management, and tenancy allocations and transfers.

The sources of government support for these expenditures are different.

Current expenditures are met out of the authorities' revenue income – most importantly rents – while most capital projects are funded by taking out a loan. Loans are used for capital expenditures because the benefits of capital expenditure will be enjoyed over a long time period, so it is fairer that the costs also should be met over a long period. Raising a loan allows repayments to be made over many years, sharing the burden between current and future tenants. Loan repayments are, however, met out of authorities' current revenues including rents. It is generally considered to be financially unsound to borrow for current expenditure.

The distinction between capital and current expenditure is not entirely clear-cut. Major repairs, for instance, might be considered to be part of the work that the landlord has to do to keep property lettable (that is, counted as current expenditure). However, as such work lengthens the life of the property, then it might equally legitimately be regarded as capital expenditure. In the 1980s, a great deal of capital expenditure was funded using the receipts that local authorities earned from selling houses, mainly under the right to buy, rather than funded by new loans. Because of the way control was exerted over capital expenditure, it was advantageous in some circumstances to 'capitalise' repairs expenditure, blurring the distinction further. However, the 1990 regime has laid down very clear definitions as to what can be legitimately considered as capital expenditure.

The government aims, in setting the framework for current and capital expenditure, to exercise control over local authorities' activities. All governments need to do this because

- they wish to ensure that overall expenditure meets the limits set within the PES system for total government spending (as outlined in Chapter 3) and
- as local government plays a major role in delivering public services, central government will often take a strong view as to how these services should be delivered and how much should be spent.

Local authorities have a wide range of responsibilities and undertake many non-housing functions, financed by central grants, the business rate payer and the general local tax (council tax) payer (discussed in more detail in Chapter 3). To make housing expenditure clearly identifiable, the government requires that housing activities should have a separate account from these other activities. In England and Wales, since the inception of the financial regime of 1990–1, government has placed particularly tight limits on the extent to which money can be transferred between the housing and non-housing accounts. Current (or revenue) income and expenditure on housing are summarised in an annual account called the Housing Revenue Account (HRA). This is kept separate from the account of other areas of local authority activity, which is called the General Fund. Local authorities require direct permission from the government *not* to keep an HRA, which really only applies when the local authority has transferred all their stock to another landlord (see Chapter 9).

CAPITAL EXPENDITURE IN ENGLAND AND WALES

It is surprising to remember that until 1976 no direct limits were placed on local authorities in relation to the amount they could borrow for new house-building, except that they were required to be able to keep their housing revenue accounts in balance. Control was exercised on a project-by-project basis over the total capital costs allowed within each scheme, and revenue account subsidies (the £x for y years outlined in the introduction) were manipulated either to encourage or to discourage local authority building, depending on the policy priorities of the time (for a fuller historical analysis of subsidies pre-1979 see Merrett, 1979; Burnett, 1986; Malpass, 1990). Since 1976, capital spending has been controlled more directly. The arrangements surrounding capital expenditure are essentially intended to fulfil two purposes; first, to control expenditure so that totals are consistent with the aggregate spending plans and, second, to enable planning so that capital expenditure is related to needs.

Definition of Capital Expenditure

The current financial regime has a tighter definition of capital expenditure than existed previously. There are three elements of capital expenditure:

(i)   the acquisition, reclamation, enhancement or laying out of land, exclusive of roads, buildings and other structures;
(ii) the acquisition, construction, preparation, enhancement or replacement of roads, buildings and other structures;
(iii) the installation or replacement of movable or immovable plant, machinery and apparatus and vehicles and vessels.

'Enhancement' is defined as lengthening the useful life of the asset, increasing substantially the market value of the asset, or increasing substantially the extent to which the asset can be used by the local authority. This has the effect of not allowing straightforward repair work to be paid for as part of capital expenditure.

Controlling Capital Expenditure

The government divides the total amount it makes available for local authority capital expenditure into broad expenditure headings for each local authority. Housing is one of the expenditure blocks. Each local authority is required to submit a Housing Investment Programme (HIP) every year to the DETR (in Wales the equivalent is the Housing Strategy and Operational Programme (HSOP)). These plans outline the authority's assessment of local housing needs and present a costed capital works programme.

HIP submissions are in two parts, a Housing Strategy Statement and a Bid for Resources. This second part has two key elements. The HIP1 form summarises needs and the HIP2 form summarises financial plans. The government also requires that authorities describe what strategy they would adopt if they were to receive the same resources as last year. Submissions are made in July. There is typically a meeting between the local authority and the Department of the Environment, Transport and the Regions to discuss bids in September or October, with the final announcement of allocations given in December. Allocations are currently made on a *competitive* basis between authorities. Until 1997–8, the total amount of money allocated to capital works in the PES system was divided, at the regional level, according to four criteria:

- the Generalised Needs Index (GNI) (see Chapter 3);
- past expenditures;
- the government's assessment of priorities for expenditures;
- the government's evaluation of authorities' efficiency and effectiveness within five major areas.

The GNI was discussed in Chapter 3. It was argued that it is impossible to construct any index which is universally agreed to be appropriate and fair. However, capital expenditure was not allocated mechanistically on the basis of the index, and the regional controller always had some discretion. From 1997–8 it was planned to move to an entirely competitive basis for capital allocations. The competition was based on the judgement of local authorities' efficiency and effectiveness in five areas of operation: (i) quality of housing strategy; (ii) enabling role in assisting the housing association and private sectors, (iii) landlord role, (iv) management of capital programme, and (v) tenant involvement and participation. Each authority receives a rank from 'well below' to 'well above' average on each of these dimensions. The Conservative government had intended that from 1997–8 capital allocations would depend entirely on success in these performance measures, but the Labour government is not committed to retaining this approach. At the time of writing it is not clear what the relative influence of the various factors will be in capital allocations decisions in the future.

Under the Conservative regimes of 1979–97, the government took considerable direct control over spending priorities, This process was popularly called 'top-slicing' the capital allocation, though the government argued that this money represented a special, separate pool of money. government did this to target money more directly towards meeting its own policy objectives. Top-slicing was first used in 1985–6, and was used subsequently for Estate Action, Housing Action Trusts (HATs), City Challenge, Housing Partnerships, Single Regeneration Budget (SRB), and the Estates Renewal Challenge Fund (see Chapter 9). Allocation of funds in each of these cases was on the basis of competitive bids submitted by local authorities.

In England, total local authority capital limits were reduced to £1356 million in 1997–8, and further falls were planned to £874 million by 1999–2000. The Comprehensive Spending Review (Treasury, 1998b) used capital receipts to boost housing capital spending £1190 billion in 1999–2000. It also allowed some growth in the (top-sliced) provision through the Estates Renewal Challenge Fund from £109 million (1997–8) to £160 million (1999–2000). However, at the same time Estate Action is being tapered down as no new schemes are declared, falling from £170 million (1997–8) to £66 million (1999–2000). In total, these two elements accounted for about 20 per cent of total capital spending in 1997–8.

It is clear that the HIP bid ultimately plays a relatively minor role in determining the final pattern of capital expenditure, and that central government priorities are able to dominate to a great extent. Formally, the annual HIP allocation consists of an annual capital guideline (ACG) and specified capital grants (SCG). The ACG is for general expenditure on public housing (although the authority has the discretion to spend the money on private housing or non-housing capital works if it wishes) and the SCG is for expenditure on the private housing stock (particularly through the repairs and improvement grants system). Particular grants available for private sector expenditure are the Private Sector Renewal Grant (PSRG) and the Disabled Facilities Grant (DFG).

Once the expenditure limits have been determined by the government, the local authority has to implement plans to spend it. Councils are guided by the priorities and plans laid down in their Housing Investment Programmes. They also work with plans and structures created within the planning framework which, for instance, establishes where developments of 'affordable' housing should be placed. A criticism of the current way capital expenditure limits are allocated to local authorities is that of annuality. Because the process takes place annually, it arguably does not facilitate good planning of capital expenditure, as many developments are likely to take longer than one year to plan and implement. The annuality of budgets commonly creates a rush to spend any remaining allocations at the end of the financial year. The problem is partly offset, because each annual allocation also contains an indicative guideline as to what the authority might (minimally) expect in the following year. The basic annual cycle may be inevitable, to the extent that the public spending process, which determines the total amount of money available, is basically an annual process (although alterations to the PES system announced in mid-1998 may ameliorate this problem to some extent).

Sources of Funds for Capital Expenditure

There are three sources of finance available for capital expenditure:

(i)   borrowing or credit arrangements;
(ii) government grants or contribution from third parties;
(iii) local authorities' own resources (including revenue contributions and cash realised from disposals of assets).

Through the 1980s, the growth of capital receipts which were received from the sale of council houses created an important additional source of money for capital expenditure.

Figure 4.1 indicates the progress of the right to buy policy in Britain. By 1996 about 1.7 million houses had been sold, about one-quarter of the 1981 stock. However, Britain's different countries showed somewhat different patterns. In England there were two peaks in sales, in 1982 and 1989, but much lower levels in the early 1990s. In 1996, sales of over 31 thousand houses were only 22 per cent of the peak 1989 annual level. Sales started at a slower rate in

Figure 4.1   Houses sold under the right to buy, 1980 to 1995

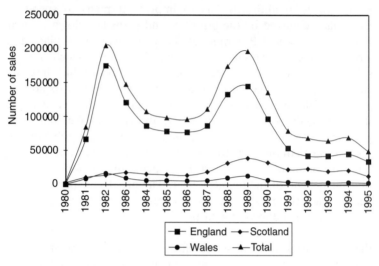

Source: Wilcox (1997a).

Scotland, but did not fall so sharply in the early 1990s. In Wales, there was a remarkably high level of sales in the first few years, which were repeated in the late 1980s. Partly in order to encourage the sales of flats, discounts available to sitting tenants increased in 1986 (and this change may underpin the following peak in sales clearly seen in Figure 4.1). Tenants of flats receive discounts of 44 per cent after 2 years, rising by 2 percentage points a year to 70 per cent after 15 years, while tenants of houses receive discounts of 32 per cent after 2 years, rising by 1 percentage point a year to 60 per cent after 30 years. Despite these significant discounts, the level of sales was high enough to generate substantial capital receipts.

In England and Wales, central government restricted the amount of these 'capital receipts' that councils could use. One of the major pledges of the new Labour government was its promise to enable the stored-up receipts from council housing to be spent. In 1997 about £800 million was released, effectively making up the cuts that had been implemented in the main capital programme. At the time of writing it is not clear *exactly* how the remaining money will be allocated, from the original estimated total of about £5 billion. It is clear that the councils that originally raised the money have not been given any 'ownership' over these resources – instead, the receipts are being used to contribute to meeting housing needs generally across the country. There is not even any guarantee that all the money will ultimately be available for housing expenditure.

Under the 1989 Act (the current regime), government controls total *spending*, whereas under the system prevailing in the 1980s it was *borrowing* that was controlled. Traditionally, capital works are funded mainly by borrowing, with a set proportion of that borrowing being allowed from the government-backed Public Works Loans Board (PWLB). Note that the list of allowable funding sources includes 'credit arrangements'. This is significant, as the spending allocation, the Basic Credit Approval (BCA), now incorporates the innovative methods by which local authorities sought to increase their *spending*, while remaining within government guidelines about *borrowing* during the 1980s. Such methods included selling and leasing back local authority assets, for instance. The inclusion of imaginative schemes into the basic spending limits means that local authorities have virtually no scope to squeeze extra money out of the system. Similarly, local authorities' own resources are included as part of the controlled spending total. The only potential additional sources are any revenue contribution to capital expenditure and the part of their own capital receipts that they are allowed to spend. The BCA covers *all* capital expenditure by local authorities, and the division between housing and other spending areas (such as libraries, schools, and so on) is at the local authority's discretion. The HIP allocation makes an assumption about how much of the BCA will be spent on housing, to give the Annual Capital Guideline (ACG).

The total amount of capital expenditure which may be financed is calculated as:

$$ACG - RTIA + SCG$$

where ACG is the Annual Capital Guideline, RTIA is receipts taken into account and SCG is specified capital grants.

That is to say, the ACG reflects the basic 'need to spend' as decided by the government in each authority. Offset against the total allowable new credit is the amount that the local authority is expected to be able to finance itself – the RTIA. Additional credit is allowed to cover expenditure on the private stock via special grants. When setting each authority's annual BCA and ACG, government will also indicate likely limits for the next two years to facilitate forward planning. Authorities that have permission to spend on the 'top-sliced' programmes receive a Supplementary Credit Approval (SCA) to cover these activities. Malpass and Warburton (1993) note that authorities that have a low assessed 'need to spend' and relatively high levels of receipts are most likely to receive a nil BCA. This means that they may spend the (prescribed) proportion of any capital receipts that they receive, but may not enter into any further borrowing or other credit arrangement.

As noted, the BCA covers all capital expenditure that is to be permitted by the local authority. There is a maximum amount stated for housing expenditure that may be subsidised within the HRA. In principle, therefore, authorities have the freedom to allocate housing and non-housing capital expenditure as they wish within this total. However, the operation of the HRA subsidy system (discussed in more detail in the next section) strictly limits the extent to which authorities are able to take advantage of this flexibility. It is basically very difficult to find alternative ways of paying for housing investment, so the limit set in the BCA for housing expenditure tends to be binding.

The PWLB remains an important source of funding for capital works. The Treasury sets the interest rate on loans from the PWLB, generally at a rate somewhat below prevailing market rates. This is because the government can borrow money more cheaply than any other body, and is able to pass the benefit of cheaper credit onto local authorities. The PWLB can lend money over any period from 3 to 60 years, and the loan may be at a fixed or a variable interest rate. Local authorities are generally allowed to borrow only part of their allocation from the PWLB, and may raise the remainder by issuing either stocks or bonds (for longer-term loans) or bills for shorter loans. These sources of money are subject to prevailing market rates of interest. Loans made to local authorities are secured on their future revenues rather than on their assets.

Capital receipts constitute a part of the overall capital allocation (as RTIA). The basic rule in England is that up to 25 per cent of the receipts from council house sales and up to 50 per cent of receipts from sales of other assets are allowed to fund capital projects. The remainder either must be applied compulsorily to debt redemption or may (less usually) be kept by local authorities if the interest received is enough to cover interest repayments on an equivalent amount of debt. This effectively prevents a problem arising from a declining number of local authority tenants bearing the whole burden of debt, including that on houses that have been sold. In Wales, a higher proportion, 50 per cent, of capital receipts from council house sales are taken into account. However, this is applied only to 'new in year' receipts, so that any unused receipts from previous years are not taken into account in spending allocations. If receipts are earned from large-scale transfers of local authority stock to another landlord then debt redemption is to be the 'first call' on that money (and there are other restrictions, discussed more fully in Chapter 9). In this way, if the size of the stock is reduced, the debt burden on remaining tenants will also be reduced.

An important electoral pledge of the Labour government in 1997 was that councils would be allowed to spend accumulated receipts. In a climate of general fiscal restraint it was seen as one of the few ways of finding extra money without tax consequences – potentially releasing an extra £5 billion. Capital receipts represent a one-off spending option as the current regime does not allow the further accumulation of new receipts. Further, as the diminution of the stock continues there will be less money forthcoming from sales under the right to buy. In 1992–3, a 'receipts holiday' allowed authorities to spend freely from accumulated receipts. Much of the money was not spent on housing. Wilcox (1996) argues that this revealed the extent to which capital receipts are seen as a corporate resource for local authorities rather than being tied explicitly to housing.

In practical terms, most local authorities keep a 'consolidated loans fund' or 'loans pool' for all their capital expenditure. In this system, all the loans that are raised (including stock issues, mortgage loans and PWLB loans) are pooled together and payments made from the pool as necessary to finance both housing and non-housing projects. The cost of all capital works made by the local authority (that is, both housing and non-housing) is then charged at an average rate of interest to the appropriate spending account (either the HRA or the general fund). Loans funds provide a flexible basis on which local authorities can both raise loans and make capital expenditures without the complex accounting and timetabling which would be required if each project were financed by raising and repaying a specific loan. It is an efficient way to manage capital expenditure, as the cheapest funds are used first.

78 *Housing Finance in the UK*

Trends in Capital Expenditure in England

Figure 4.2 shows the trend in capital expenditure from 1979–80 to 1996–7. It shows that total spending has been held at a consistently lower level in the 1990s than during the 1980s. It also shows how important capital receipts have been in funding works. In the latter half of the 1980s they consistently funded most of the total, while in the 1990s capital receipts funded about half of it. In 1996–97 the estimated outturn capital expenditure was £2.5 billion, of which local authorities 'self-financed' £1.16 billion – or 46 per cent of the total. Within the total 'new' credit provision, 55 per cent was for general capital expenditure, 24 per cent for capital grants and the remaining 20 per cent top-sliced for Estate Action and Estate Renewal Challenge Fund (and, therefore, concentrated in a few areas). (Funding urban regeneration is discussed in more detail in Chapter 9).

Figure 4.2   Local authority housing capital investment in England, 1979–80 to 1996–7

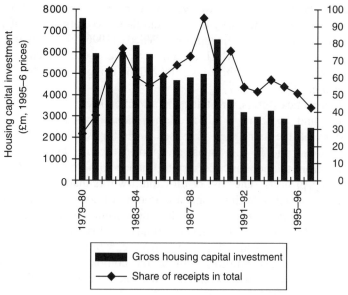

Source: Wilcox (1997a).

Malpass (1990) points out that it would be wrong to interpret the decline in investment in the 1980s in new council housing purely as a result of central government suppressing the aspirations of local authorities to build new housing. It should be remembered that many local authorities shared the political outlook and policy priorities of central government during the 1980s. Many took advantage of capital receipts to generate surpluses on their housing revenue accounts and to transfer money from their housing accounts into their general funds. Similarly in the 1990s, many English authorities were persuaded to take the Conservative government's preferred route of divesting themselves of the landlord role and transferring all their stock. This was, for many, a pragmatic move, as the financial 'rules of the game' are such that it can be possible to fund large-scale rehabilitation, and typically the housing authorities get much more financial autonomy following transfer (see Chapter 9).

Evaluating the System of Controlling Housing Capital Expenditure in England and Wales

The system introduced by the 1989 Act had four key aims:

(i)   to provide effective government influence over aggregate levels of local authority capital expenditure and borrowing;
(ii) to bring about a distribution of capital expenditure reflecting both national and local needs;
(iii) to promote the government's aim of reducing the size of the public sector
(iv) to provide a sound basis for local authorities to plan their capital programmes with confidence.

Have these aims been met? There can be no doubt that the rules on capital expenditure are much tighter, which should enable a more rational distribution of housing expenditure across the country, though moves towards competitive, performance-based allocations do not reflect needs at local level. However, the ground is shifting again. Partly as a result of the increased control, an increasing number of local authorities are escaping the traditional boundaries imposed on their housing activities by transferring their stock to housing associations or arms-length companies. For these bodies, the rules on expenditure are different again. So, the division between traditional social rented organisations and these 'new style' ones will come to constitute an increasingly important divide in patterns of investment and revenue-raising (these issues are discussed more fully in Chapter 9). Such changes directly contribute to the third aim above, namely that of decreasing the size of the public sector and transforming local authorities into 'enabling' rather than provider bodies.

Another important factor in determining expenditure outcomes will be the extent to which there is a continued success in transferring housing stock through the right to buy. Even though the use of receipts has been strongly controlled, they have been a very important source of finance for capital expenditure. However, as the remaining stock becomes increasingly concentrated in less desirable housing types and estates, and as remaining tenants are increasingly dominated by those who are economically disadvantaged (a process described as residualisation), it seems inevitable that receipts will continue to fall.

Local authorities have exploited the freedom of action in the system in a way not originally envisaged by the government. In particular, some authorities have increased rents by more than government guidelines to increase the extent to which they can pay for capital works out of revenue and to offset declining capital receipts income. In the Housing Act 1996, the government noted that rents in the sector should not be allowed to rise unchecked, particularly as a majority of such rises are met from the public purse – albeit from a different pocket – through Housing Benefit. Rent rises since 1996 are to be pegged to the general rate of inflation.

The recent trends in expenditure on local authority housing indicate that tight control is now effectively imposed. The question as to whether it is better targeted towards local needs has not yet been fully analysed. The concentration of resources on major urban regeneration schemes has allowed some central direction of effort to those problems deemed most significant by the government.

CURRENT EXPENDITURE IN ENGLAND AND WALES

The 1989 Act introduced parallel measures to control local authority current (or revenue) expenditure in England and Wales. Current expenditure (and income) had not typically been subject to direct control by the government. Instead, the current accounts of local authorities had been manipulated through the use of subsidy to the Housing Revenue Account to achieve changes in revenue expenditure or income. The key problem that arose under the financial regime operating throughout the 1980s was that the old subsidy regime ceased to deliver effective control. Huge discrepancies evolved through the 1980s between different authorities in England, and there was no consistency in determining which authorities received support in meeting the costs of running their housing service. This section first presents the current revenue regime and then evaluates the extent to which the new regime delivers more consistent and targeted subsidy.

Local authorities are obliged to set an HRA budget in January for the following financial year, and it must not be in deficit at the financial year end. The basic idea of the HRA is that it acts as the account covering all landlord activities. As described in Chapter 1, income from rents (and any subsidy) must cover the costs of being a landlord – repaying the loans for past developments and running the service. The most significant change implemented in 1990 was to introduce Housing Revenue Account Subsidy, which replaced the three previously separate elements of central government support to local authority housing, namely, Housing Subsidy (previously paid to balance the HRA), contributions from local authorities' general funds (which contain implicit subsidy because of the grants given to local authorities – see Chapter 3), and the rent rebate element (paid as Housing Benefit). At the same time, a tight 'ring-fence' was placed around the HRA, making any other transfer of money out of or into the account very strictly limited. In order to understand the significance of these changes it is important first to outline in more detail the components of the HRA.

Understanding the Housing Revenue Account

Table 4.1 presents the national housing revenue account. The items on this account are now described in more detail.

Expenditure

Supervision and Management
This item covers the staff and office costs required to allow the authority to act as a landlord. It is the smallest of the major

Table 4.1   Total HRA in England, 1997–8 (percentages)

Expenditure	
Supervision and management	16.6
Repairs	19.3
Revenue contribution to capital	4.4
Charges for capital	19.4
Gross rebates	38.5
Other	1.8
Income	
Gross rents from dwellings	61.7
Other rents from dwellings	1.6
Housing revenue account subsidy	33.4
Interest income	1.0
Other income	2.8

Source: Wilcox (1997a, table 65).

expenditure items. It has always included the general expenditure that effectively benefits all tenants, such as costs of administering waiting and transfer lists, as well as some items of more specific expenditure that benefit only some tenants (such as lifts, or the provision of caretakers in some blocks of flats). The tight ring-fence introduced in 1989 created an increased scrutiny on exactly what is being charged to the HRA and consequently borne by tenants. Particular issues have arisen in the context of care in the community, where the division between expenditure on a pure *housing* service and what might be considered to be a *care* element has proved controversial and difficult. This has raised fundamental issues about the role of housing and the appropriate way of paying for the support that some individuals need (see Chapter 9). The more general concern to control the growth in Housing Benefit expenditure also turns the spotlight on what tenants' rents cover. It is clearly unfair if tenants pay for services that effectively benefit everyone in a local authority area, for instance services for homeless people. It is now broadly established, for instance, that the HRA should not cover the costs of placing homeless people in temporary accommodation, but the costs of running the homelessness and advice services are typically split between the HRA and the general fund. It must be expected that the rules on charging items to the HRA will continue to be scrutinised.

Repairs and Maintenance

This item basically covers the running repairs and maintenance required to keep properties lettable. It does not include more major 'improvement' works, which are capital expenditure. There are notional allowances for the amount that local authorities are expected to spend on repairs and maintenance, calculated by the government as part of the evaluation of what rental levels ought to be in different authorities. However, these allowances are argued to be out of date, and again are under considerable scrutiny (discussed in more detail below).

Revenue Contribution to Capital

This is the amount of capital expenditure funded by revenue income, and is a relatively minor sum. It might cover preparatory or feasibility work, perhaps when a full scheme did not go ahead. As discussed above, some authorities have funded more major capital works from revenue in the past.

Charges for Capital

This is a relatively complex item. Its main element is loan repayment costs, that is, the interest cost and repayment of principal incurred on traditional loans taken out for new developments in the past. As discussed above, the system is designed to control all capital spending, not just borrowing, so this item also includes the costs incurred on any other devices used to undertake capital expenditure. It includes:

- transfer payments – to new landlords when councils dispose of their stock;
- interests on negative cash balances;
- charges on older credit arrangements;
- a notional cost for using internal funds;
- HRA set aside – local authorities must 'set aside' a sum to cover credit liabilities at a rate of 2 per cent of outstanding balances.

Gross Rebates

This is usually the biggest item in a local authority's HRA expenditure. It shows the amount spent on rent rebates through Housing Benefit. The majority of local authority tenants receive some Housing Benefit and, in aggregate, 64 per cent of all rental income was paid as Housing Benefit in 1997–8.

Other Transfers

As discussed above, the HRA is ring-fenced, which means that there are very tight restrictions on the flows allowable between the HRA and other funds of the local authority. Authorities are obliged by the DETR to transfer to another account the amount by which HRA subsidy is negative (the notional HRA surplus). Any authority that does not receive subsidy may transfer all or part of any credit on the HRA to another account. However, the HRA cannot receive contributions from the General Fund, and nor can authorities that receive subsidy transfer money out of the HRA into the general fund. Authorities also have to make provision for bad debts – mainly rent arrears that they will never recover.

Income

Gross Rents from Dwellings

Rents are the main source of income for authorities, over 60 per cent of which are paid by Housing Benefit. Local authorities have had the right to set rents as they wish since 1975. The current financial regime sets a guideline rent for each local authority. It is difficult for authorities to charge less than the guideline rent even if they wish to do so. In fact, the average increase was markedly higher than the guideline during the first half of the 1990s. The guideline rents apply to the overall average level of rents within an authority, and the authority remains free to decide how that total rent bill is to be apportioned between different houses within its stock. (Different rent schemes are discussed in Chapter 9.) Guideline rents generally exerted upward pressure on rent levels, particularly in the more expensive parts of the country. However, as authorities increasingly chose to increase rents above that level, the government became concerned about the impact of high rents on the Housing Benefit bill and sought to restrict rent rises above guideline from 1996–7. The Conservatives introduced a 'subsidy penalty' for authorities changing more than the guideline rent from 1996–7. As a result there has been a much wider compliance in keeping rent rises within the general rates of inflation. Labour expects that council rents should rise in real terms by 1 per cent in 1999–2000, and 2 per cent in the following two years.

Housing Revenue Account Subsidy
This subsidy was introduced in 1990 and is at the very heart of the control regime. It is calculated to bring a notional (that is, not the actual) HRA for each authority into balance. For each local authority, a notional account is prepared which consists of the following items:

Expenditure	*Income*
Management and maintenance	Rent
Charges for capital	Other reckonable Income
Rent rebates	
Other reckonable expenditure	

If this notional account is in deficit, the government pays an amount to make the account balance. If there is a notional surplus, the authority must transfer an amount equal to that sum into another fund. The notional account is calculated using the guideline rent for each authority; management and maintenance allowances set by government; and the allowable charges for capital based on existing commitments and any new capital allocation given. The implications of the subsidy mechanism are discussed in the following section.

Other Income
There are very few other items of income allowed into the HRA. There are some 'other rents' received, such as from garages or commercial promises. The item also includes any 'bad debts' that had been written off, but are subsequently recovered, or the repayment of mortgages granted to purchase HRA properties. Interest payments on outstanding balances are also received into the account.

Local authorities should not make a deficit on the HRA. Any deficit that *does* occur is carried over the following year.

The Operation and Impact of HRA Subsidy

The major change brought in by the 1989 Act is the inclusion of
rent rebate subsidies into the HRA. The cost of Housing Benefit is
explicitly counted as part of the subsidy to the HRA. Because all
authorities have a considerable proportion of their tenants in
receipt of Housing Benefit, this effectively means that almost all
local authorities receive some subsidy and are affected by the way
the regime operates. What this did was to give central government
leverage on rents and the operation of the HRA for the great
majority of authorities.

The key feature is that the 'housing subsidy' element – namely
that required to balance the housing account – can be negative. This
allows the basic 'landlord' operation of the housing stock effectively
to make a surplus, which is then offset against the total subsidy
granted to the HRA.

Basically:

Housing subsidy = Reckonable expenditure –

Reckonable income

If the estimated expenditure is *greater* than income, housing subsidy
is given to cover the difference. If, however, estimated expenditure
is *less* than income then there is a *negative* entitlement to housing
subsidy. Before the introduction of the 'subsidy penalty' (discussed
below), the final entitlement to housing revenue account subsidy
was calculated as:

Housing revenue account subsidy =

Housing subsidy + Actual Housing Benefit expenditure

So, authorities that get a positive entitlement to housing subsidy
receive all of that amount plus their expenditure on Housing
Benefit. Authorities that are assessed as making a surplus on their
notional HRA – and that therefore have a *negative* housing subsidy
entitlement – have that amount *subtracted* from their Housing
Benefit expenditure.

In bald terms, where a local authority has a surplus on its
notional HRA, giving rise to a negative entitlement to housing

subsidy, income in the HRA pays part of the Housing Benefit bill in that authority. As most income comes from rents, it is effectively those rents that are funding part of the Housing Benefit bill. Only a minority of such payments come directly from tenants that are paying their own rent (but even so, the very principle is arguably unfair). This is significant as, in 1997, only 27 councils in England still received a positive entitlement to housing subsidy. The estimate of total rent surpluses across all other local authorities was £1,146 million in 1996–7.

When the new revenue regime was introduced in 1990, it had three main aims:

- to bring all authorities into a consistent subsidy regime;
- to use the leverage provided by the subsidy regime to increase rents; and
- to control the growth of Housing Benefit.

The first aim can be said to have been met. Although there are flaws in the system and some inconsistencies based on historic differences in rents (particularly looking across regions), overall the system *does* successfully bring authorities into a more consistent regime. Incorporating Housing Benefit also brought virtually all authorities into this nationally consistent scheme.

The second aim has also been met. Rents in the local authority sector increased rapidly in the early 1990s, growing faster than general prices and incomes (see Figure 4.3).

Figure 4.3 shows:

- The very rapid increases in rents in the early 1980s – produced as an intention of the new subsidy regime introduced by Thatcher's first administration – gave way in the mid-1980s to much more moderate rises in average rents.
- The new regime of 1990 also produced rapid rent rises, as intended. Rent increases have been significantly faster than general price inflation through the 1990s.
- Through the 1980s, actual rents charged were less than those used to estimate subsidies – many local authorities explicitly sought to keep rents for their tenants lower.
- In the 1990s, rents became *higher* than subsidy guideline rents – in 1996 actual rents were 15 per cent higher than the guideline.

Figure 4.3   Local authority rents in England, 1980 to 1996

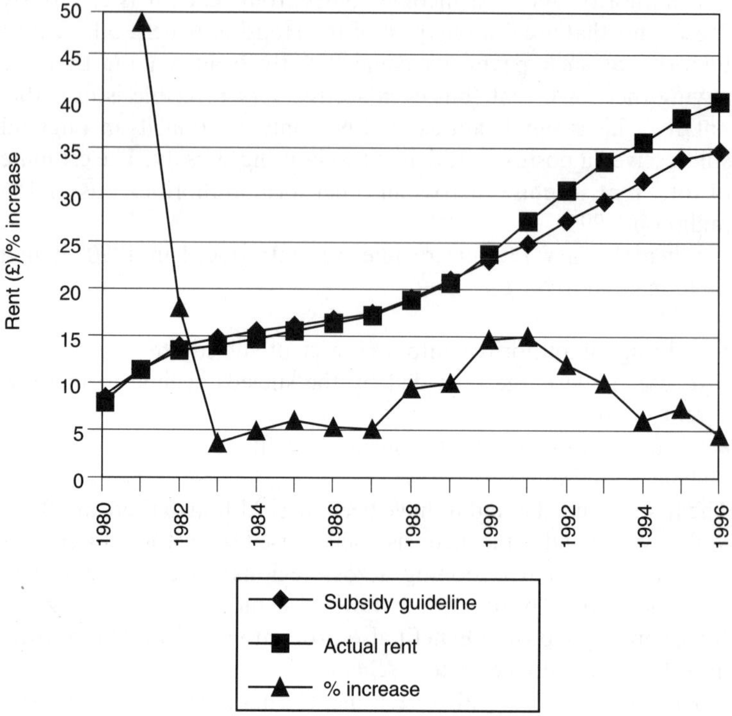

Source: Wilcox (1997, table 67).

Why Did Rents Increase Faster than the Guideline in the 1990s?

It is believed that many local authorities have traditionally sought to maintain low-rent policies. It could be seen as politically popular and fair to tenants who are typically on relatively modest incomes. However, the financial regime in the 1990s produced major incentives to set larger rent increases. A couple of examples will illustrate how this worked.

AN EXAMPLE: ANYTOWN: BASELINE POSITION

Anytown is an authority with negative housing subsidy entitlement. In 1995 this was −£600 per house, with the guideline rent at £1 800. Two thirds of its rent payments come from Housing Benefit.

Housing subsidy was calculated on the following notional account:

Reckonable income		*Reckonable expenditure*	
Gross Rents	1 800	Capital Charges	500
Other	500	Other	1 200
Total	2 300	Total	1 700

That is, Anytown is expected to receive £2 300 per house in income and spend £1 700 – giving a *negative* housing subsidy of −£600.

Consider what the consequences of setting rents either at or above the guideline rent are.

Example 1   Anytown sets guideline rents

If Anytown sets the average guideline rent of £1 800,

$$\begin{aligned} \text{HRA Subsidy} &= \text{Housing subsidy} + \\ &\quad \text{Housing Benefit expenditure} \\ &= -\pounds600 + (\text{two thirds} \times \pounds1800) \\ &= -\pounds600 + \pounds1200 \\ &= \pounds600 \end{aligned}$$

Its *actual* HRA is therefore

Actual Income	£	*Actual Expenditure*	£
Gross Rents	1800	Capital Charges	500
Other	500	Other	1200
HRA Subsidy	600	Housing Benefit	1200
Total	2900	Total	2900

Key points to note are that:

• capital charges are fixed at £500;
• other expenditure on the stock is as estimated by the government – at £1 200;
• HRA subsidy covers half of the cost of total Housing Benefit, with the remainder coming from within the HRA (that is, £600 average per house paid towards Housing Benefit by the tenants).

Example 2   Anytown sets higher than guideline rents

Suppose the council desperately want to undertake some refurbishment and upgrading work to the stock, so they set rents higher – at an average of £2 100. Their entitlement to housing subsidy remains the same –£600, (remember it is calculated on the *notional* HRA account). The calculation of HRA subsidy becomes:

$$\text{HRA subsidy} = \text{Housing subsidy} +$$
$$\text{Housing Benefit expenditure}$$
$$= -\,£600 + (\text{two thirds} \times £2100)$$
$$= -\,£600 + £1400$$
$$= £800$$

The final HRA account is therefore:

Actual Income	£	*Actual Expenditure*	£
Gross Rents	2100	Capital Charges	500
Other	500	Other	1500
HRA Subsidy	800	Housing Benefit	1400
Total	3400	Total	3400

The key things to notice when the authority in the examples sets rents *higher* than guidelines are:

- HRA subsidy is now higher (£800 compared with £600).
- Capital charges are as before – they are fixed because they are repaying previously incurred loans.
- The increase in rent (of £300) creates the direct opportunity to spend £300 per house *more* on the stock (£1500 compared with £1200).
- Two-thirds of this increase (that is, £200) is funded by the government, through Housing Benefit (as HRA subsidy has increased).
- HRA subsidy now actually covers a *bigger* proportion of total Housing Benefit expenditure (as the same amount – £600 per house on average – is paid towards Housing Benefit by the tenants).

It should be clear from this simple example that there were clear incentives to increase rents for the many councils that wanted to spend more on their housing stock than was allowed under the strict new capital regime or was estimated in their notional HRA. And because such a significant proportion of local authority income comes from Housing Benefit, much of the cost of this strategy was forced onto central government and the Housing Benefit bill. For many councils this was an attractive outcome, despite the increasing real burdens placed on those tenants who pay all or part of their rent from their own income.

The Conservative government quickly became more concerned about rents rising *too fast*, with the consequent rapid increase in Housing Benefit expenditure, than with continuing to try to force rents upwards. What has become clear, then, is that the last two aims of the 1990 financial regime (outlined above) are mutually incompatible. It is not possible to increase rents while at the same time containing the Housing Benefit bill – even though part of that bill is offset by 'surpluses' made by local authorities. This resulted in the Conservative move to control rents to the Guideline level. In 1996–7 a 'subsidy penalty' operated, whereby subsidy is payable only up to the guideline rents. The Labour government may remove this control, and it will be evident that this is a harsh regime for local authorities. When rent rises over the guideline are no longer covered from Housing Benefit, a rent rise of £1 will allow only 33p more spending on improving the service to tenants (as about two-thirds of rents is covered by Housing Benefit).

Moves to limit subsidy still further have also turned the spotlight sharply on the accuracy of local authorities' *notional* HRA accounts (because they will increasingly be forced to stick to the spending as described in that account). A particular problem arises with the expenditure notionally allowable for management and maintenance expenditure. Local authorities have long argued that the allowances are unrealistically low and in 1996–7, when the average allowance was £964, local authorities actually spent £203 on average *more* than this per house. Downward pressure on this spending will effectively be exerted because of the subsidy penalty, and this is likely to be very unpopular among local authorities and their tenants.

LOCAL AUTHORITY FINANCE: IN RETROSPECT AND PROSPECT

The two major recent reforms in local authority finance, the first at the beginning of the 1980s and the second a decade later have demonstrated some important lessons. First, there is no doubt that the financial regime can have a profound effect on outcomes in the local authority sector. Figure 4.3 above showed how successfully rent leverage had been applied. Table 4.2 compares the average English HRA at the beginning and end of the 1980s regime and in 1996–7. That direct comparisons are not straightforward with this later year is due to the significantly different treatment of rent rebate expenditure in the 1990s system shown in the 1997–8 account.

Despite the difficulties in comparison, some very clear trends emerge from this table:

- Income increasingly comes from rents – both as paid by tenants and as paid through the Housing Benefit system.
- The general 'bricks and mortar' housing subsidy of the early 1980s has been replaced by the targeted, mean-tested Housing Benefit. The overall reliance on government subsidy has not changed very much, however.

Table 4.2   Trends in the English HRA, 1980–1, 1989–90 and 1997–8 (percentages of total)

	1980–1	1989–90	1997–8
Expenditure			
Loan charges	61.6	46.6	19.4
Repairs and maintenance	19.6	28.4	19.3
Supervision and management	13.3	20.6	16.6
Other expenditures	5.5	3.8	6.2
Transfers to general funds	—	2.5	0.0
Gross rebates	n/a	n/a	38.5
Income			
Rents[a]	36.6	35.3	61.7
Exchequer subsidy: Housing	31.9	5.5	} 33.4
Exchequer subsidy: Rent rebates[a]	8.0	36.7	
Interest receipts from council house sales	4.4	14.1	1.0
Other income	6.5	3.9	2.8
General fund contribution	12.6	4.5	0.0

Note:
[a] Before the new regime, *gross* rental income was often shown together –
   that is, both rents direct from tenants and rents paid via Housing Benefit.
Source: Bucknall (1991, table 1); Wilcox (1997a).

- The major change on the expenditure side has been the fall in the proportion spent on loan/capital charges (which continues even after taking out the effects of gross rebates). This fall reflects the low levels of new capital expenditure in the local authority sector over the 1980s. Outstanding debts are falling and being eroded in real terms.

There remains a central dilemma at the heart of local authority finance. While general 'bricks and mortar' subsidies can be criticised as being too untargeted, their obvious benefit is that they keep rents low. This allows more people to pay at least part of their rent and does not create the same disincentives to take up low-paid work (this so-called poverty trap is discussed in detail in Chapter 8). The systematic shift towards higher rents has inevitably led to a higher Housing Benefit bill and there will continue to be real concerns about whether rents are really 'affordable' to those in low-paid work – as they are intended to be. There is no simple solution. However, it seems inevitable that there will continue to be downward pressure on public spending, which will mean that restraint in the Housing Benefit bill will remain an important policy target. At the same time, there are pressures to meet housing need and to squeeze the maximum housing output from a given level of public resources. This tends to exert some opposite pressure towards ensuring that tenants pay for a greater proportion of the costs. It also creates incentives to involve the private sector in development, which suggests that housing associations will remain favoured developers with a continued reason to transfer housing stock out of the local authority sector (see Chapters 5 and 9).

LOCAL AUTHORITY FINANCE IN SCOTLAND

The system for managing capital and revenue spending in Scotland was different in detail from that in England and Wales during the 1980s. However, these details caused significant differences in outcome, to the extent that Scotland experienced far fewer inconsistencies in funding local authority housing than England. So, there was less pressure to reform the system in 1989. In Scotland, therefore, there has been no reform to date, and the system operating bears more similarity to the English system of the 1980s than that of the 1990s. It is, therefore important to analyse the Scottish situation separately, although recognising that there may well be reform in due course.

Capital Expenditure in Scotland

In some respects, capital expenditure is allocated in a similar way to that in England. Councils are required to submit four-yearly housing plans that lay out proposals to undertake capital expenditure (except Glasgow, which must submit plans every two years). Net new money is allocated at the discretion of the Secretary of State for Scotland, whereby each local authority's gross permission to spend is made up of net new borrowing and an estimate of the amount of capital receipts that will be available to supplement that expenditure. Scottish local authorities have been allowed to spend *all* of their capital receipts until 1996–7 – which means there has been a lower accumulation of receipts in Scotland. From 1995 to August 1998, Scottish local authorities had to use half of any non-housing capital receipts to redeem debt – the same proportion as in England, but they were left free to spend the remainder. In

1997–8, local authorities spent £385 million on capital works (a considerably lower amount than in any year in the previous decade), and over 60 per cent of that spending was funded by capital receipts. From 1997–8, Scottish local authorities had to put 75 per cent of housing receipts to debt redemption. This will clearly restrict future spending, and no significant resource boost resulted from the Comprehensive Spending Review.

Current Expenditure in Scotland

The central revenue account is the Housing Revenue Account (HRA). Most of the main items are exactly as the English counterpart, with the exception that Housing Benefit expenditures on rent rebates do not feature in the calculation of subsidy. Table 4.3 presents the aggregate Scottish HRA for 1996–7.

The items on the HRA are largely self-explanatory, and, despite differences in presentation, of a proportional distribution similar to that in England. It is striking that almost all income now comes from rents on dwellings (rents from garages, and so on, are included as other income), although as in England most of it comes from Housing Benefit. As in the rest of the UK, there has been a clear policy drive to reduce the amount of general 'bricks and mortar' subsidy. The situation as shown in Table 4.3 contrasts sharply with that of the early 1980s, when (in 1980) just half of total income came from rents, 37 per cent from the general Housing Support Grant and 13 per cent from the General Fund (that is, local

Table 4.3 The Scottish HRA, 1996–7 (%)

Expenditure	
Loan charges	46.9
Supervision and management	14.8
Repairs	31.8
Other	6.5
Income	
Rent	91.5
Housing Support Grant	1.8
General Fund contributions	0
Other	6.7

Source: Derived from Wilcox (1997a, table 79); figures are as budgeted.

Figure 4.4   Local authority rents in Scotland, 1987–8 to 1995–6

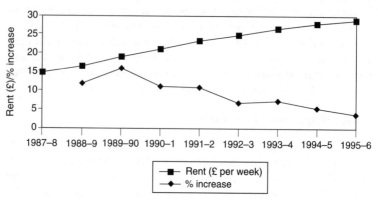

Source: Scottish Office (1998).

taxpayers). In Scotland as in England, the withdrawal of general housing subsidy has caused increasing rents and an increasing Housing Benefit bill. Figure 4.4 shows the recent pattern of average rents, and rent increases.

'Housing Support Grant' is the main central government support to local authority housing in Scotland. It is very different from HRA subsidy in England, though more similar to housing subsidy, which preceded it. It was introduced in 1979 and the first HSG allocations were made in 1979–80. It was intended to unify and simplify the previous, complicated, system of giving assistance to local authority housing. It is calculated by the Secretary of State and, like housing subsidy in England, it is a 'deficit grant' that is, it is calculated so that it makes up the shortfall of income over expenditure on a *notional* HRA for each authority. Initially it was to cover 85 per cent of the deficit, but since 1983–4 it has met 100 per cent of any notional deficit.

The basis of the calculation that is made for HSG is to compare each authority's assessed expenditure and its basic income, as follows:

- Assessed expenditure is actual loan charges, plus allowances for management and maintenance (with some adjustment for the number of high rise flats in the area);

- Basic income is calculated on a 'notional' rent (that is, the government evaluation of what rents ought to be), plus the allowed amount for the local contribution from general funds.

The level of grant is then simply determined by the difference between these two basic elements.

A consequence of the ability to use capital receipts is that income from interest on balances has never become a significant part of the income accruing to authorities in Scotland – just over 1 per cent on average. It is also interesting to note that very few authorities in Scotland have made surpluses on the HRA, and there are no significant transfers from the HRA to the general rates fund.

While an authority receives subsidy, the Secretary of State can exert considerable influence over rent levels. During the 1980s, this leverage was used to increase rents. As subsidy is withdrawn, authorities faced very little scope to avoid rent rises, because there are few other sources of income (and, since 1985, the Secretary of State has been able to determine what transfer from the general fund is allowable – almost always set at zero for most authorities). However, that leverage is lost as HSG is withdrawn. In 1996, very few authorities remained entitled to any HSG at all – a couple of major urban areas (including Glasgow) and some remote rural areas. Effectively, then, most areas in Scotland are free to set their own rents and manage their HRAs with no influence (or inter-ference?) from central government.

It will be interesting to see whether the subsidy system will be changed in line with changes in England and Wales. The different detail of the system did prevent the worst inconsistencies that emerged in England. In Scotland there was no 'cascade' of capital spending, and there was no widespread inconsistency in the alloca-tion of subsidy as apparent in England. Consequently, subsidy to Scottish HRAs was more consistent and better targeted than in England. However, the situation in 1996–7 is that there are major rent differentials between councils in Scotland that are largely arbitrary and due to historical accident. Rents are determined by the decisions of the councils, but also by when subsidy was finally withdrawn, and, perhaps most significantly, the historic pattern of debt holdings and repayments. There is, arguably, no rationale for differences that see rents of £22.34 in Midlothian and £40.57 in its neighbour Edinburgh (in 1996) – over 80 per cent more. While there may be arguments for reviewing the subsidy system in Scotland with a view to producing more coherent rents (as Wilcox, 1997b, argues), it is likely that any reconsideration will now wait for the Scottish Parliament.

CONCLUSION

The regime for local authority housing was arguably hostile through the 1980s. The hostility was underpinned by an ideological agenda that was seeking to diminish the scale and scope of the public sector allied to a frequent political hostility between a right-wing government and left-wing councils. In addition, there was a continued downward pressure on public spending that limited the scope of local authorities to incur expenditure without the agreement of central government. With the election of a Labour government in 1997, it might be expected that some of that ideological and political hostility would be eased. However, there is no sign of any retreat from strong constraint on public expenditure.

Local authorities are far from being residual landlords. They remain responsible for the largest rental sector and, particularly in urban areas, continue to house a very substantial proportion of the population. For these reasons it remains important to understand the arrangements for financing local authority housing. However, central tensions between limiting public expenditure, producing affordable rents, and meeting the needs of those who cannot look to the private market remain critical. In the current climate, the answer is seen to be increased private sector involvement in social rented housing and, with the existing conventions for public expenditure, this is likely to mean that organisations *other* than local authorities will be expected to undertake future housing developments.

FURTHER READING

Looking at the wider literature, rather more has been written about the English and Welsh systems than the Scottish system. Malpass and Murie (1999), Malpass (1990) and Merrett (1979) all give a longer historical perspective to the development of the present system of housing finance. Aughton and Malpass (1994) is useful for an introductory summary of the English position. An excellent summary of a lot of financial information, along with fairly brief commentaries, is to be found in Wilcox (1997a) and other editions.

QUESTIONS FOR DISCUSSION

1. Identify the main ways in which central government can control local authority housing capital spending in Britain. How effective are they?

2. Local authorities have been encouraged to become business-like in all their activities. What are the key similarities and differences of private-sector business and running council housing?

5 Financing Housing Associations

INTRODUCTION

This chapter provides a review of the means by which the voluntary housing sector in Britain is financed. The sector – of housing associations and co-operatives – plays a vital role in housing policy and in the housing finance system. The chapter

- explains the importance of voluntary provision to the British housing system;
- examines the allocation of public moneys to the voluntary sector;
- examines the main changes that have occurred to capital and revenue funding for housing associations and co-operatives;
- looks at how the landlord organisations in the sector set their rents.

Housing associations and co-operatives have been relatively favoured as providers and managers of social rented housing over the last fifteen years. (In the rest of this chapter, they are simply referred to as 'housing associations'; readers should note that in England, they are part of a wider category called registered social landlords (RSLs)). The Conservative governments of 1979–97 sought to restrict the role of local authorities to enabling the provision of social rented housing, and housing associations have taken an increasingly important role as developers of new housing and as managers of transferred housing. Although the sector is growing it remains small; in 1995 about 3.7 per cent of British households were housed by a housing association, compared with 2.1 per cent in 1981. The absolute number of houses in the sector almost doubled between 1989 and 1996. Despite being the smallest tenure, it is important because of its dominant role in new housing investment. This is shown in Figure 5.1, which indicates that across Great Britain, new investment by housing associations has for

Figure 5.1 Capital expenditure on housing and housing associations' share

(a) England and Wales, 1986–7 to 1996–7

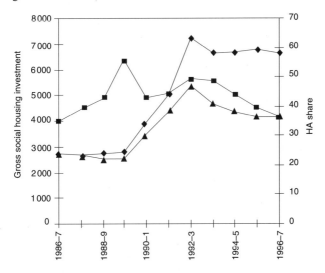

(b) Scotland, 1986–7 to 1996–7

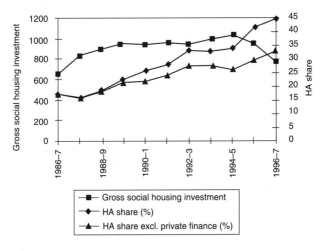

Notes
Volumes of investment in cash terms.
Figures for England and Wales include local authority HAG.
Source: Wilcox (1997a, tables 53a, 55).

much of the past decade been about forty per cent of all social housing investment. The charts also show that much new investment in social housing is directly *private* in origin, rather than being public-expenditure-financed.

HOUSING ASSOCIATIONS: THE CONTEXT

The Beginnings

Housing associations have grown over the last 150 years or so, from charitable housing trusts, often associated with industrial philanthropists, to the broad-based movement existing today. Throughout the first half of this century, they relied mainly on private and charitable funding for their work and later on loans from local authorities. The description of housing associations as 'voluntary' results from their management by voluntary, unpaid committees. Larger associations hire professional staff to manage their properties, to organise the development process and to oversee the financial arrangements. The staff remain accountable to the voluntary committee, which is elected by the members of the housing association and may consist of tenants, local professionals or other people committed to the work of the association. The description of housing associations as a 'movement' reflects their history. It also reflects their grouping into collective bodies – for England, the National Housing Federation (formerly NFHA, the National Federation of Housing Associations), in Scotland, the SFHA (Scottish Federation of Housing Associations), and in Wales, the WFHA (Welsh Federation of Housing Associations).

Housing associations occupy a middle ground between the public and private sector and they have at various times been treated as both in legislation. They do not distribute profits and they can be placed in the public sector as:

• they are largely reliant on public funding, and
• they are committed to providing social housing to meet housing need.

However, reform over the past twenty years or so has increased the importance of private funds and consequently the discipline of operating with private, profit-making enterprises.

The formation of the Housing Corporation in 1964 heralded the start of the modern housing association movement. The Housing Corporation had responsibilities for housing associations throughout Britain, with some limited decentralisation, including a regional Board for Scotland. In the early years, housing associations provided housing at moderate (cost-based) rents and also in co-ownership schemes, funded by Housing Corporation loans. The Housing Act 1974 was the catalyst for a major growth in housing association activity. There was all-party support for the new system of loans and grants established under the Act. The new system increased markedly the depth of the subsidy available to housing associations, enabling much lower rents than had been possible previously, and the total amount of money made available to the Housing Corporation increased greatly. The movement continued to provide general housing, with specialist housing associations providing housing (and sometimes associated support) for people with a wide range of special needs (such as frail older people, homeless people, those leaving prison and people with physical or mental disabilities). A further important area of growth was in area renewal through the rehabilitation of older houses. As a so-called 'third arm' of housing policy, housing associations were not truly in either the public or the private sector and so commanded cross-party support.

The 1980s

The Housing Act and Tenants' Rights, etc, (Scotland) Act 1980 marked an important landmark in housing association activity. In this act, low-cost home ownership (LCHO) schemes opened up new activities for housing associations. The most significant of these activities were:

- Shared ownership schemes – occupiers contribute a share of the equity of their house and pay a reduced rent for the remainder. (England and Wales also had a variant of this in leasehold schemes for the elderly, aimed particularly at sheltered housing.)
- Improvement-for-sale schemes – run-down houses are improved and sold on the open market, normally as part of a wider area renewal programme.

The Acts introduced the right to buy for tenants of non-chari-
table housing associations (in England and Wales) as well as for
local authority tenants, with similar discount entitlements (see
Chapter 6). Scottish housing associations implemented a voluntary
sales scheme until 1987. These measures resulted in widespread sales
of housing association houses, including a large transfer into
owner-occupation of the earlier co-ownership houses. The Housing
and Building Control Act 1985 extended the right to buy to give
discretionary home ownership discounts to tenants of charitable
housing associations (HOTCHA) (in England and Wales, but not in
Scotland). This allowed tenants of charitable housing associations
to take the monetary equivalent of a discount towards buying a
house in the ordinary private market. It was replaced across Britain
by the tenants' incentive scheme (TIS), which allowed associations
to give a transferable discount to their tenants to buy in the private
market. The main condition is that the move must contribute to the
alleviation of housing need.

The 1988 Acts and Beyond

The Housing Act 1988 and Housing (Scotland) Act 1988 reflected
the government's fears that the housing association movement was
becoming too much a part of the public sector. It embodied a desire
for a more private-sector-oriented independent rented sector, as
part of a broader policy aimed at increasing private sector involvement in rented housing. Disquiet was underpinned by the depth of
the subsidy available to housing associations and the consequent
cost to the public purse of housing association developments. The
1988 Acts set in place new financial arrangements, aiming to
encourage housing associations to bear a greater share of the risk
of their developments and to reduce direct subsidy levels. In order
to implement the new financial regime, changes were required in
tenancy conditions, to ensure that there was enough flexibility in
rent levels and to reduce the risk of losing properties through the
right to buy, in order to provide security for private sector investment. Consequently the secure tenancy that had been introduced in
the 1980 Acts for housing association tenants was superseded in the
1988 Housing Acts by assured tenancies. New housing association
tenants, whose tenancies commenced after January 1989, no longer
were given the right to buy, nor 'fair rents' previously accorded by

the Rent Act 1974. The 1988 Acts restructured the Housing Corporation, with separate organisations both in Wales (Tai Cymru – see Chapter 1) and in Scotland (Scottish Homes, formed from amalgamating the Housing Corporation in Scotland and the Scottish Special Housing Association (SSHA).

In England and Wales, a Housing Act was passed in 1996. Chapter 1 of this required registered housing associations to be registered as social landlords. Chapter 3 clarified that Social Housing Grant would be the principal public capital subsidy to their organisations – replacing Housing Association Grant.

In 1998, also for England and Wales only, government replaced TIS and shared ownership with a single package, Homebuy, which allowed RSLs to use recycled social housing grant to buy back part or all of occupiers' equity. This scheme of 'staircasing down' was generally welcomed.

Housing associations are a diverse group of organisations. Partly because of the transfers of what was previously local authority housing (see Chapter 9), associations have grown markedly in the last decade. In 1989, associations owned some 510 000 homes, but by 1996 this had increased to over 1 million. In England between 1988 and June 1998 no fewer than 70 large-scale voluntary transfers (LSVTs) had transferred over a quarter of a million local authority houses to housing associations. To date (June 1998), only one Scottish council has transferred all of its stock (Berwickshire, in 1996, prior to local government reorganisation), although this may well change following Labour's promotion of transfer under the auspices of New Housing Partnerships (see Chapter 9). Alongside growth, there has in parallel been a shift in the types of household occupying housing association property. Particularly noticeable is an increased proportion of new lettings to families with children, who, in England in 1997, accounted for 41 per cent of all lettings, compared with just 29 per cent in 1989 (National Federation of Housing Associations, 1989; National Housing Federation, 1998). Nearly half (45 per cent of lettings) were to people nominated by local authorities in 1997, again a proportion that has grown from 25 per cent in 1989.

There are many distinct types of housing associations: some operate within tightly defined geographical boundaries (and may be community-based) while others operate nationally or regionally; some provide housing for general needs, others only for particular special needs (see Chapter 9). Many have been created specially to manage ex-local authority stock (frequently using the same staff). Why, then, have governments preferred investment through this disparate group of organisations over local authorities?

- For the Conservative administrations of 1979–7, the non-monopolistic and 'non-political' housing association movement was preferable to larger and generally politically non-sympathetic local authorities.
- The diverse housing association movement has been able and willing to respond to the changes in the emphasis of housing policy through the last twenty-five years.
- The nature of the funding system gives the government very direct control over the development programmes in terms of location and house type.

Capital Funding for Housing Associations: The Approved Development Programme (ADP)

The ADP is agreed each year by the Secretary of State for the Environment (in England, in the Scottish and Welsh Offices for Scotland and Wales). It sets out for the Housing Corporation and Scottish Homes (and Tai Cymru/Welsh Housing Department) the overall planned spending for the following year. Housing Corporation borrowing is also planned in the ADP. (Note that Scottish Homes receives grant in aid and does not borrow.) Individual housing associations bid for funds for proposed developments and only registered housing associations can receive funds from the Housing Corporation or Scottish Homes (or Tai Cymru/Welsh Housing Department). In England, housing associations typically compete with each other for the opportunity to undertake a particular development. In Scotland, housing association bids for funds are judged in relation to their own development strategy, contained in their strategy and development funding plan. In 1996, amid some resistance and scepticism, Scottish Homes introduced a few competitive schemes in Scotland, testing out a pilot before wider implementation.

In England, a Housing Needs Index (HNI) is used to distribute the planned expenditure in the ADP between regions. This index attempts to measure the need for housing expenditure objectively,

based on indicators of housing condition and population characteristics. In Scotland, the distribution of money is in relation to the
overall Scottish investment strategy framed by Scottish Homes.
This strategy has no rigid formula, and is intended to have regard to
measures of need and housing shortage. Within English regions,
funding bids are judged in relation to overall investment priorities,
and the target levels of Social Housing Grant funding (see the next
section). Ultimately, the Housing Corporation and Scottish Homes
(and Tai Cymru/Welsh Housing Department) have considerable
discretion as to which associations are given development money.
Successful bidding is also increasingly tied to a good performance
rating in relation to a series of management and financial performance measures returned annually by associations and to the
regulators' monitoring reports. Regulation of the voluntary housing sector helps to ensure that public funds are being spent where
they should be – that there is an effective allocation of resources.
They also help to improve investors' confidence in the association.

Figure 5.2 shows the planned 1997–8 split of the ADP in England
and in Scotland. Recall from Figure 5.1 how the total volume of
spending on social housing, and how housing associations' share in
that total has changed over the past decade. There has also been
some redistribution within the total. The most notable element of
this has been the growth of the Low Cost Home Ownership
mechanisms – from a tenth to just under a quarter of the budget
in England between 1989–90 and 1997–98, and from about a
twentieth to a fifth of the Scottish budget in the same period.

CAPITAL FUNDING

Housing associations, like all landlords, have to cover the two key
elements of the cost of providing housing for rent – the capital cost
of providing the houses (either building new houses or rehabilitating older ones) and the current (or revenue) costs of repaying loans
and managing and maintaining those houses. In the social rented
sector, rents have traditionally been kept below the full cost by
subsidy. In the case of housing associations, the subsidy has been
paid largely on the capital costs of provision. There is a difference
between Scotland, England and Wales in the ways in which capital
funds are made available.

Figure 5.2   Approved development programmes for England and Scotland, 1997–8

(a) England: percentages of gross capital expenditure (£692m)

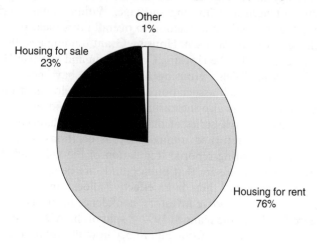

Source: Wilcox (1997a, table 60).

(b) Scotland: percentages of gross capital expenditure (£201m)

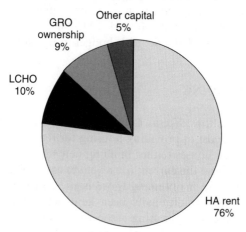

Source: Scottish Homes (1997).

- In Scotland, housing associations registered with Scottish Homes are eligible for Housing Association Grant. They bid for this subsidy on the basis of costs against agreed limits for certain types of development and an acceptable rent level. Funding can be made available on a streamlined basis, minimising the amount of Scottish Homes' scrutiny. This is applicable according to associations' performance and regulation ratings. The rest of the capital cost is raised in loan from a private institution, like a bank or building society.
- In England and Wales, housing associations are eligible for Social Housing Grant, principally on the basis of 'mixed funding'. This is essentially similar to Scotland, in that associations make bids on the basis of their costs for particular development types. However, there are two important distinctions:
  - South of the border, associations also bid on a competitive basis against a published target subsidy rate. They have access to a specialist organisation, the Housing Finance Corporation, enabling lending from the capital market. Like Scottish associations, those registered in England can also borrow direct from banks and building societies.
  - The distinctive position of the small associations is recognised. Many of these do not have a portfolio of properties or an asset base that would provide suitable security for a private investor. If they cannot raise private finance, they have to bid for 100 per cent SHG.

As well as the total volume of investment having changed (Figure 5.1), and there having been a shift in programme distribution (Figure 5.2), SHG and HAG rates have shown steady decline. The average figures are shown in Table 5.1, though it is important to remember that averages mask a lot of variation. Some of the most important sources of variation are:

- that grant rates, and capital costs, are higher for rehabilitation than new-build schemes;
- that grant rates tend to be higher for supported housing projects;
- that capital costs can be higher in remote rural areas and islands, which puts an upwards pressure on grant rates;
- that capital costs can be higher in London and the South-east than elsewhere in England.

Development Risk

The capital funding system exposes the housing association to risk of various types, which is intended to act as a spur to greater efficiency in the organisations.

(i)   Private Finance   Because private investors have to be convinced that the organisation can meet loan repayments, they must be confident in the financial viability of the organisation, its ability to survive unexpected financial blows, its systems for monitoring and controlling developments, and the structures of management and accountability within the organisation.

(ii) Financial Viability   An investor needs to be convinced of the financial viability of the particular scheme in which the loan is to be used. The assured tenancy conditions are an important element of reducing financial risks as it entails freedom in rent-setting and no right to buy. There is still some risk to associations' financial planning through tenancies being awarded to people who retain their rights, but as, typically, the private loans cover only a minority of the costs while being secured against the whole scheme, this risk is slight. Subsidy calculations are based on costed scheme development plans, approved by the Housing Corporation and Scottish Homes (and Tai Cymru/Welsh Housing Department) prior to development starting.

Table 5.1   **Average HAG and social housing grant rates, England and Scotland 1990–1 to 1997–8**

Financial year	England	Scotland
1990–1	75	82
1991–2	75	80
1992–3	72	80
1993–4	67	78
1994–5	62	75
1995–6	58	73
1996–7	56	65
1997–8	56	66

Source: Scottish Homes (various dates); Housing Corporation (various dates).

(iii) Development Process   The amount received in subsidy is fixed, so that any cost overruns have to be borne by the housing association. In these circumstances, the association can:

- Increase rent levels;
- use reserves to subsidise the scheme;
- sell assets;
- apply for supplementary grant and/or loans.

Only in exceptional circumstances will extra grant be forthcoming, and associations are expected to stay within the approved cost of the schemes in the great majority of cases. Even if there appears to be no alternative but to give extra grant, associations will receive no more than the original grant rate percentage of the overspend, so the association will have to find a part of the cost overrun in all cases.

Major Repairs Provision

The 1988 Acts withdrew HAG funding from major repairs. Housing associations must set aside a portion of their income for a sinking fund intended to cover the expected future need for major repairs. In England, guidelines state that this should be 0.8 per cent of current construction costs and fees for new build, or 1.0 per cent of reconstruction costs and fees per year for rehabilitation schemes (in Scotland it is 0.7 per cent for all schemes). These levels are reviewed and can be changed from time to time.

In Scotland, no schemes approved under the post-1988 HAG scheme are eligible for major repairs HAG funding. Schemes funded under the pre-1988 HAG regime retain eligibility for major repairs HAG, subject to surpluses accrued.

Raising Private Finance

Private institutions do not 'invest' in housing associations in the sense of buying and holding part of the equity in a scheme. In the first years after the 1988 Acts, most of the finance raised was simply borrowed directly from high street banks and building societies. However, this was a relatively expensive way to raise money, particularly in England where low-start finance was commonly sought. In England in 1994, banks and building societies still provided the greater part of private funds (at 36 and 35 per cent respectively) but capital markets provided 27 per cent, a share that had grown. Capital markets are an important source of long-term cheaper lending, but the amounts of money dealt with are large and most commonly have been accessed by groups of housing associations forming themselves into 'clubs', where members have to be acceptable to all in terms of size or asset base. A specialist organisation, The Housing Finance Corporation (THFC),was set up with the explicit aim of acting as an intermediary to raise funds for housing associations on the capital market. It is an unfunded organisation and has to lend money on as soon as it is raised. Only a very few of the largest associations have raised money on their own behalf.

In Scotland, the greater part by far of private finance has been raised from a narrow range of institutions – banks and building societies. THFC had no business in Scotland until March 1998.

It is a significant departure for social rented housing to attract money from large-scale, institutional investors, through the capital markets. Such investors prefer to hold tradeable assets, such as stocks and bonds, than to be directly tied to lending to a particular association or scheme. Since 1991, capital market funds have been issued as fixed-rate securities (bonds), with the security based on the assets of the association. There are different mechanisms to repay the debt, but most commonly the associations cover interest payments only, with a single repayment of capital when the bond matures. This means that associations must build up a fund to cover the final repayment. It appears there is scope for new instruments to be developed to meet demands from associations and as the institutions become more confident of this area of activity.

In England in particular, housing associations have had to bear some sharp criticisms recently relating to the quality of their new developments. The downward pressure on grant rates, cost levels and competitive bidding between associations is giving some reason to suppose that quality standards (previously seen to be somewhat higher than those of local authorities) are under threat. The Page Report contained an indictment of much new housing association development of the late 1980s and early 1990s. It suggested that quality was low and that pressure to build in larger estates at high densities was threatening the neighbourhood environment of the new developments. The fear was that housing associations were being pushed down a road whose destination is sadly familiar from the local authority experience – the creation of poor, densely packed communities containing high proportions of children, whose housing may well become the difficult-to-let and difficult-to-live-in estates of the future (Page, 1993). Using data for 1996, research by Pawson and Kearns (1998) showed that the problem of difficult-to-let housing was as pervasive in the housing association as in the council sector. In the voluntary sector, however, it was not always let to the most severely disadvantaged people. Karn and Sheridan (1994) reported evidence for the early 1990s that space standards were being severely compromised. The fact that such concerns have not emerged so strongly in the higher grant regime in Scotland lends support to suggestions that quality problems are caused by working within tight financial limits.

REVENUE FUNDING

The main elements of revenue income and expenditure of a housing association are summarised in the Property Revenue Account, which is equivalent to a local authority's Housing Revenue Account. It should be clear that housing association subsidies work basically on the capital side of the equation. For new schemes it is part of the bidding process that associations show that, after taking account of the grant requested, the proposed scheme is financially viable. Effectively, they must set rents at such a level that they cover:

- the costs of repaying private or public loan;
- the provision for major repairs;
- the Management and maintenance costs in running the scheme;
- the provision for the possibility that some tenancies are taken up by those who have preserved rights to fair rent and that some such tenants take up the right to buy;
- the risk of voids, bad debts and so on.

The freedom that associations gained to set their own rents enshrined in the 1988 Housing Acts is vital in making scheme

finances viable. This freedom replaces the previous arrangement by
which housing association rents were set as 'fair' rents by the rent
officer. Tenants from before 1989 retain their right to have such a
determination. Rents are supposed to be set with regard to 'affordability', a concept discussed later in the chapter.

However, associations face more controls on the revenue side
than this description would suggest. As well as more or less complex
arrangements for schemes originally provided for under the old
funding system, there are further controls to ensure that there is no
'profit' derived from public subsidy.

The Rent Surplus Fund

The rent surplus fund (RSF) replaces what was formerly known as
the Grant Redemption Fund (GRF). The need for such a fund is
relatively simple to understand. Housing associations receive their
subsidy as a capital lump sum at the time of first development.
Typically, over time, inflation will erode the real value of their debt
(whether to a private or a public agency). So, the real size of their
loan repayment will also become less (like an ordinary mortgage).
In some sense, therefore, the initial subsidy becomes 'too much', as
keeping rents at the same real level would enable an increasing loan
to be repaid. Government is anxious that this money should not be
allowed to act as a cushion for inefficient practices within housing
associations, that any potential surplus should not be used to keep
rents 'artificially' low. Therefore it requires that these accumulating
surpluses should be identified within housing association accounts.

A major consequence of this policy is that the government has to
become involved in the details of housing association expenditures
on the revenue side of the equation. To judge whether diminishing
real debt is being used to keep rents 'too low', the government does
not simply need to know about rent levels, but also has to take a
view as to whether expenditure on management and maintenance
by the association is 'too much' or whether the provision for
unanticipated losses is 'too much'. All such aspects of housing
association activity and accounts are therefore open to scrutiny,
and the Housing Corporation and Scottish Homes (and Tai Cymru/
Welsh Housing Department) must set acceptable levels of expenditure on these items.

The 'surplus' is calculated at gross rental income minus:

- four per cent allowance for voids and bad debts;
- actual loan charges;
- management and maintenance (M & M) allowances;
- service charges;
- rent loss from tenants entitled to fair rents;
- miscellaneous items.

Any schemes funded with low-start finance are deemed to be unlikely to accumulate surpluses, and such schemes will not fall within the RSF arrangements. This provides some incentive to seek low-start finance, but, as was noted above, there is relatively little use of low start finance among associations.

Management and Maintenance Allowances

These define what the Housing Corporation and Scottish Homes (and Tai Cymru/Welsh Housing Department) view as reasonable management and maintenance costs. Associations must also be able to plan, knowing their own likely position with respect to the RSF. Any movement in M & M allowances has a direct impact on the amount of money available to associations to provide housing management services. Reduced allowances provide a further downward impetus to HAG levels, for at any given rent level a greater amount is available to repay a private loan, after taking account of allowed costs if allowed costs are lower. Both the Housing Corporation and Scottish Homes have committed themselves to reviews of their allowance systems.

Revenue Deficit Grant (RDG) and Seed-Corning

Revenue Deficit Grant is paid only in very exceptional circumstances for a scheme making a loss. It is not paid where an association has reserves that could be used to cover the deficit. Small, new associations whose costs outweigh their income are eligible for a small up-front grant called 'seed-corning' to help with the initial set-up costs of associations.

RENT SETTING

It will be clear that a vital element in determining the grant levels and financial position of an association is the rental income that it receives. A central concept in the guidance that associations have been given is that rents should be *affordable* to those in work. For instance, the circular HCiS 3/89 says:

> 'The introduction of the new funding procedures should not be taken as a signal to the movement that it should move away from its traditional purposes . . . the government intends that associations will continue to be able to provide for their existing client groups: and that grants will be set at levels which will enable associations to set rents at levels which are affordable to those who can be expected to look to the movement for their housing requirements.'

Government has not, however, given any explicit definition of what it believes affordability to mean, and there has been debate around possible interpretations. For much of the late 1980s and early 1990s, as Figure 5.3 shows, housing association rents increased, putting strain on the Housing Benefit system (see Chapter 8). The last Conservative administration recognised the difficulties that high rents caused, and sought to apply a break to increases in its 1996 Housing Act (in England and Wales only).

In the absence of government dictum, the housing association federations have used CORE and SCORE data (systems by which new tenants are monitored) to assess the composition of the tenure's consumers, and particularly their relative poverty. They have offered guidance to their members on what constitutes an affordable rent:

- In England – 'if the majority of working households taking up new tenancies are not caught in the poverty trap (because of dependency on Housing Benefit) or paying more than 25 per cent of their net income in rent' (National Federation of Housing Associations, 1994).
- In Scotland – for households with at least one member in work that rent should take no more than 25 per cent of household income and leave a household with at least 140 per cent of the appropriate Income Support level of income (Scottish Federation of Housing Associations, 1993).

Figure 5.3 Housing association rents in Scotland and England, 1981 to 1996

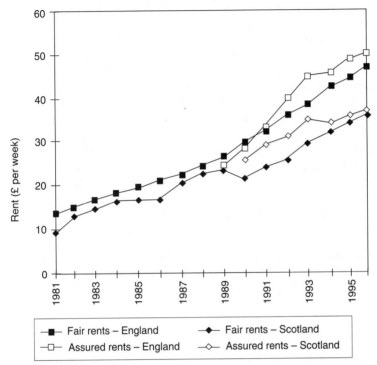

Source: Wilcox (1997a, tables 67 and 81).

So, both countries refer to households in work and use a composite measure of affordability. The reference to working households is needed because those households with no-one in work are fully protected from rent levels and rent changes by Housing Benefit. The affordability test combines a ratio measure with a measure of residual income. This allows for both a straightforward check on the average position, and for examination across the range of household circumstances. The residual measure also allows a check on whether people have enough to live on, after having paid their rent.

Using its measure, the National Housing Federation estimated that 68 per cent of new lets to working households in England in the first quarter of 1997 were unaffordable – 18 per cent above the target threshold (National Housing Federation, 1997). In Scotland, 32 per cent of new lets to working households in 1996–7 failed one or both of the affordability tests (Scottish Federation of Housing Associations, 1997). Analysis confirms that a great majority of new tenants are relatively poor. In both Scotland and England, only one household in four had its head in employment (full- or part-time). Over half of the households had no income apart from state benefits. Weekly incomes in 1996–7 averaged £120 net in England, £97 in Scotland (with incomes for working households about 50 per cent higher). Average rents for new lets were £48 per week in England, £32 per week in Scotland.

Public funding to housing associations is made on the basis of associations having considered rent levels in their development bids. In Scotland, registered associations are expected to comply with their approved rent policy. The rent policy sets out how the association plans its income according to the criteria of:

- viability – to ensure clear revenue covers costs;
- comparability – to ensure that rent levels are inline with other local social housing landlords;
- affordability.

Rent policies are less well developed in England.

In summary, a housing association seeking public finance for development has to:

- ensure that the type of development proposals fits with its strategy and the funder's programme;
- ensure that it can demonstrate a need for the type of development proposed;
- ensure that its development can be made to acceptable limits;
- ensure that it can raise a private loan for a negotiated proportion of development costs;
- ensure that it has a satisfactory system for managing the development programme itself, and particularly scheme costs;
- ensure that the rent levels charged fit with its rent policy.

HOUSING ASSOCIATION ACCOUNTS

Any organisation may call itself a housing association (although there is a legal definition), but it must be registered with the Housing Corporation, Scottish Homes, or Tai Cymru/Welsh Housing Department, before it is eligible to receive the public funding described above. Associations may also be eligible to be charities. Until recently, registered housing associations have also been able to claim tax relief (relief of corporation tax and income tax; for charitable housing associations this relief is full). With these rights come an obligation to keep accounts as required by the regulator and to maintain the appropriate standards of auditing and accounting procedures. Following the 1994 Statement of Recommended Practice for Accounting, the requirements for housing association accounts are similar in a style to those required from public companies. This reflects their close relationship with private financial institutions and the management of the risk and reserves that they carry.

CONCLUSIONS

As organisations like many others, housing associations are under constant change. Their roles are diversifying significantly – and they have made major contributions to the provision of housing required for care in the community needs and to bringing private finance into social housing by taking over stock from local authorities (see Chapter 9).

The housing association finance system described in this chapter is one that clearly has many government controls, much more so than might be expected from a regime that was ostensibly designed to reduce the public-sector – bureaucratic ethos, in favour of creating a freer, more entrepreneurial, risk-taking sector. A key issue for the future will be the level of investment that can be secured from the private sector. If such investment saves government money and increases the investment in housing overall then it is surely to be welcomed. Conversely, however, to the extent that associations are simply providing some private institutions with profit-making business, which ultimately comes in large part through the benefit system, the advantages are less obvious.

As the scale of the voluntary housing sector has increased, so too have the pressures on it to demonstrate its accountability. This has been targeted on standards of member behaviour (the Nolan Committee and Hancock Panel of the early 1990s) and on financial prudence. Both transparency of accounting practice and openness to scrutiny can be expected to increase over the next few years.

Although it has been favoured in public funding, the voluntary sector has not escaped restraint. Budget tightening has heightened the quest for greater operational efficiency, and commentators within and without the movement have questioned whether a very large number of small organisations is a sustainable way of managing provision and development. The likelihood is that mergers and the formation of group structures of association will consolidate the sector. Finally, associations seem likely to continue to diversify their activities beyond the strict bounds of housing provision. For community-based organisations, the renewed emphasis on social and physical regeneration may mark a welcome return to roots, and, for others, the agenda of what has been called 'Housing Plus' calls for a new direction, new skills and new programmes.

FURTHER READING

Housing associations are markedly less well documented than local authorities. Full details of the financial regime and the requirements placed on housing associations can be found in Chartered Institute of Public Finance and Accountancy (1994), which although basically a guide to the English regulations provides much that is broadly applicable in Scotland. Hills (1991) contains useful, detailed analysis of the operation of the housing association finance system. The book by Cope (1990) although almost exclusively English in detail, can be recommended for further information on the housing association movement generally, but is now dated in relation to policy details. Malpass (1997) usefully updates some elements. Dealing well with housing associations and private finance are the publications by Saw *et al.* (1996) and by Chaplin *et al.* (1996).

The CORE and SCORE systems produce regular updates on the characteristics of the new tenants in the stock. A detailed understanding also requires keeping up with recent research material and the housing press, notably the journal *Social Housing*. Also of interest are the outputs from the research programmes of the Housing Corporation and Scottish Homes.

QUESTIONS FOR DISCUSSION

1. What aspects of their finances make housing associations unlike other small businesses?
2. Assess the extent to which government checks on housing association finances allow it to ensure that public money is being spent wisely.
3. What are the factors that housing associations should take into account in setting their rents?

6 Mortgage Finance, Housing and the Economy

INTRODUCTION

Chapter 2 looked at the underlying principles of the economics of the housing market. It indicated that there has been considerable instability in the UK owner-occupied market. In this chapter, we explore two dimensions of this instability. First, we look at the market for mortgage finance, which underwent revolutionary deregulation in the 1980s. This was an important contributory to the 1980s boom and bust. The second, related theme concerns the relationship between owner-occupied housing and the UK economy. Chapter 2 indicated that rising incomes and demographic change affect the housing market. In the 1980s and 1990s, a number of links between housing and the economy became increasingly apparent:

- Housing market wealth affects total spending and inflation.
- Rising housing prices affect labour market mobility and wage inflation.
- Falling prices and sales deepen and lengthen recession.

The fundamental policy question addressed in this chapter is whether the most recent cycle has been the result of structural change (mortgage deregulation) and policy mistakes, or whether the process is cyclical and future instability is inevitable.

THE UK HOUSING MARKET AND MORTGAGE FINANCE: EVIDENCE

The UK Housing Market

The key features of the UK owner-occupied housing market in the period since 1970 have been:

- long-term growth, in terms of overall market size and increased turnover;
- house price growth after inflation (that is, real terms) of by more than 1 per cent per annum;
- real and nominal house price instability, evident in three house price cycles since 1969;
- the rapid growth in.the importance of housing equity as a form of wealth; and,
- in the early 1990s, the most severe downturn in house prices and transactions since the war.

Figure 6.1 illustrates the two most recent cycles in real house prices. The diagram compares UK nominal house prices with general price inflation (defined as the GDP deflator). When analysts talk about 'real' terms they are subtracting the effects of inflation from the nominal (or cash) change in prices. This is always important in an inflationary world. Mortgages are set in nominal terms and this

Figure 6.1   House price and general inflation, 1974 to 1996

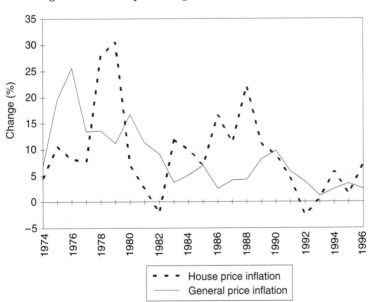

Source: Wilcox (1997a).

means that, as time goes on, the real cost of the mortgage repayment falls as incomes rise (approximately) with inflation. This
benefit of inflation also means, however, that housing costs the
most at the initial point of purchase (known as front-end loading).

Let's look at some possible linkages between house prices and
inflation:

- House prices may simply follow the general rate of inflation.
  Home owners may feel better off, because their asset (their home)
  has gone up in value. But so has everything else. This is called
  money illusion.
- Alternatively, house prices may generally go up faster than the
  rate of inflation. We say that the relative price of housing
  increases. Here home owners may be better off.

  - Owners will get a real benefit if they can use some of the
    increased value, to buy other goods and services. They would
    do this by taking out a loan, or selling their house. However, if
    they sold, they would probably have to buy a new home. And
    they would have to pay more as house prices rose.
  - Other people who might find things difficult are people looking
    to buy their first home. Some people's budgets make them
    what we call marginal home owners – people who can just
    afford entry into owner-occupation. This becomes harder as
    house prices rise faster than general inflation.

What these examples show is that inflation and rising house prices
have different effects on different households. They can be good,
they can be bad. It depends on where a particular household is in
the market. It is a mistake to say price rises are **always** good or bad.

We all know that house prices have increased massively in cash
terms. Yet more people find housing affordable. This is because
incomes have also been rising in that period. To see how much more
expensive houses really are, we have to take away the effect of
general inflation, which increases all prices, social security benefits
and (usually) incomes via wage increases. When house price inflation is greater than general inflation, *real* house prices are rising.
When house prices are rising less quickly than general prices, the
real value of housing is falling. Looking at the Figure 6.1, we can
see periods where house price increases have exceeded those in

general prices (for example, 1978–80) and vice versa (for instance, after 1990). Taking the period as a whole, real house prices have risen considerably, averaging more than one per cent real gain per annum (see Figure 6.2). However, within any one cycle (that is, a period from peak to trough in price change), there has been considerable variability. Not only have households experienced falling *real* house prices, but in the downswing after 1990 house prices have actually fallen in nominal as well as real terms. People always thought that house ownership was a good investment, a reliable hedge against inflation. This was an important reason for the growth in owner-occupation, but it disappeared in the early 1990s. Many households (estimated to be between 1 and 2 million at its height) found at that time that the value of their property fell below the value of the loan secured on it by mortgage lenders (so-called negative equity).

Figure 6.2   House price, earnings and retail price indices (1993 = 100), Q1s 1986 to 1997

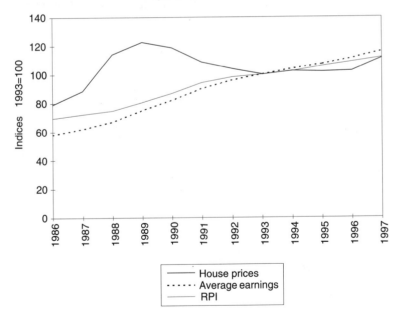

Note: House prices are here drawn from the Nationwide Building Society series.

Figure 6.2 shows the relationship over time between house prices, average earnings and the general level of inflation. Part of the house price increase may actually reflect quality improvements rather than simply price effects. In other words, people may be consuming more or better quality housing and therefore paying more for it, rather than, for example, general house prices rising. For many households, especially those with large mortgages, the downturn in the housing market was disastrous. Where before, if a borrower got into difficulty, they could sell up, this option was ruled out by the state of the market of the early 1990s. Falling prices meant that potential sellers could not achieve the minimum price required to pay off accumulated debts and meet the costs of moving and a down-payment on a new home. Figure 6.3 shows the pattern of housing transactions between 1980 and 1996. Transactions peaked with prices, but by 1993 had fallen to only 55 per cent of the 1988 level. This had severe repercussions for the housing exchange industry, such as lenders, surveyors, estate agents, removers and so on, who depend on turnover for incomes. It had knock-on consequences for furniture sellers, decorators and the like, whose

Figure 6.3   Property transactions (England and Wales) and mortgage advances, UK, 1980 to 1996

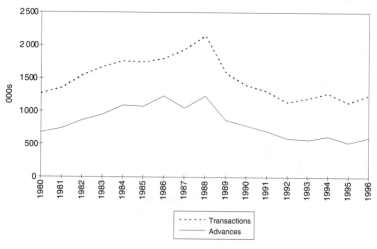

Source: Wilcox (1997a, table 46).

trade is often linked to house purchase. For the first time since records began, transactions fell for four years in a row from 1990 to 1993. They have since levelled out, and in 1997 with real house price inflation re-emerging, there were signs of another house price boom.

Figure 6.4 shows:

- the rapid growth in repossessions and serious mortgage arrears from 1981 to 1993 (and subsequent tailing off thereafter);
- how repossessions (the lender taking legal possession of the home because of non-payment of debt) peaked in 1991 at more than 75 000 but remained at more than twice the previous cyclical peak through the early 1990s;
- that both 6 to 12 month arrears and longer-term arrears have fallen back after peaking in 1993.

The market downturn introduced the term 'negative equity' into common usage. When mortgage debt is more than the present value

Figure 6.4   Mortgage arrears and repossessions, UK, 1981 to 1996

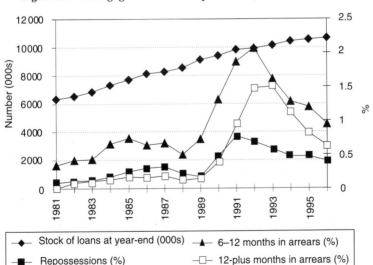

Source: Wilcox (1997a, table 46).

of the property it is difficult to move house, and borrowers may also have to find ways of making additional debt repayments in the short term. All of those who experience house price falls may feel their wealth being eroded and a loss of confidence in their economic security. This arguably depresses consumer spending (the 'feel bad' factor). Estimates suggested that in the summer of 1995 between half a million and two million households had negative equity (see Wilcox, 1997a). Subsequent increases in house prices have virtually removed the most significant problems of negative equity. House price increases also change the housing market psychology of potential movers by giving them confidence about the future, encouraging more transactions.

So far, the focus has been on the UK housing market. However, to look at that picture on its own is not enough. Within the UK, there are considerable variations both in house prices and in the rates at which they change. Table 6.1 indicates the extent of this variation. We can see a 'ripple effect' in regional house prices, where southern prices rise first and furthest, followed later by more northern regions. The downturn has followed a similar pattern, with price falls occurring first and most substantially in the south (while prices continued to rise in the north).

Table 6.1   House price levels across the UK, 1980 to 1996 (£)

Country/Area	1980	1985	1990	1996
North	17710	22786	43665	52184
Yorkshire and Humberside	17689	23338	47231	57368
East Midlands	18928	25539	52620	59755
East Anglia	22808	31661	61427	62790
Greater London	30968	44301	83821	94575
South East (excluding Greater London)	29832	40487	80525	86308
South West	25293	32948	65378	68408
West Midlands	21663	25855	54694	64606
North West	20092	25126	50005	58207
Scotland	21754	26941	41744	57476
Wales	19363	25005	46464	55328
Northern Ireland	23656	23012	31849	47980
UK	23596	31103	59785	70537

Source: Wilcox (1997a, table 42a).

The Mortgage Market

Figure 6.5 shows the average advance for first-time buyers, all buyers and former owner-occupiers buying new homes from 1981 to 1996 (Q3). In 1996, first-time buyers borrowed 89 per cent of the purchase price on average, while former owners borrowed less than 65 per cent. There is some evidence of a cyclical trend in borrowing ratios, which become higher as prices accelerate. Among former buyers in particular, there appears to have been a significant upward shift in the proportion taken. Although income data are less reliable, average advance-to-income ratios also show a structural change since 1980. First-time buyers in 1980 had an average ratio of 1.67 and this rose to a peak of 2.21 in 1991 before falling back slightly. In 1996, the figure stood at 2.23. Former owner-occupiers had comparable figures of 1.54 in 1980, peaking at 2.12 in 1989 and subsequently falling back to 1.97 by 1996 (Council for Mortgage Lenders, 1994, tables 7 and 8; 1997, tables 17 and 18).

Figure 6.6 shows the relative proportion of lending by lender types in the 1990s. This is dominated by building societies.

Figure 6.5   Advance-to-price ratios, 1981 to 1996

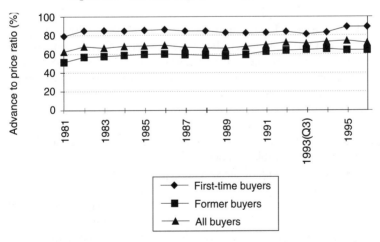

Note: Discontinuity in data presentation between 1993 and 1994.
Source: Council for Mortgage Lenders (1994, tables 6, 7 and 8; 1997 tables 16, 17 and 18).

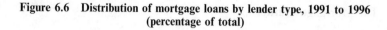

**Figure 6.6   Distribution of mortgage loans by lender type, 1991 to 1996
(percentage of total)**

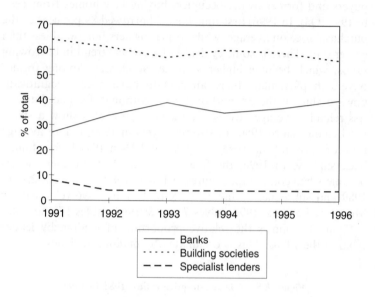

Until the early 1980s, building societies completely dominated the
mortgage market, but then they began to face effective competition
from the banks. In the housing market recession (post-1988) bank
lending grew again, particularly at the bottom end of the market.
There were five main reasons for the entry of the banks into the
mortgage market:

- First, the growth of home ownership made mortgage lending a
  large and profitable business.
- Second, the ending of the special deposits 'corset' in 1980 allowed
  banks more freedom to lend.
- Third, the collapse of the building societies' mortgage rate cartel
  in the early to mid-1980s encouraged the banking sector to enter
  the mortgage market as it enabled direct price competition.
- Fourth, the ending of the societies' tax advantages for savers also
  helped banks compete in the savings market and thus increase the
  flow of funds to lend to mortgagors (borrowers).

- Lastly, the Building Societies Act 1986, the Financial Services Act 1986, technological change and the deregulation of financial institutions (the 'big bang' in the City) changed the banking, mortgage and savings markets beyond recognition, making all financial activities more subject to open competition.

If one examines the distribution of mortgage lending, a number of points emerge:

- Public sector loans have declined and become insignificant.
- There was a large-scale but essentially temporary market entry by specialist lenders in 1987, which has since receded.
- The major market share battle has been between banks and the previously dominant building societies. Deregulation brought the banks in on a massive scale in 1981 and 1982 (24 per cent of the total in 1981 and 36 per cent in 1982). They had another successful period in 1987 and 1988, before the societies re-established their dominance. In the downturn, the banks' market share has again grown. As a result of society caution and the consequent decline in society advances, the banks stepped in to fill the gap, particularly for more marginal owners. To some extent, this development reversed their previous tendency to aim further upmarket.

Mortgage lenders operate by borrowing money themselves to advance to house buyers. So, lenders require sources of funds, which they must pay for at the market rate. They make profits by charging rates on their mortgages that are higher than those they pay out to savers or other lenders. This 'margin' has been whittled away by competition. Building society net funds come from two major sources: individual savers and wholesale funding (borrowed money). At present (1998), gross receipts can only have a maximum of 50 per cent funded from wholesale sources. Societies face fierce competition for savings from banks, from national savings, pension and insurance companies and privatisation share issues. They are also affected by tax changes such as the introduction of VAT on fuel (which change household outgoings). To guarantee having enough money to fund mortgages, they require access to alternative sources of funding. However, lending regulators have concerns about prudence and set limits to societies' exposure to wholesale money.

Table 6.2 Building societies, 1910–95

Year	No. of societies	Shareholders (000s)	Depositors (000s)	Borrowers (000s)	Mortgage balances (£m)	Total assets (£m)	Advances in year (000s)
1910	1 723	626			60	76	
1920	1 271	748			69	87	
1930	1 026	1 449	428	720	316	371	159
1940	952	2 088	771	1 503	678	756	43
1950	819	2 256	654	1 508	1 060	1 256	302
1960	726	3 910	571	2 349	2 647	3 166	387
1970	481	10 265	618	3 655	8 752	10 819	624
1980	273	30 636	915	5 383	42 437	53 793	936
1990	117	36 948	4 299	6 998	175 745	216 848	1 397
1995	94	38 998	6 307	7 178	233 358	299 921	1 047

Source: Council for Mortgage Lenders (1994, table 24; 1997, tables 31 and 32).

For most of the modern period, building societies have dominated mortgage finance (until the demutualisation that followed
deregulation – discussed below). Table 6.2 summarises the twentieth-century development of the building society movement. A
number of trends stand out:

- The number of societies has been dramatically reduced by merger
  and take-over,
- As a consequence, assets (and liabilities) have become more and
  more concentrated in the hands of less than ten major lenders. In
  1910 there were more than 1700 societies; today, the number has
  fallen to fewer than 100 much larger institutions.
- The numbers of depositors and shareholders have grown rapidly.
- The number of loans advanced in each year has grown seven and
  a half times, from 159 000 in 1930 to more than a million in 1995.

We saw earlier that there is a strong regional dimension to the
UK housing market, and this carries over to the mortgage market.
Statistics for building society lending in the third quarter of 1996
suggest that the highest shares of loans to first-time buyers, at 52 to
53 per cent, are in the lower house price regions of England
(Yorkshire and Humberside, the North West) and Northern Ireland. The percentage of advance to value is relatively stable across
regions (70 to 77 per cent) with Northern Ireland having the highest
percentage (77) and East Anglia and the South East the lowest (70).
More than a third of all loans were made in the South East. The
other striking variation is in the average income of borrowers.
Remember that income averages are affected not only by wage
differentials but also by age and the regional proportion of first-
time buyers. Incomes in London and the South East are significantly above those in the rest of the UK, and, indeed, those are the
only regions where incomes are above the UK average.

MORTGAGE PRODUCTS AND HOUSE PURCHASE

So far in this chapter we have looked at broad aggregates. However, both the actual product, the mortgage, and its availability
have undergone considerable change in recent years. In order to
explore this process of change we must first look more closely at

what we mean by a mortgage. A lending institution lends an agreed sum to be repaid over a number of years (normally, at least twenty). A mortgage is a way of making house purchase affordable. The cost of a house is generally several times what someone earns in a year. So it is more than most potential purchasers might be able to save. The loan calculation is based on an estimate of what the buyer is assumed to be able to pay per month. Despite this, some borrowers can get into difficulty, facing loan repayments that they cannot afford – a situation that has increased significantly since the late 1980s.

The mortgage is actually held by the lending institution. It is an *asset* of that institution, whereas the savings accounts deposited in the institutions and other funding sources such as wholesale money are its *liabilities*. They are liabilities because savers or lenders are paid interest on accounts and have the right to take out their money when they wish. This is why specialist institutions like building societies are often called *financial intermediaries*, that is, because they link the different markets for savings and for mortgages. Building societies borrow 'short' from savers. In other words, savers have the right to withdraw their savings relatively quickly. They lend 'long' to borrowers in the mortgage market (borrowers are given loans of 20 to 30 years). Because of this, mortgage lenders have to be 'safe', a requirement sometimes called 'conservative'.

Deregulation has led to a greatly increased choice of types of mortgage for the home-buying public. Mortgages come in two basic forms: annuity (or repayment) and endowment mortgages. With the *Annuity* version, the total cost of the mortgage (principal and interest payments) is calculated into equal monthly payments on the assumption of a constant interest rate. The principal is gradually paid off over the life of the mortgage. In the early years, the repayment is primarily interest, whereas towards the end of the mortgage the repayment increasingly consists of principal. Over the life of the mortgage, increases in earnings and general price inflation tends to erode the real value of the mortgage debt. This leads to a *front-end-loading* problem. That is, there are relatively high repayment burdens in the early years of the mortgage. However, interest payments attract tax relief. So, payments in the early years of the mortgage are substantially lower in net terms than later on. This counters the problem of front-end loading to some extent. The declining real value of payments also gives borrowers potential scope to bear changes in their financial circumstances once the mortgage is a few years old.

Alternatively, with an *endowment* mortgage the home owner takes out a life assurance policy. This will mature at the end of the mortgage term to provide a lump sum, which is calculated so that it should (at least) cover the initial sum borrowed. During the mortgage term, the household pays only interest (net of tax relief) plus the endowment policy premium. These payments are constant throughout the life of the mortgage (for a given mortgage rate), so giving rise again to front-end loading. One of the reasons for a borrower to take out an endowment mortgage is the expectation of a profit on the policy, in addition to the expectation of a real capital gain on the dwelling. Lenders also receive commission on each endowment policy sold, which gives them an important supplementary source of income. Experience in the 1990s suggests that endowment policies have less flexibility than the traditional annuity mortgage for existing borrowers. A mortgagor with a repayment mortgage can lengthen the period of repayment and top up the loan in a straightforward way. Endowment loans do not have this flexibility. But no type of loan provides complete protection for the house buyer whose income falls. In any case, if loan repayments are not made, the lender is entitled to repossess the property. Furthermore, an endowment policy depends on its performance as an investment. There is no guarantee that the (often low-cost) dividend will return enough to pay off the mortgage debt, particularly where the policy is very low-cost. At the other end of the spectrum, some (higher-cost) endowment policies are associated with the expected provision of much larger returns – for instance, being linked to pension provision.

A range of new mortgages has been designed to overcome some of the front-end-loading problems. They include:

- 'Low-start' deals in which payments rise over time (as expected income also rises).
- Deferred principal payments, or substantial, temporary, interest discounts.
- Low-start endowment policies.
- Fixed-rate mortgages.

This variety has arisen because of deregulation, increased profitability and increased competition in the mortgage market. Perhaps the most interesting development in recent years has been the growth of fixed-rate mortgages. Here, the interest rate payable on the loan is frozen for a specified term (rarely more than three to five years). The growth of fixed-rate mortgages (which peaked at 60 per cent of all new loans in the third quarter of 1993 but subsequently fell back) can be attributed to a number of factors. Most importantly, lenders have been facing more and more competition for new lending, following a sustained period of low interest rates. Buyers are attracted to low fixed rates, taking the gamble that rates will generally rise in the future. Some buyers will be attracted to a deal that gives them the security of knowing exactly what they will be paying over the next few years. For the buyer, the fixed-rate mortgage seems a good idea, *provided* variable-rate mortgage interest rates do not fall below the fixed rate of interest. However, the buyer must make up any difference in the long run. And they may face a significant increase in payments at the end of their fixed term, depending on general movements in interest rates. The decision is a matter of fine judgement, one that is increasingly difficult as buyers are swamped by literally hundreds of different mortgage product options. These vary by interest rate (variable, fixed for different periods, capped, discounted and so on) and by mortgage type (interest-only, endowment, annuity repayment, pension-tied, and so on) while market interest rates may change without notice. Recent evidence has shown that a buyer in this complex world will not always make the right choice and cannot count on unbiased or appropriate advice from their lender. A final point is that some commentators have argued that a reliance on fixed-rate mortgage products could reduce housing market volatility by making borrowers less reliant on variable-interest-rate mortgages and therefore less exposed to macroeconomic fluctuations in interest rates.

There is no doubt that there is wider financial choice open to more households than ever before. This is not to be dismissed, since it widens lifetime savings and consumption opportunities, as well as making the financial system far more accessible than in the past. However, financial liberalisation and efficiency gains (see below) have also been associated with new costs. This is most obvious in the greater risk of default, borne out by the growth in mortgage arrears and repossessions and homelessness, all to record levels. For a balanced judgement on the net effect of deregulation, we need longer for the full impacts to work through.

The House Purchase Process

House purchase is a complex and worrying experience for most households. This is not surprising, because:

- It is the largest purchase made by most households. It involves relying on a series of third parties who act as the household's agent (for borrowing money, taking out insurance, buying and selling homes, conducting legal matters).
- It involves significant additional costs. The full costs of buying a house may add up in total to 10 per cent of the value of the property. Not only is the property expensive relative to income, but also it is difficult to 'know' the property without living in it. Prospective buyers therefore have to rely on specialist agents to use their expertise and local knowledge in the buyer's interest.
- It is thus important that competition regulates standards of behaviour to ensure that these agents act professionally for their clients. At the same time, sellers are trying to find the buyer who is willing to pay the most for the property. Sellers may use specialist agencies (estate agents) to market the property as widely as possible. The way the property is sold – negotiated in England and auctioned by sealed bid in Scotland – attempts to maximise the 'profit' for the seller. A study in Glasgow (Gibb, 1992) found that competition between buyers increased prices significantly.

The need for professional surveying and conveyancing, and the problems of linking buyers to sellers, mean that third parties are an unavoidable part of buying a house. These parties act as the *agent* on behalf of the *principal* (either the buyer or the seller). The principal, however, faces an *information asymmetry*. That is, he or she does not have the capacity to undertake these tasks efficiently or quickly and has to trust the agents in terms of the quality and value of their service. This is an important issue because of the increasing integration of buying and selling services. Although competition might be expected to ensure a good service, in small markets there may only be a few specialist agents and competition may be weak. Conflicts of interest can arise within integrated agencies where estate agents sell mortgages and insurance as well as properties to prospective buyers.

Search costs, professional fees and relocation costs can be formidable hurdles to households, most obviously for those that possess limited savings. Lawyers no longer charge recommended rates but quote competitively and face competition from licensed conveyancers. The costs of surveys are more standardised and any variation that does exist tends to reflect the scope and detail of the survey. However, many estate agents are paid on a commission basis, thus relating their cost to the general level of house prices and the cost of selling property in the area in question. Moving house incurs further costs such as refitting the new house, and indirect costs such as those imposed by moving away from a familiar neighbourhood.

DEREGULATION AND CHANGE IN BUILDING SOCIETIES

It used to be that one could define building societies as non-banking financial intermediaries. The legal difference originates in the statutory mutual (non-profit-making) basis of building societies (they are legally owned by their depositors and do not distribute profits). Banks, conversely, are private or public limited companies owned by their shareholders. Although nominally non-profit-making, building societies can make 'surpluses', which can be reinvested in the building society. The bank–society distinction remains useful for small and even medium-sized societies. The distinction is, however, somewhat redundant for the bigger high street societies, because, as a result of enabling legislation and stiff competition, almost all have converted into banks (with the few remaining virtually indistinguishable from banks in terms of the services they provide). The transfer of status became a major national issue because transfer involved converting reserves into shares for members of the transforming societies. This gave cash windfalls to savers and borrowers, often in excess of £2000 per account. These were seen by some as a bribe, by others as an important injection of spending into a sluggish retail economy and by others still as potentially inflationary for the macroeconomy.

In economic terms, the changes instigated since the early 1980s (the deregulation of mortgage and personal finance) represent a structural change in the mortgage market. This section briefly identifies and assesses the main features of radical change in the mortgage and savings markets in a comparatively short period of time.

Non-price competition largely dominated building societies' competitive behaviour until the late 1980s. It took the forms of a mortgage rate cartel, regulations that prevented bank competition, tax advantages in the personal savings market, massive entry costs to deter competitors, manifested in large advertising expenditures and, primarily, branch expansion. The number of branches grew from just over 2000 in 1970 to around 5700 in 1980 and to nearly 7000 in 1988 (Council of Mortgage Lenders, 1990). However, this was economically inefficient.

Following the massive deregulation, societies found that their eighteenth-century statutory basis of mutuality was not compatible with their late twentieth-century needs. The financial viability of the movement was threatened and they needed to (and wanted to) be able to operate like banks. For several decades, societies had been sitting on a mountain of assets (the stock of mortgages). These were economically dormant because building societies were legally obliged to have most of their assets as first mortgages and were not allowed to engage in other businesses. This stock had a vast credit potential if only enabling legislation existed to free up the institutions that could make use of them. Deregulation of the societies meant removing some of the restrictions and putting them on a more even footing with the rest of the financial sector.

It was not only in the mortgage market that societies faced new competition. There was also increased competition in attracting savings. National Savings, the banks and the building societies had fought over the market for decades, but from the late 1970s onwards banks competed more effectively for clients. In addition, the government had begun a more varied assault on personal savings through for instance privatisation shares, PEPs and granny bonds.

Another factor important in precipitating the changes of in the Building Societies Act 1986 was the uncertainty created by the rapid and radical developments emerging in banking technology. The customer saw this most clearly through 'hole-in-the-wall' automated tellers. The industry was most concerned with the wide-ranging consequences of technology enabling the electronic transfer of funds. Society managers wanted the freedom to exploit these innovations. The important point is that the building societies *wanted* change – deregulation was not imposed on a reluctant industry.

The Building Societies Act 1986

The key change in the Act related to the redefinition of building society assets. Prior to the legislation, building societies were allowed only a very narrow portfolio of assets, namely mortgages and assets necessary to conduct their business (such as premises). The 1986 legislation allowed three types of asset:

- *Class I* – traditional first mortgages for owner-occupation.
- *Class II* – are other forms of secured lending such as second mortgages and loans for home improvements.
- *Class III* – unsecured loans and investments in property and land ownership.

The freedom to hold Class II and III assets is only given to bigger building societies and, even for them, the proportion of total assets held in these relatively less secure loans is controlled by the government. By the mid-1990s, the upper limit on non-Class-I activities was expanded to 25 per cent, and Class III assets, for qualifying societies, to 15 per cent. It is Class III assets that are most significant, as they allow societies to trade, to create current accounts (which require the potential for unsecured lending because of the potential for overdraft facilities with cheque guarantee cards) and to engage in a number of competitive functions, such as estate agency. Lending funded by wholesale money (money borrowed from other financial institutions) can take up to 50 per cent of new lending. The remaining building societies argue for more freedom and less tight restrictions, while others escape the legislation by becoming banks.

De-mutualisation

Mortgage lenders now seek to diversify their activities beyond the housing and mortgage markets. However, this diversification process is hindered by the rules governing the regulation of building societies. In the absence of further deregulation legislation, the main route taken by lenders to achieve diversification and liberalisation has been through a wave of mergers and acquisitions, and conversion to banks – sometimes called 'de-mutualisation'.

After the Abbey National's successful conversion to plc status in 1989 it was 1994 before there were further moves in this area. Subsequently, changes occurred at a very rapid pace. First, one of the big ten societies, the Cheltenham & Gloucester, was taken over by one of the major clearing banks, Lloyds, who then took over the TSB, a network of mutual savings banks across the UK with a large mortgage book. In 1995, the largest mortgage lender, the Halifax Building Society, took over one of the other big ten societies, the Leeds Permanent. The Abbey took over another of the big societies (the National & Provincial). All of this activity was the precursor to a sudden wave of conversions, with most of the big societies becoming banks in 1996 and 1997 (Halifax, Woolwich, the Alliance & Leicester, Northern Rock, Bristol & West), the last-named being taken over by the Bank of Ireland). At the end of 1997, only the Nationwide and the Bradford & Bingley societies remained as larger institutions committed to mutuality (for the time being).

Does demutualisation really matter in terms of the mortgage market and housing finance? To make conversion happen, the majority of members have to vote for the change. This was made possible when societies realised that their reserves were in effect owned by the members and decided to convert them into shares or cash – meaning that account holders could receive a windfall of £1000 to £2500 per account. The blatant appeal to self-interest of this approach was very popular, and indeed many thousands of people attempted to join societies likely to convert in order to be eligible for any subsequent issue. The succession of these conversions is likely to have had some sort of inflationary impact on the economy (depending on the marginal propensity to consume the windfalls). From the point of view of the housing market, these large financial institutions are now more free to operate, though interest rates may be higher as a result of having to pay shareholders' dividends. It is difficult to predict the future in this volatile industry, but it does seem that the era of building societies is passed and that the consolidation of these large financial services organisations will continue.

TAXATION AND HOME OWNERSHIP

An important question in analysing any housing finance system is whether it is fair in terms of the amount of financial support people receive towards their housing costs. In this section and the next, the subsidies received by owner-occupiers are considered. The most significant of these are called *tax expenditures*. A tax expenditure is a failure to levy tax on an activity that would be taxed under normal circumstances. For instance, if the government introduces a savings programme allowing people to pay no tax on the annual interest earned, the amount of tax lost is called a tax expenditure because it reduces government revenues in exactly the same way as direct public expenditure. Tax expenditures are difficult to measure, because it is hard to define a 'normal' tax system to use as a benchmark. This is especially a problem in the case of owner-occupied housing. There are four distinct ways in which such housing has been considered to be exempt from 'normal' taxation or treated more favourably than in a 'neutral' tax regime, and these are now examined in turn.

Mortgage Interest Tax Relief

Mortgage loans are the only form of borrowing that is granted tax relief on interest payments (on the first £30 000 of the mortgage). To put it another way, income earned to pay interest on mortgages is exempt from income tax. From 1983–90, this tax relief was deducted at source at the basic rate (25p in the pound in 1990) by the lender (and hence known as MIRAS – mortgage interest tax relief at source). Higher-rate tax payers had to claim back any extra relief to which they were entitled. The subsidy therefore operated as a reduction in the interest paid. Since 1990, a number of policy changes to mortgage interest tax relief have made it pretty clear that the long-term policy aim is to eliminate the tax break; the ceiling of £30 000 has been maintained, despite the fact that it is only now around 50 per cent of the average UK house price, while changes in and after the 1993 Budget progressively reduced the tax rate applied to 10 per cent in 1998–9. Because interest rates have been relatively low, expenditure on MITR has fallen correspondingly (see Figure 6.7).

Figure 6.7   Mortgage Interest Tax Relief and Income Support Payment of Mortgage Interest Benefit for borrowers, 1979–80 to 1997–8

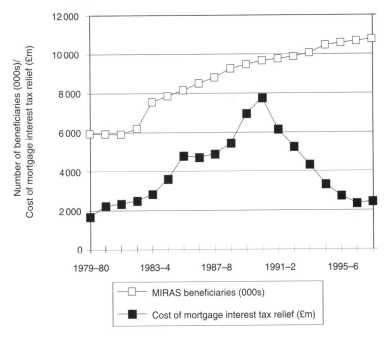

Source: Wilcox (1997a, table 122, p. 179).

The Absence of Imputed Rental Income Tax

The old schedule A income tax was based on the principle that the owner-occupier is simultaneously owner (landlord) and occupier (tenant). The housing asset yields income, which is consumed as housing services by the occupier. It is argued that, strictly speaking, this stream of real income should be taxed, valued as the rent that would have been paid had the occupier not owned the house. There is a direct parallel in the private rented sector, where the landlord is taxed on the rental income received, but gets tax relief on money borrowed for the investment. The tax base for schedule A was the rateable value of the property in question and was taxed at the owner-occupier's marginal tax rate. It was abolished as a result of pre-election pressures on the Conservative government in 1963, together with the unpopularity of schedule A in the revaluation of properties in 1963 (the first revaluation in the post-war period). In 1963 the offsetting mortgage interest tax relief was retained. When tax relief was ended on all other personal loans in 1974, the preferential treatment of home ownership became therefore more marked.

The preferential tax treatment of owner-occupation can be considered to be either the absence of an imputed income tax or mortgage interest tax relief. Both views have their supporters, but the argument turns on whether the neutral or normal tax system would treat owner-occupied housing as a consumption good (and thereby MIRAS is the subsidy, since it departs from the treatment of other consumption goods) or as an investment good (failure to tax investment returns therefore constitutes the subsidy). In practical terms, it is hard to imagine a politically persuasive case being made to reintroduce a tax on imputed income – it would be hard to persuade people that it was a reasonable and fair way of raising taxes.

Exemption from Tax on Real Capital Gains

Since 1982, the UK has taxed most real capital gains at the appropriate marginal tax rate for income tax, as assets are bought and sold, provided that the individual tax unit's annual exemption of £6500 has been exceeded. The most important exemption from this form of capital gains tax is owner-occupied housing.

The Non-taxation of the Consumption of Housing Services

VAT is charged on most goods and services and could, in principle, apply to the taxation of the flow of housing services in each time period in which they are consumed. It is frequently argued by those opposed to VAT on housing that housing is a necessity in the same way that food and children's clothing are vital to life, and that therefore, like them, housing should escape VAT. Economists often argue, however, that there should be as little exemption from a commodity tax as is possible because different treatment distorts behaviour. Furthermore, the wider the overall tax base, the lower is the marginal rate required to raise the same amount of revenue.

The UK tax treatment of owner-occupied housing is not typical of developed economies. The United States is even more lenient than the UK, because it allows tax relief on property tax payments as well as mortgage interest up to $1 million dollars of mortgage loan (and the absence of imputed rental income tax). Other countries that follow the same principles as the UK include Germany, France and Japan. However, there are just as many countries that have a system of imputed income taxation combined with mortgage interest tax relief.

CAPITAL GRANTS TO OWNER-OCCUPIERS

Not only do owner-occupiers receive help through the tax system to meet their housing costs, but some are also eligible to receive grants towards improvement and repair work from the local authorities. These grants are part of the local authorities' armoury in improving house conditions. They are awarded

- in response to owners applying for them,
- following local authority encouragement to apply (for instance in association with area-based schemes);
- in response to local authorities forcing some types of improvement work on owners (including landlords) by issuing compulsory notices requiring that action be taken.

Part of the expenditure is met by capital grant from the government to the local authorities and part, like other local authority capital expenditure, is met by a permission to borrow. Costs are shared between central and local government.

Grants to help owner-occupiers (and private landlords) to improve the quality of their houses have existed since the Housing Acts of 1969. The basic framework remained broadly in place between 1969 and 1990. The basic principles of the system are that grants are available to meet a proportion of the costs of specified works – such as installing basic amenities. The allowable costs are predetermined for the various types of works. There were two peaks in grant-funded activity, stimulated by temporarily higher grant rates, first in the early 1970s and second between 1982 and 1984. Leather and Mackintosh (1994) estimate that over 3.5 million properties in the UK have been given grant assistance.

However, despite the long history of improvement and repair grants expenditure, successive house condition surveys in England and Wales and the first two house condition surveys in Scotland indicated a significant degree of disrepair. Over the longer period, this has proved quite stubborn despite policy initiatives. A major change in approach was instituted in the Local Government and Housing Act 1989. The government argued that the grants system was never meant to effect a wholesale shift in the responsibility of maintaining private property onto the public purse and consequently they proposed that better targeting of grants, through a system of means-testing, should be implemented.

In Scotland, although the same broad principles for reform were set out, first in a Green Paper in 1985 and then in a further consultation document, parallel legislative change was not enacted. This may have been because of the difficulty with introducing means-testing in Scotland arising from the common ownership and shared responsibility for repairs which exists within tenements, typically the most problematic and worst-maintained part of the private sector stock. Scotland therefore retains a variant of the system that operated in England through the 1980s, and both the present Scottish and English systems will be briefly described.

The post-1989 English and Welsh system defined a higher standard of fitness than had existed before (similar to the Scottish tolerable standard, though different in detail). A ten-point standard has been set, and houses are to be considered to be below standard if they fail on any one of these elements. Grants became *mandatory* for work required to bring properties up to this standard level, and local authorities were given discretion to provide grants for further work – to put the dwelling in reasonable repair, to provide adequate insulation or heating or to make adequate the internal arrangements in the house. All types of grants are now means-tested, with respect to income and savings, for both owner-occupiers and private landlords. The government contribution was set at 60 per cent of the cost of providing these mandatory grants, under the so-called Specified Capital Grant (SCG) arrangements. Under the arrangements, local authorities made a substantial contribution to the costs of grant work. Leather and Mackintosh (1994) estimate that this contribution was about £0.5 billion in 1993. Local authorities were anxious about the expenditure implications of mandatory grants, despite the rationing effects of the means-testing requirements. They were not keen to publicise the new arrangements strenuously for fear that the demands would be overwhelming. Despite this, the demands for mandatory grants was more than local authorities could meet. In the interest of controlling expenditure, all awards have been at the discretion of local authorities since 1996.

A key problem with the old systems and the new is a lack of uptake among private landlords. This is important, because the private rented sector contains a disproportionately high level of the very worst housing conditions. Means-testing is unlikely to improve the attractiveness of the grants system for private landlords, and will make many ineligible for grants in any case.

As indicated, improvement of the privately owned stock can also be prompted by local authority action. They have the power to issue notices to require that individual properties be brought up to standard. They are also able to tackle improvements on an area basis. In England and Wales, the means are known as 'renewal areas'. These can be declared where properties in an area are in poor condition and the problems can best be tackled on an area basis, subject to conditions determined by the Secretary of State. Within these areas, authorities can provide grants and loans, or devolve responsibility to housing associations. Authorities may apply for permission to give more than the usual grant help to owners in these areas.

In Scotland, area renewal has been slightly differently arranged. There are three types of Housing Action Area, which distinguish explicitly between those areas that will require improvement work only and those where demolition is more appropriate. Scotland is not covered by the 1989 Act and has retained its non-means-tested system. Scottish Homes is able to give grants as well as local authorities. There are three types of grant available in Scotland. Mandatory improvement grants are available for fitting standard amenities, discretionary improvement grants are for work that will improve the quality of a house or provide houses by conversion, while repair grants are for repairs works alone (whereas improvement grant works must contain some element of improvement or enhancement of the house). They are discretionary except where the house is in area improvement scheme (Housing Action Area) or where there has been a repairs notice served. Generally these grants are given for a proportion of works cost (which has varied through time and depends on the status of the area in which the property is located) up to a maximum expenditure limit.

The abandonment of a separate capital allocation to local authorities for the private stock (see Chapter 4) caused some concern that the improvement programme in Scotland would become less active. Much work on the older stock is now coordinated by housing associations (which often work with owner-occupiers in buildings they are rehabilitating).

GRO Grants

In Scotland, specific grants have been available from Scottish Homes to stimulate home ownership (and private renting) in priority areas, including rural housing markets. Grants for rent and ownership (GRO) provide developers with a deficit subsidy, which allows them to earn a normal return (8 to 12 per cent internal rate of return) in areas where low demand, high development costs, other market failures or simple non-affordability make traditional home ownership non-viable.

Typically, subsidies of 25 to 40 per cent of development costs have produced new private housing in hitherto mono-tenure public housing estates, older urban neighbourhoods and rural markets. Not only has this targeted subsidy boosted tenure mix and introduced home ownership into new locations, but it also helped to sustain the business of property developers in the early 1990s recession. Although the smaller GRO for market rent projects have now ceased, GRO for owner-occupation remains a potential tool to develop new housing markets.

This brief explanation of the grants available to owners has given no more than a flavour of the range of measures that exist. For more details, see the recommendations under 'Further Reading'. Some local authorities have pursued housing condition problems very vigorously, and the success of the measures is witnessed by a general improvement in housing conditions as well as a very visible transformation of many inner-city areas. There are concerns that the current system is neither sufficiently well-funded nor broad-ranging enough to solve some of the most significant problems of poor condition that remain. It must, however, be recognised that grants *have* made a significant contribution to solving earlier problems – such as the absence of basic amenities. Even so, most work to improve the owner-occupied stock continues to be a privately funded activity. In the context of this chapter, however, it is important to note that many owner-occupiers have benefited from fairly significant levels of expenditure on improvement and repair work over the last twenty years, and this, along with the support from the tax system, counters the notion that owner-occupiers are 'unsubsidised' or 'independent from the state' in financial terms.

HOUSING AND THE ECONOMY

Equity Withdrawal

A consequence of financial deregulation is the release of housing equity and wealth, and its use for general consumer spending. Consumption arising from housing equity withdrawal leaks into higher non-housing spending, more imports and lower levels of savings. Equity withdrawal arises in three major ways:

- First, when owners die, and pass wealth on as an inheritance, most is probably *not* recycled back to the housing market, as recipients are typically middle-aged, with a well-established housing career.
- Second, when households trade down or leave the owner-occupied sector. This is typically associated with older owners – perhaps pre- or post-retirement.
- Third, when mortgage borrowing covers non-housing expenditure.
- Fourth, in relation to borrowing behaviour, via the 'feel-good' effect: owners witness their housing wealth increasing as the relative price of housing rises. This knowledge, as well as the implicit accumulation of savings, increases consumption and reduces savings.

In the late 1980s, there was growing concern about the increasing use of borrowing on the strength of capital appreciation, which was seen as a direct result of housing finance deregulation (Miles, 1994).

Evidence suggests that equity withdrawal was being used to fund holidays, school fees, car purchase and, increasingly, to pay for care of older family members.

The future stability of the housing sector, however, is threatened by the increase in house prices. This has left asset values at around four times the value of mortgage debt. This represents a vast sum (£700 billion of loanable funds), which, because of deregulation, can potentially be released. The point is that it will be very difficult for any government or institution to control credit on this massive scale because of the freedom financial institutions have following deregulation (Spencer 1990). Even a small leakage of 2 per cent per annum would imply a consumption injection of £14 billion. House price inflation is therefore one of the Treasury's target variables that they try to keep within control.

Explaining the Boom and the Bust

Maclennan and Gibb (1993) identify a number of trigger and reinforcement effects that pushed the housing market, particularly in the South East, into an unsustainable boom in the mid to late 1980s. In explaining why this boom occurred, it is helpful to distinguish between long-term housing policy measures, one-off policy triggers, real economic factors and financial elements.

Long-term Housing Policy Measures

On both demand and supply sides, housing policy forced house prices upward. Housing demand increased, particularly among first-time buyers. This was due partly to the absence of tenure choice, as a result of rising social sector rents, a contracting private rental sector, and fewer opportunities in the social rented sector following the right to buy. At the same time, tax expenditures acted to lower the effective cost of home ownership. On the other side of the market, housing supply faced tight land planning release strictures, and significant lags in house-building. These made for a climate of inelastic housing supply, particularly in the South.

Real Economic Forces

After the 1980–1 recession, the 1980s were characterised by a long period of real income growth. The UK's economy outperformed its main economic rivals. Remember Chapter 2's estimate of the income elasticity of demand for housing as being around 1.0. This underpinned a long-term expansion in housing demand as real incomes expanded. Long-term real capital gains of 2.0 per cent per annum in the South and more than 1.0 per cent per annum in the North fuelled *asset demand* for housing. That is, housing was expected to remain a 'gilt-edged' asset worth investing in to beat inflation. Demographics also pushed housing demand upwards. In the mid-1980s the post-war baby boom household cohorts entered their peak-earning phase, and the 1960s cohort of 'boomers' moved into their first owned homes.

Financial Effects

Deregulation of financial products, mortgage and consumer credit in the 1980s allowed personal sector indebtedness to increase. In fact, it did this at an unprecedented 19 per cent (compounded) per annum in the 1980s. Mortgage-to-income and loan-to-value ratios increased significantly. Also, greater access to lending facilitated turnover and transactions in the market. The demand for consumer credit was also boosted by equity withdrawal (see the above discussion).

Specific Triggers

A number of specific policy changes were important triggers in 1987–8. First, income tax reductions in 1988 reduced tax relief for the highest earners, and also added to aggregate demand by increasing disposable income. Second, one consequence of the 1987 October stock market crash (Black Monday) was sharp reductions in interest rates, while at the time there was little recognition of the inflationary impact that this might have on the economy via housing wealth. Third, the government chose to stop allowing unmarried couples to claim two sets of tax relief on a single property. Unfortunately, it left a five-month gap between the announcement of this change and its coming into effect. This created an artificial bubble as these households moved to benefit from the last months of double tax relief. Finally, the government abolished the property tax (domestic rates) and replaced it with the per capita poll tax. This reduced the relative cost of housing, further increasing housing demand.

The combination of these one-off and longer-term policies led to the housing market price increase described earlier. In turn, the upward dynamic of the housing market created macroeconomic repercussions. Increased housing market activity (nearly 2 million transactions in 1988 alone) fuelled several related industries: estate agents, conveyancing solicitors, mortgage and insurance sellers, removals' firms, repair and improvement construction activity, DIY, decorating, interior design, landscape gardening, electrical goods and other consumer durables all benefited directly from the volume of transactions in the housing market.

There were also demand- and supply-led inflationary pressures originating from the owner-occupied sector. On the demand side, housing wealth effects increased consumption through equity withdrawal, through the additional consumption that follows moves, and from the 'feel good' factor associated with rising real house prices. All served to increase aggregate consumption and worsen the trade balance. At the same time, housing prices raised the cost of living. It pushed wage demands up as a response to affordability difficulties, creating cost-based inflation. So, housing contributed to the economic boom and helped create inflationary pressures. These forced the government in 1988 to raise mortgage rates sharply to combat inflation and slow the housing market down.

The Housing Market and the Economic Downturn

Higher mortgage rates, followed by lower levels of economic activity (and increased risks of unemployment), are liable to promote reinforcing negative effects on the economy and the housing market. They affect all types of buyer:

- First-time buyers reduce their demand for homes as mortgage rates rise, and this slows down turnover, with depressing effects on housing construction.
- Both they and recent movers spend less on consumer durables and the housing exchange professions lose work.
- Non-movers face higher mortgage repayments, reduce non-housing consumption, and may even face repayment problems.

Further, the house-building industry had to cope with a lack of demand just at the time when borrowing was becoming more expensive. Because of lags in the building process, there was an overhang of unsold property started in more buoyant times. Employment and output fell in the construction sector. The recession was associated with downward pressure on consumption, house-buying, house-building and house prices. The situation was further worsened by growing arrears and mortgage default. The economic psychology of rising real house prices became increasingly replaced by that of negative equity, high levels of unemployment among owner-occupiers and financial losses for lenders and insurers. Lenders had been willing to make such large loans in the 1980s because they were protected by mortgage indemnity guarantee insurance (MIG). This was paid by the borrower and meant that the upper part of the loan (normally the unsecured part) would be insured were the loan not recoverable because of a default or price fall. However, this led to the major insurers taking the brunt of the housing market collapse. Following these significant losses, insurers now insist on lenders sharing the risk. Lenders are therefore reluctant to take on such big risks as they did in the 1980s.

In short, not only did the unstable housing market heighten the economic boom, but it prolonged and deepened the subsequent recession. So, the fundamental question is: is this cycle likely to be repeated or was it caused by one-off and structural changes in the British economy?

Many commentators have argued that structural change in the financial system and one-off policy mistakes in the housing and economic sphere made the late 1980s and early 1990s unique (Miles, 1994). Some have argued that a low-inflation environment requires stable house prices and the mass housing tenure has become more *consumption-oriented* and less *investment-oriented*. What is the evidence for this?

- Lower levels of MIRAS and the reduction in the availability of income support for mortgage interest payments for owners in difficulty have increased access costs to home ownership and reduced the comprehensiveness of support should things go wrong (see Chapter 8).
- Fixed-rate mortgages, lifestyle and flexible products are all more consumer-oriented and consumption-oriented. At the same time, the voluntary tightening of lending and the introduction of risk assessment through credit scoring techniques has tried to reduce the risks for lenders.

- The increase in non-traditional employment contracts (part-time, temporary and fixed-contract employment) plus more spells of unemployment is changing the environment for home ownership. In particular, it is making the issue of *sustaining* home ownership, rather than simply gaining access to it, the key focus for lenders as well as for policy-makers.

All of these factors indicate a more cautious system, which may be better able to protect the housing system from extreme volatility. Some commentators, however, consider this 'industry' position to be over-optimistic. There have been three cycles in the period since 1970, all associated with income and monetary growth. Housing remains, in the long term, a good hedge against (even lower) inflation. The preference for home ownership – within government and with the public – if consumer preference studies are to be believed, remains. And relative subsidisation continues to discriminate against renting.

> So, the fundamentals of the market, its inelastic supply and positive income elasticity of demand suggest that volatility is an inevitable feature of the housing market.

People's financial behaviour also depends on confidence. One would expect equity withdrawal and wealth effects to reimpose themselves should significant price inflation return. It is, of course, the nature of things that volatile markets should attract the speculator. It is not yet clear whether the fundamentals have changed in the housing market. In the long run, it remains perfectly possible that the conditions associated with another boom and bust in the housing market will reappear.

CONCLUSIONS: THE COST OF HOME OWNERSHIP

Owner-occupation is the mass tenure of Britain, and the chief source of personal sector wealth and debt. It also makes a significant contribution to the real economy. So, owner-occupation now casts a large shadow over macroeconomic performance and the capacity of the economy to sustain real and non-inflationary growth. This means that the reform agenda focuses on economic and efficiency-based arguments to put in place a more 'flexible' housing system. This would allow mobility, choice and access linked to the current imperatives of the labour market. It would also sustain existing home owners in the context of the changing labour market and economy.

But reform must take account of the factors that have destabilised the housing market and led to unnecessary damage to the real economy. Deregulation and financial liberalisation will not be reversed. They may be rationalised in a more sober economic climate through some form of controls on the capital market and through more conservative lending and insurance of mortgages. The housing market with its distortions will continue to play an integral part in the macroeconomic and microeconomic future of the UK economy. Plans to reform the owner-occupied sector on the grounds of efficiency and/or equity must pay close attention to these wider impacts. This implies a broader, system-wide appeal for housing reforms that will encourage wider choice and flexibility in housing, simply to allow the labour market and competition policy and regional policy to work with the grain of British housing and not to be immobilised by its immensely destabilising effects.

FURTHER READING

A substantial literature exists on the material covered in this chapter. Forrest *et al.* (1990) is a useful introduction to the complexity of modern home ownership. An introduction to many of the financial topics raised can be found in Bain (1992) and Buckle and Thompson (1992). Mortgage finance is discussed in several articles in each edition of the quarterly *Housing Finance*, published by the Council of Mortgage Lenders. Stephens (1993a; 1993b) provides two useful surveys: one of European mortgage finance and one that tells the deregulation story. Maclennan and Gibb (1993) and Maclennan (1994) set out the housing and economy linkages that emerged in the 1980s and explain the most recent boom and bust. Chapter 5 of Maclennan *et al.* (1991) sets out the distribution and methodological issues central to the housing tax debate. Ermisch (1990) and Maclennan and Gibb (1993) are wide-ranging collections covering much of the housing finance and housing and national economy literature. McCrone and Stephens (1995) deal with many of the issues contained in this chapter, but widen the discussion by putting Britain in a European context. Finally, Maclennan *et al.* (1997) project forward the housing market to see what levels of home ownership will be sustainable long-term.

QUESTIONS FOR DISCUSSION

1. Does de-mutualisation of the mortgage industry matter?

2. Has the housing industry learned from the 1980s and 1990s?

7 Private Rented Housing

INTRODUCTION

Sixty years ago, private renting was numerically the most popular tenure in Britain. Today, it is a truly residual part of the housing system. The private rented sector (PRS) does, however, seem to be experiencing a small reversal of fortune (see Figure 7.1 and below).

Figure 7.1   Private renting's share of tenure, 1981 to 1996

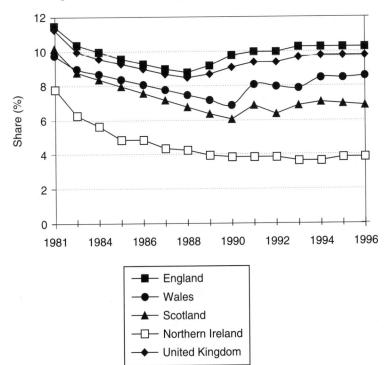

Source: Wilcox (1997a); Department of the Environment, Northern Ireland (1998).

In this chapter, a number of issues critical to the PRS are addressed:

- the causes of nearly continuous decline;
- the role that private renting still plays and its continuing significance for housing policy;
- evaluation of recent policies aimed at reviving the sector, including rent and tenancy deregulation, the Business Expansion Scheme (which ended at the end of 1993) and, most recently, housing investment trusts;
- reforms to private renting finance.

Why Are We Interested in Private Renting?

The Conservative government enacted two tranches of legislation aimed at the private rented sector, in 1980 and 1988. The aim of these policies was to deregulate the tenure, removing restrictions on rent levels and reducing tenure security, thereby allowing new and existing investors to have much more freedom to enter and exit the market and to make better returns on their investment. The objective, therefore, was to create the market conditions that would allow quality private renting to flourish in an environment of minimum regulations (apart from some element of direct financial assistance to encourage landlord investment through grants, subsidised loans and tax reliefs for specific forms of investment). The mechanisms used to achieve these objectives were the creation of new forms of tenancies in 1980, the assured and shorthold tenancies, and the extension to *all* new tenancies of a modified form of assured tenancies in 1988. The Housing Acts of 1988 extended the assured tenancy principle of market rents and privately negotiated tenancy rights and obligations to *all* new lets.

The second plank of government policy for the private rented sector was financial – giving local authorities limited powers to assist capital investment by landlords and widening the Business Expansion Scheme to provide generous tax relief for investors in rental companies (though the scheme ended in 1993). In Scotland, the housing agency Scottish Homes used additional powers to provide grants called GRO-Grants (Grants for Rent and Ownership), subsidising the cost of new provision or rehabilitation for private landlords. For instance, over £6.5 million was spent in 1993–4 to subsidise new rental housing in Scotland. The GRO-Grant for market rent has now ended and has not been replaced.

The PRS remains an important part of the housing system, both as easy-access housing for economically active, mobile households and as a form of short-term and student accommodation. In addition, it continues to house a declining number of older tenants who have always lived in the private rented sector. It also acts as accommodation of last resort. This part of the PRS is typically the focus of policy on standards, tenant harassment and other problems associated with private renting. The variety of household types that demand private renting, and the different motivations of the various landlords, undoubtedly create a diffuse set of housing arrangements, which are not readily amenable to simple policy instruments.

The sector is also very diverse on the supply-side. Apart from employer landlords, who make supply decisions largely on the basis of demand for their economic activities, it is possible to divide landlords into two basic types: investor landlords and those not primarily motivated by financial factors. Investor landlords are in the business of letting to make a profit and earn income. Whether they are individuals or larger corporations, the important point is that they will in all likelihood respond to economic signals, new subsidy mechanisms, and market deregulation. Non-economic landlords, including individuals, charities and other organisations (who are often sideline landlords) cannot be guaranteed to respond to economic signals. This is a significant constraint on the capacity of housing policy to impact on the private rented sector.

Evidence from the English House Condition Survey in 1991 and the Census in the same year suggests that both the size of the tenure had increased since 1986 and that turnover had increased. This appears to have been the result of rent deregulation, the Business Expansion Scheme (BES) and the downturn in the housing market which has encouraged some owners to rent their houses following a move rather than leave the house empty (Crook and Kemp, 1996). However, when BES finished in 1993 no property-based replacement for it was made, and the recovery of the housing market will reduce the stock of unsold property. To capture the potential benefits of a more healthy private rented system will require more durable reform in the form of some kind of subsidy mechanism.

Creating an efficient and fair financing environment for land-lords and tenants alike is central to overall housing finance reform, and should not be conceived of as only something of a sideshow. The recent downturn in owner-occupation has demonstrated that furnished private renting can compete with home ownership, particularly for new, younger households and recent graduates with accumulated debt. Furthermore, support for this form of renting may generate macroeconomic benefits. If younger households can be persuaded to rent in the early stages of their housing career, deposits can be built up and the dangerous dependence on very high mortgage-to-value and mortgage-to-income ratios may be lessened (see Chapter 6). If housing policy-makers are to be serious about housing flexibility, then the positive stabilising impact that private renting can have on mass home ownership ought to be required. Innovative ways of using private landlordism in the social sector are discussed below.

Although there is a tendency to contrast the dominance of private renting in 1914 (90 per cent) with today (less than 10 per cent), this can give a misleading impression of the scale of recent decline. As recently as 1961, the private rented sector accounted for just less than a third of all British housing. In 1970, the sector contained a fifth of all housing. Figure 7.1 shows tenure shares in the UK countries from 1981 to 1996.

RENT CONTROLS AND THE PRIVATE RENTED SECTOR

The imposition of restrictions on the maximum level of rents go back to 1915. It was in Glasgow that rent strikes and civil unrest during the First World War precipitated the government's efforts to hold back escalating rents, by introducing rent ceilings on a 'temporary basis'. Prior to 1914, 90 per cent of households were tenants of primarily unfurnished accommodation. Since the 1915 Act, there has been some form of rent control continuously, periodically strengthened by legislation concerning security of tenure for sitting tenants. Rent control is a peculiar form of subsidy, which acts like a tax on the return of the landlord – because it sets a maximum revenue and therefore profit per unit of housing, and it also implicitly subsidises the tenant, who pays less than in a 'free market'. This 'tax' effectively redistributes income between landlord and tenant.

The contraction of private renting has commonly been explained solely by the succession of Rent Acts. Landlords make a return on their investment in two ways: from the rental income and from any capital gains on their property. Rent controls reduce both types of return; the rental income is directly reduced and the asset value of the property is also reduced, since it is determined by the flow of rents that it will yield, while security of tenure (which normally co-exists with rent controls) further holds down the asset return to the landlord. This is because occupied dwellings sell for less than vacant properties, and landlords are less able to remove tenants to get higher rents or sell into owner-occupation (the capital value can be thought of as the capitalised stream of rents, the sum of which will be lower with rent controls). If the net return (the sum of the rental and asset rate of return after taking account of costs) is lower than the return on offer in other investments then the supply of rented accommodation will fall in the long run. In the short run (where the property has a sitting tenant) the rational landlord will reduce costs by minimising repair, maintenance and management in order to make up their lost profits. The argument runs further: the stigma attached to private landlords derives directly from the security of tenure problem. Landlords have a poor reputation because they have had recourse to unscrupulous means to evict tenants and thus realise their asset value by selling into owner-occupation. LeGrand *et al.* (1993) argue, further, that not only is a policy of rent control inefficient, it is also inequitable in that it benefits present tenants at the expense of potential or future tenants who find that choice is circumscribed. The policy also notionally transfers income from landlords to tenants as compared with the free-market situation, and since most landlords are not wealthy, have only a small portfolio and are drawn from the skilled manual class, it is oversimplifying to assume that such redistribution is inevitably equitable (LeGrand *et al.*, pp. 105–9).

The standard argument identifying rent controls as the main factor in the decline of this sector, however, simplifies a complicated chain of cause and effect. This has created problems because the simple model has been naïvely applied to policy towards private renting (Kemp, 1990). The damage inflicted by rent controls has produced the argument that by *deregulating* rents (that is, removing rent control legislation), rental and asset returns will rise to their 'proper', market levels and new supply will respond to these profit opportunities. While there is little doubt that rent controls cannot have had a positive effect on private renting, a simple policy of deregulation has failed, because the source of decline is in fact more complicated than the simple model would imply. Further, it is quite another thing to imagine that deregulation, even if it encourages new supply, will create *demand* from potential tenants.

Kemp (1988) points out that before 1914, investment in the form of rented housing was the second most popular form of saving (after stocks and shares) in the United Kingdom. The attraction of this form of residential capital was simply that it offered low risk and a stable return. In addition to the effects of rent controls and tenure security, which progressively made private renting both a higher risk and a lower return opportunity, there was a general improvement in the range of alterhative investment opportunities and the returns available. This was the result of the centralisation and coordination of the nation's capital markets, the development and increased sophistication of the City and the stocks and shares markets, and the increase in the volume of personal savings as a consequence of rising real incomes. As both the relative and absolute profitability of renting fell, the availability of more attractive opportunities grew.

A second factor to consider is that rent controls have never applied a simple, single ceiling, but instead were determined by different pieces of legislation (at least 14 since 1915) that have varied in coverage, scope and intent. Broadly, according to whether the government was Conservative or Labour, policy involved either limited deregulation or reimposition of controls (respectively). For example, the Conservative Macmillan government pursued a comprehensive policy of deregulation in 1957, which, ironically, led to the largest disinvestment of stock this century and the addition of 'Rachmanism' to English usage. The following Labour Wilson governments reimposed and then extended rent controls in the 1965 and 1974 Rent Acts, extending security of tenure across the whole sector and introducing 'fair rents'. Fair rents were to be rent officers' assessment of a rent that would not discriminate against either the tenant or the landlord. Throughout this period, therefore, the practical significance to landlords of rent controls has varied markedly, but the very uncertainty over future legislation arguably reduced both demand and supply in the private rented sector throughout the post-war period. The negative impact of this 'political risk' can be seen as resulting in a need on the part of the landlord to earn a higher rate of return, simply because of the likelihood that a future government might reverse present policy. Until there is political consensus about the future of private renting, it will be much more difficult for the sector to earn competitive returns as a longer-term investment (this is a point recognised and, some would even argue, accepted by all of the major political parties in the 1990s).

The existence of loopholes in the Acts always allowed some tenancies to be created outside any rent control legislation. The cumulative impact was to create a situation in which a majority of existing contracts and an estimated 80 per cent of new ones were not covered by rent controls in the late 1980s (Kemp, 1988b). The impact on new supply cannot be very significant if landlords are not actually affected by the controls in the first place. This is why it is probably more helpful to think of deregulation as a necessary rather than a sufficient condition for the revitalisation of the sector.

The third key element in explaining the demise of private renting is the growth in demand for other tenures. Again, this is a relative point about imperfect substitutes operating under different financial arrangements. While landlords saw little incentive to upgrade their old, small and poor-quality dwellings, their tenants were moving steadily to the new, higher-quality local authority housing. Furthermore, real income growth and affordable prices (beginning in the inter-war period) allowed a sustained growth in owner-occupation. The relative attractiveness of these other tenures, caused partly by subsidy to local authority housing and the tax expenditures accruing to owner-occupiers, *must* have reduced the relative demand for private renting. The fiscal arrangements operating in the other tenures have, therefore, long discriminated against the private landlord. In the context of wider economic change, it is not surprising that this resulted in a shrinking private rented sector and a massive disinvestment in the stock (in the period since 1945, four times as many properties have been sold into owner-occupation by private landlords than by public ones; this *includes* RTB sales). To conclude this section, the basic argument that rent controls alone have caused the collapse of the tenure is much too simple. It follows that policies based on the idea that the sector is inhibited mainly by government intervention may well not achieve their objectives (the revitalisation of the PRS).

THE PRIVATE RENTED SECTOR TODAY

Although greatly reduced in size, the private rented sector today still caters for a number of identifiable groups, and continues to perform an important function in the modern British housing system. It is difficult, however, to be precise about the size and characteristics of the tenure, because the data that exist are relatively poor compared with other tenures. Data are very difficult to collect because of the small size and frequent informality of the tenure. Here we use survey evidence to supplement official statistics. For tenancies outwith the Rent Acts, that is, the market for assured tenancies (free market tenancies), much of what will be said is based largely on *ad hoc* and limited sources. This is particularly unsatisfactory because it is in this area of new lettings that policy reforms are targeted.

The Stock

In 1996, around 10 per cent of the UK housing stock was in the PRS. At a more local level this figure masks a large variation across Britain and between urban and rural areas. In rural areas, for example, there is a greater tradition of tied housing. In the urban areas, quantitatively, there is more demand for private lets because of employment and student requirements. This is particularly true in South East England, where demand pressures are strongest. Table 7.1 indicates the distribution of private renting in volume and percentage terms. Not surprisingly, this is numerically dominated by the South East and London, in particular. The other part of England to have a large proportion of houses privately let is the South West. Scotland and Wales have lesser rates of private renting, with Northern Ireland's share being about a half of the rest of the UK.

The 1996 English House Condition Survey (EHCS) indicated that the private rented stock was much older than owner-occupied housing (53 per cent of the private rented stock was constructed before 1919). The stock is predominately made up of converted

Table 7.1 Private renting across the UK 1996 (000s, percentage of total stock)

	Units (000s)	% of stock in country/region (of England only)
England	2,095	10
Greater London	458	15
Eastern	218	10
South West	251	12
South East (except Greater London)	347	11
Yorks and Humberside	196	9
East Midlands	154	9
North East	80	7
North West	178	8
West Midlands	158	7
Merseyside	54	9
Scotland	152	7
Wales	104	8
Northern Ireland	22	4
UNITED KINGDOM	2,373	10

Source: DETR, Scottish Office Environment Department, Welsh Office (1998).

flats. There is evidence of growth in the sector and of increased turnover, plus considerable exit of stock into the owner-occupied sector (but some 23 per cent of the private rented stock in 1996 had been in owner-occupation in 1991 – Department of the Environment, Transport and the Regions, 1998). There were 62 000 bedsits (or 'traditional' Houses in Multiple Occupation) in England, down by about a fifth since 1991.

As to conditions, the EHCS found that poor housing conditions were heavily associated with private renting. Poor housing conditions were defined as statutory unfitness, or the house being in substantial disrepair, or requiring essential modernisation. 31 per cent of private tenants lived in poor housing conditions, compared to 14 per cent of households across England. In Scotland, the Scottish House Condition Survey found that for all dwellings, 1 per cent were below tolerable standard but that this figure rose to 4 per cent for the private rented sector (Scottish Homes, 1997a). Again,

Table 7.2   Average cost of comprehensive repairs, private renting and all housing, England and Scotland, 1996 (£)

Country	Private renting	All properties
England	5030	3420
Scotland	4137	2598

Source: DETR (1998); Scottish Homes (1997a).

however, the data suggested general significant improvement over the 1991 situation.

Table 7.2 summarises the average cost of repairs for private renting against all properties. For both England and Scotland, repair costs are higher for private renting than for housing as a whole.

Although much of what was the British private rented sector has been removed in successive slum clearances, the current stock is predominantly unimproved pre-war housing and is in relatively poor condition. We discuss below the reasons for the lack of investment in this stock, but two of the consequences of relative depreciation can be noted. As a result of its vintage, the stock will generally be smaller than more modern housing and, consequently, the stock will be more likely to lack basic amenities.

The private rented sector is not uniformly of poor quality. BES investment led to more than 40 000 units being added to the private rented sector after 1988 – the largest investment in commercial rented housing since 1945. Given that most of this investment (in Scotland, certainly) was in new build, it must be expected that this part of the stock is generally of high quality.

The Tenants

Private tenants can be divided up in two ways: according to the functional character of the stock (furnished, unfurnished and tied housing) or according to tenant characteristics. Since 1945, there has been a relative contraction of the unfurnished sector and growth in the furnished sector over time. It is possible to identify four discrete tenant types (Bovaird *et al.*, 1985):

- There are those tenants, typically now elderly and relatively poor, who have always lived in the tenure and probably enjoy protection under one of the Rent Acts, and who typically live in unfurnished accommodation.
- There are tenants with employment and tied accommodation who may make up as much as a fifth of the tenure.
- There is the all-encompassing category of easy access renting. This group, the main focus of the new lettings sub-market, is composed of business and executive tenants, transient owner-occupiers, students, single-person households and other mobile households.
- Finally, the tenure also performs a residual role for those households unable to gain access to the majority tenures, including some of those groups identified above, such as people leaving care or leaving a partner.

The relevance of this categorisation can be confirmed by looking at data from the 1996 English and Scottish House Condition Surveys. In Scotland, 38 per cent of heads of household in the furnished sector were aged under 25, and 39 per cent of those in the unfurnished sector aged over 65. Tied housing accounted for 22 per cent of households in the private rented sector (Scottish Homes, 1997a). In England, private renting provided housing for one minority ethnic household in six, compared with 10 per cent of all households (DETR, 1998).

It should be clear from this brief summary that the private rented sector performs a number of specialist functions in the housing system. It is also possible to distinguish between demand sectors: market-renting households that can be thought of as rent–buy households on the margins of ownership; those on Housing Benefit; and those, normally with low incomes, who are just above benefit levels, such as the low-paid or students (Kemp, 1997).

Landlords

Information is generally at its weakest when considering the modern landlord, especially when one is concerned with the objectives and motives of the investor. What is clear is that the portfolios of landlords are typically small-scale. Landlords can be divided into three groups: 'classical' small landlords (that is, non-resident landlords with a small portfolio of usually less than five properties),

Table 7.3   Distribution of landlords by type, 1978 to 1993–4 (%)

Landlord type	1978	1982–4	1986–7 Recent mover	1986–7 Established tenant	1993–4 All tenancies
Resident individual[a]	6	5	4.4	4.6	8
Non-resident individual	58	56	74.2	59.6	67
Employer or institution	22	21	16.2	16.2	13
Property company	10	18	6.1	19.7	8
Other or don't know	4				5

Note: a Resident individuals include relatives who are landlords to the tenants surveyed (authors' categorisations).
Source: Todd *et al.* (1982; 1986); Whitehead and Kleinman (1990); Survey of English Housing (1993–4).

resident landlords, and property companies. Table 7.3 examines the breakdown of landlords by type.

The main points in the table are:

- the recent growth in resident landlords;
- the importance of non-resident individual landlords;
- the decline of employer landlords;
- reduction in property company landlords.

The small landlord still appears to provide most new lets, although favourable legislation has helped property companies to expand their role at the expense of traditional landlords (Todd, 1986). In a review, Kemp (1988) found a wide diversity of reasons for investing in rented property, making it difficult to generalise about landlord objectives, and, therefore, to weigh up the effects of innovative legislation for the sector. A quarter of non-resident landlords let primarily to meet their own housing costs in one form or another. Around the same proportion let to provide an income, while more than a third were landlords to make a return on their capital. The variations widened between different types of landlords (Kemp, 1988, reviewing Todd, 1986). Intuition, however, would suggest that property companies with their economies of scale in management and investment may well react in more predictable fashion to tax exemptions and subsidies. It was emphasised above that commercial renting as an investment was left behind by the centralisation of savings and investment in the latter part of the last century. The deconcentrated structure of landlordism was a major cause of this withdrawal of investment. Discussion of reform tends to assume that the 'new' landlords who will invest in private renting will be larger institutional investors. Such landlords, however, never significant in numerical terms, left the sector in droves in the 1950s and 1960s (Hamnett and Randolph, 1988). It is not apparent that many have yet returned to the rental market in the deregulated 1990s (see Crook *et al.*, 1995).

Kemp and Rhodes (1994) conducted a survey of landlords in Scotland. In many cases, their findings reinforced the earlier points – heterogeneity; a small-scale activity; a variety of reasons for letting (not all of them commercial); and a general satisfaction with their role. Yet, many landlords reported that rental income was insufficient to cover the current costs of letting and give a reasonable return. The rental rates of return earned averaged 6.5 per cent gross (of any repair and maintenance) and 4.6 per cent net. Interestingly, individual landlords were able to average a higher net yield (4.9 per cent) compared with organisational landlords (4.2 per cent). Crook *et al.* (1995) suggest that rental returns for Britain as a whole are too low. At a gross level of 7.6 per cent average return and a net level of 5.6 per cent, they require an increase of 3.4 per cent (average) to compare favourably with alternative investments. However, they do indicate that different forms of market rental investment offer different returns: the gross return on a furnished letting is 10.3 per cent, compared with only 5.7 per cent on an unfurnished letting; before 1989, letting earned only 4.4 per cent, whereas after 1988 it earned 9.2 per cent. Interestingly, Crook *et al.* indicate that individual landlords earn a higher gross return (8.8 per cent) than do corporate landlords (5.7 per cent).

Recent research in Scotland (Gibb, 1994) contrasts the Glasgow and Edinburgh rental markets in 1988 and 1992, using large data sets drawn from newspaper adverts on rent offers, location, property type and supplier. Several conclusions emerged:

- The volume of properties advertised grew significantly.
- There was a significant shift in the location of and types of property advertised.
- Glasgow evidence suggested more competition between landlords.
- In real terms, rents were flat in Glasgow; they fell in Edinburgh.

Subsequent work by Bailey (1996) confirms these findings. The implication of this research is that the Glasgow furnished rental housing market has become more competitive in the face of a significant supply expansion, at least in the sense of more providers and pressure on rents. Change in the more mature Edinburgh housing market has been less radical, but in the same direction. It is not possible to disentangle the effects of BES and rental deregulation, but it would appear that, for the furnished part of the sector, opportunities for rental growth do exist. Bailey (1996) extended this approach to looking at rents in all four Scottish cities for the period 1987–94. He found that the supply of accommodation (proxied by the volume of adverts) grew by 40 per cent across the cities. Rents were highest in Aberdeen, higher in Glasgow than in Edinburgh and much lower in Dundee. In real terms, rents had remained constant in Glasgow despite the apparent expansion of supply. In both Dundee and Edinburgh, rents had risen slightly in real terms between 1987 and 1994.

RECENT REFORMS TO THE PRIVATE RENTED SECTOR

Recent legislation has sought to revitalise this disparate part of the housing system. The main changes have been deregulation, the Business Expansion Scheme, financial assistance from local authorities to landlords, and the possibility of social rented housing being sold to approved landlords. In addition, the Building Societies Act 1986 has provided the larger of the societies with the opportunity, taken up by Nationwide Anglia, to become private landlords (more have been involved in BES schemes). It has been argued that deregulation will have a limited effect on a market for new lettings, as it is practically a free market in any case (Bailey, 1996). Evidence from Scottish Homes suggests that financial assistance through GRO-Grants in Scotland (a deficit subsidy averaging more than 30 per cent of scheme costs to developers, which enables affordable new construction at an acceptable rate of return to be built for owning or private renting) has led to substantially more support for home ownership rather than private renting (the Grants are supposed to provide critical development finance in approved areas where private investment would otherwise take place; this is much easier to sell for starter homes than it is for rented housing estates).

In this section we gauge the impact of the Business Expansion Scheme (BES) initiative and the recent Housing Investment Trust proposal on the deregulated PRS.

Business Expansion Scheme

This initiative, introduced in 1983 but at first not applicable to schemes involving property, was amended in the 1988 Budget to allow full tax relief on investing in shares of newly formed companies who would make a long-term commitment to investing in approved private renting. The initiative was intended to attract new investment into private renting and to provide pump-priming for the rental market. A maximum annual investment of £40 000 could be set against taxable income (at the tax unit's highest marginal tax rate) in addition to the absence of capital gains tax on the first resale of shares (Crook and Kemp, 1995). The initiative was led by the Inland Revenue rather than a housing agency and has, in many quarters, been seen as a tax avoidance scheme rather than a purposeful housing policy.

To qualify, BES companies had to let properties for at least five years. After this period, the companies identified a number of 'exit' options that allowed them to realise their gains. BES firms could then either continue as trading landlords (but without special tax status) or sell their properties, either to other private landlords, or for owner-occupation, or to social landlords – such as housing associations. The attractiveness of different options depends on prevailing market conditions, but doubts as to the long-term survival of the BES companies as private landlords were borne out in research and subsequent experience after the end of the first companies' qualifying period in 1993 (Crook and Kemp, 1996). Several of the companies entered into contracted 'exit' options with universities and housing associations, guaranteeing a purchaser at the end of the five-year qualifying period (often using sale and leaseback arrangements). Because the market turned down, many of the firms that did not enter into such cast-iron agreements found themselves with property that did not earn the projected returns and was difficult to sell at prices acceptable to investors (see Crook *et al.*, 1995).

Nonetheless, BES was an important demonstration that subsidy can make private rented housing an attractive investment. It suggests that appropriate subsidies (with a much longer life) could make private renting profitable. With a working life of only five years, BES was a more generous subsidy to investors than, for example, HAG, which has a higher percentage subsidy but a working life of between 30 and 60 years (see Chapter 5). BES also has had an important impact on housing markets, urban renewal and the built environment. This is simply because the subsidy offered an opportunity to guarantee cash flow. Builders, developers, surveyors, lawyers and property companies could develop schemes that were often managed by the same people and allowed certainty to be built in to cash flow projections. As much as a quarter of Glasgow's new build in 1988 was BES-funded. With much of this on brown-field sites in inner urban areas, the regenerative benefits of the funding should not be dismissed.

Whitehead and Kleinman (1990) argue that, in London, new furnished sector rents and rates of return prevailing in the London furnished rental market would need to rise by 30 to 50 per cent to attract new investment (even though it would raise problems of affordability). Even at existing rents, more than a third of tenants were paying more than 20 per cent of their incomes in rent. Further, the calculation of required returns is modest; the authors point out that the (6 per cent) assumed return does not allow any extra return to compensate for the risks of the uncertain legislative future or of the volatile levels of capital gains on vacant property. If we acknowledge the need for a thriving, quality rental sector catering for a wide range of demands, then generous short-run tax concessions to individual investors are not the answer. It is questionable, moreover, whether BES produced a long-term increase in the supply of new lets.

The BES ended in December 1993, and has been replaced by a new tax-based investment programme that excludes rented housing (existing schemes had to be wound up by the end of 1998). Crook *et al.* (1991) examined the impact and the nature of BES companies. For these new landlords, investment had been motivated by post-tax returns, not the desire to be a landlord, although most sponsors of the companies had had previous experience of commercial rented housing. In almost all cases, these companies were looking to short-run capital gains and not income from renting as the way to earn economic returns. Crook *et al.* also found that BES landlords saw 'little prospect of raising finance ... without the benefit of a subsidy like BES' (p. 63). Crook and Kemp (1996) summarise their extensive research into the BES:

- Exit options meet investor requirements, but mean that there will only be a short-run fillip to the PRS.
- Nearly two-thirds of investment took place in the South East. It was estimated that BES property companies received a subsidy on average of 48 per cent of acquisition costs.
- Net rental returns were actually below the rest of the deregulated sector, partly because of high operating costs, although larger firms did better, suggesting the existence of scale economies (falling costs as output rise).
- Interviews with company directors painted a pessimistic picture for the future of the BES companies as a result of low returns and technical difficulties associated with modifying a company's structure after the qualifying period.

Housing Investment Trusts

A significant gap in the PRS in the UK is the absence of any sizeable investment by the major financial institutions (pension funds, life assurance, and so on). The institutions have always played a significant role in funding commercial property, on the basis that property helps to diversify the portfolio of assets and thereby spread risk, has historically been a good hedge against inflation, and can, if managed and organised properly, overcome the problems of illiquidity and discontinuity associated with large properties. The PRS, however, would require extensive management with correspondingly high operating costs. For this reason, the solution came to be seen as providing a vehicle that would allow the institutions to invest *indirectly* in property companies. Such a vehicle would need tax-exempt or reduced tax liability in order to maintain the tax-privileged position of the institutions. From this basic idea was born the concept of the housing investment trust (HIT), which is now legislated for under the Finance Act 1996.

The Conservative government developed HITs to take the following basic form. Financial institutions would be able to invest in specially developed investment trusts designed exclusively to own and manage privately rented housing based on assured or shorthold assured tenancies. They would be exempt from capital gains tax and would pay corporation tax at the lower, small-companies rate. Individuals who buy shares in HITs will pay tax, whereas gross funds (those from the financial institutions) will not, thus creating tax transparency (that is, keeping institutional funds on the same tax basis in or out of HITs). As Crook *et al.* (1996, p. 6) argue: 'The intention, therefore, is to draw in financial institutions, create a tax transparent vehicle and to make private renting a more liquid investment by creating a market in tradable securities in HITs (which will be a more liquid form of investment than ownership of the dwellings themselves).'

To date, the evidence on the efficiency of HITs is not encouraging. It is possible to identify a number of potential constraints. Crook *et al.* (1996) argue that the PRS is in the main a cottage industry where only the BES firms show a (short-lived) capacity for larger firms to make competitive returns. Second, they reason that the returns made by private landlords are well below the opportunity cost returns required by financial institutions, and that the planned tax concessions are unlikely to bridge the yield gap (approximately 10 per cent, compared with 6.5 per cent). A subsidy would still be required. They conclude (p.18) that 'until they are sufficient in size to realise the economies of scale that will reduce their operating costs significantly, it is unlikely that they will draw in institutional funding.'

ALTERNATIVE REFORM FOR FURNISHED PRIVATE RENTING

In great part owing to the inability of many home owners to sell their property in a collapsed housing market, and their then being forced to let out the unsold accommodation, there has been a cyclically based growth in private renting in the 1990s. One cannot be confident that this will endure beyond an upturn in the housing market. However, many commentators argue that a more flexible, fast-entry furnished private rented sector would secure benefits for the housing system and the economy. This would widen choice for potential first-time buyers and may reduce some of the pressure felt in that segment of the housing system. And by allowing newly forming households the opportunity to save, it may also reduce the need to take on risky, high-exposure mortgage loans at an early age. This section considers some of the ways in which the furnished private rented sector can be made more attractive to that market niche.

It should be clearly understood that one does not expect (or desire) the return of mass private renting, in which private unfurnished lets could compete with the social sector. To make it work, it has to be financially viable. At present, countless research studies indicate that it cannot earn a reasonable rate of return that will be sufficiently high to attract new investment. What are the options? There are three elements of feasible reform and these are discussed in turn:

(i)   depreciation allowances;
(ii) the fair rent system and licensing;
(iii) durable subsidy mechanisms.

Depreciation Allowances

For tax purposes in the United Kingdom, it is assumed that private rented housing has an infinite life with zero depreciation. Not only is this unusual internationally, but it is inconsistent with the UK treatment of housing associations in the new financial regime, which *does* imply the need for a sinking fund to counter depreciation. Housing may be a very durable asset, but it does depreciate. A depreciation allowance would enable the landlord to offset some recurrent costs against tax. Alternatively, it may be possible to design a tax on the profits of landlords that can be earmarked for modernisation expenditure for specific private lettings. Chapter 5 indicates that sinking funds for repairs and improvements are now a normal part of housing association funding. In Britain, to add to the inconsistency, private landlords do receive tax allowances on expenses for repairs and other similar work. They cannot, however, impute expenses from the work that they do themselves. The tax system is, therefore, at present stacked against the small private landlord.

Fair Rents and Licensing

Many tenants are still protected by Rent Act legislation and have their rents controlled by the Fair Rent system which fixes rents for a fixed period of time (two to three years) on the basis of a rent officer's assessment of an appropriate rent for the property. It is important to recognise that there is no economic basis for these calculations. Fair rents are calculated by first using 'comparables' of a closely located market or existing fair rent and then taking account of 'scarcity'. However, this is not the economic notion of shortage or scarcity, but a crude percentage reduction (of as much as 60 per cent) in the rent to reflect 'lack' of supply (whereas in economics scarcity simply means that a commodity commands a price). Indeed rent assessment tribunals tend to operate on the basis that this 'scarcity factor' has always to be applied. Note also that by using existing fair rents as comparables, any previous mistakes, arbitrary calculations and so on, are compounded in the new assessment. The scarcity measure is both misleading and arbitrary.

At the same time, low-income tenants receive support in the form of Housing Benefit (see Chapter 8). The long term decontrol of the remaining and dwindling supply of properties let out under the Rent Acts would put an end to the inconsistencies created by the present system. Income-based assistance in the form of a transitional allowance or income supplement would be a more sensible way to help tenants than distorting rents in an arbitrary and misleading way.

There is nothing intrinsically wrong with a free market in quality rented housing, provided that tenants have basic rights of access to information, and to inexpensive legal assistance in the case of landlord–tenant disagreements (landlords and tenants do have directly conflicting interests), and can depend on an effective binding guarantee for contracts drawn up over tenancy. These might be achieved through three relatively simple measures. First, tenant relations officers (TROs) in local authorities could be provided with statutory policing powers for private tenancies and be responsible for the enforcement of information rights and binding tenancy agreements. Second, all tenancy arrangements would be of a standard written form that need not be in legal jargon or a disincentive to letting. Third, all landlords should be approved by a licensing agency (which could be the TROs themselves), with powers to penalise abuses from either side of the letting contract. Since the licence would provide the landlord with respectability, the ability to charge market rents and official sanction as a 'good' landlord, it would be worth paying for.

The combination of these three reforms would create an enforceable licensing system for all new tenancies. It must be accepted that harassment and intimidation (on either side of the letting contract) can be very difficult to prove. This is not just a problem in the private sector. Nonetheless, these measures would certainly help to narrow the range and frequency of these unhappy outcomes. This would have substantial imitative and beneficial effects, which should enhance the reputation of the market and its landlords.

Recent proposals to reform the treatment of Housing Benefit in the private rented sector have changed the ways in which rent officers determine the maximum eligible amount a tenant can claim on the basis of their rent, locality and type of accommodation. These reforms (see Chapter 8) are likely to restrain the growth of the private rented sector by imposing a new form of local rent ceiling for properties likely to attract private tenants who may require Housing Benefit. The interaction of the rent officer and the rental market continues to distort the sector.

Durable Subsidy Mechanisms

The evidence suggests that, without subsidy, returns are not generally high enough to encourage investment in the private rented sector. The first requirement of a new subsidy system is therefore to increase post-tax real returns to private renting to a competitive level. The second major requirement is that the subsidy should attract long-term investment and not be based on short-run capital gains, as was the case with BES. Crook and Kemp (1993) review four sets of subsidy proposals: the National Federation's Inquiry into British Housing (NFHA, 1991); that of Hills (1991); that of Maclennan *et al.* (1991); and their own proposals. All of these involve tax reliefs (respectively, harmonising with owner-occupiers or business; depreciation allowances; tax harmonisation and competitive tender for lower levels of HAG; and tax relief for individual investors in property companies and limited capital allowances). There are a number of points that can be made. Capital allowances in the first year of a development are attractive, because they encourage investment, although this does not necessarily support long-term investment. Tax relief for the landlord focuses subsidy on rental returns and is sustainable. Tax relief for investors in property companies explicitly favours this type of landlord (reflecting the belief that property companies would be a good landlord because of their financial strength and economies of scale). Tendering for HAG is a different issue. In this case, landlords are being offered capital subsidies of 30 to 40 per cent in return for social responsibility – they would act as social landlords for finite periods of time (for instance, 15 years) before having the opportunity of reverting to a commercial role (although this requires some further consideration, namely as to what safeguards existing tenants would retain). All of these proposals imply an exchequer cost, but it is important to distinguish the first-round cost to the Treasury from the second-round benefits from a vibrant private rented sector (in terms of housing flexibility, wider choice and greater economic efficiency). Given the increased turnover in the sector, it is all the more apparent that an effective commercial rented sector does not need necessarily to be a large sector.

CONCLUSIONS

Private renting continues to suffer from policy overkill. Tenants and landlords have a legitimate concern over possible future Housing Acts that may change or reverse current practice. This uncertainty contributes to a low level of new investment, because it raises the risk element of the required return. Private renting, however, continues to be important, first, because it performs a series of specialist functions in the housing system, and, second, because a well-ordered rental market would assist the supply side of the economy, and, third, arguably, help stabilise the owner-occupied sector. Under current policy, private renting cannot break out of the current long-standing housing policy trap. A housing policy for private renting based on a durable subsidy, depreciation allowances and landlord licensing – in the context of wider housing finance reform – would help to stem the tide. It probably could not hope to return Britain to the levels of private renting common thirty or more years ago, but it is not clear anyway that this would be appropriate.

FURTHER READING

The economics of rent controls are well covered in Maclennan (1982) and Black and Stafford (1988). Kemp (1988) provides a comprehensive analysis of the decline and implications of deregulation to private renting. Whitehead and Kleinman (1986; 1988; 1990; 1994) develop an illuminating if pessimistic picture of future long-term demand for the tenure. Kemp (1990) examines the logic and the prospects of what he calls the 'reprivatisation of rental housing' in England and Wales. Crook *et al.* (1991) provide an in-depth study of the first two years of the Business Expansion Scheme. Gibb (1990; 1994) and Bailey (1996) discuss many of the issues raised in this chapter in more depth. A special issue of *Housing Studies* (vol. 11 no. 1, January 1996) is devoted to the PRS and provides several different perspectives. Crook *et al.* (1995) is a possible alternative.

QUESTIONS FOR DISCUSSION

1. To what extent does the economic explanation of rent controls account for the decline of the private rented sector in the UK in the twentieth century?
2. Imagine you are an investor with funds that could be directed into the private rented sector. Outline the main financial and economic factors (both positive and negative) that would influence your decision to invest in residential property.
3. 'The evidence therefore supports the view that rent deregulation was a necessary but not a sufficient condition for achieving a viable revival of private renting' (Crook and Kemp, 1996). Do you agree with this conclusion? What conditions might be sufficient to revive the PRS?

8 Help with Housing Costs

INTRODUCTION

This chapter provides an introduction to the Housing Benefit system (HB). Housing Benefit is extremely important for Britain's housing finance system, as it is the main person-oriented housing subsidy in the social and private rented sectors. The chapter

- discusses the development of the system and the way it operates;
- looks at the coherence, effectiveness and fairness of HB;
- examines ways in which the system's faults might be remedied;
- assesses the 1996 reforms to HB and income support for mortgage interest.

State support to meet housing costs has a long history in Britain. Income-related assistance for people in all housing tenures was established in the 1930s in the form of Unemployment Assistance, and voluntary local authority rent rebate and differential rent schemes were introduced from 1930. The number of authorities providing such schemes declined after the Second World War. In short, the growth of schemes aimed at helping people with their housing costs was *ad hoc*, and only became systematic as part of the government's response to the disintegration of the post-war consensus that existed around the Beveridge social security system proposals. As this chapter will indicate, this has had profound consequences for the housing component of income maintenance policy, now funded separately and known as Housing Benefit. Income-related housing assistance is a central part of any well-functioning housing finance system. Yet, in the UK, apart from all the practical problems created by the introduction and administration of Housing Benefit, there is still a fundamental tension between the income maintenance and housing policy objectives of the scheme. This tension underpins the discussion of affordability and the use of income-based subsidy to relieve the burden of housing payments.

HOUSING BENEFIT IN PRACTICE

The Present System

Housing Benefit provides low-income tenants with an *ex post* rebate of their rents. In other words, the rebate depends on the actual level of rent chargeable, rather than an *ex ante* allowance, which gives the recipient a predetermined sum that can be used to bid in the market-place. Housing Benefit is administered by local authorities, but, at least until the introduction of ring-fencing (see Chapter 4), virtually all Housing Benefit expenditure could be reclaimed from central government. The new system, introduced in 1988, followed the Fowler Review of Social Security in the mid-1980s and tried to coordinate the three existing means-tested benefits (Supplementary Benefit, Rent Rebates, later Housing Benefit, and Family Income Supplement) around the household's eligibility to Income Support (which replaced Supplementary Benefit; Family Credit replaced Family Income Supplement).

Housing Benefit is structured around the Income Support system so that if the claimant is eligible for IS then 100 per cent of their eligible rent is met. For incomes above this threshold, the amount of support is reduced by 65 pence for each additional post-tax pound, ultimately reducing to zero. The actual outcome for the claimant depends on the combination of household circumstances, rent levels and the Income Support framework. Household circumstances are mediated through the system by several factors. Based on the assumption that non-dependents make a financial or unpaid contribution to the household, non-dependent deductions are used, varied by the income of the non-dependent. To cover the expenses associated with working, households may earn a small amount (a 'disregard') without their benefit being affected. Income is assumed to be earned on savings in excess of £3000 ('tariff income'), which reduces entitlement to Housing Benefit by increasing the income figure in the calculation. Savings of more than £16 000 exclude the claimant from receiving Housing Benefit (which is especially important for non-IS-claiming pensioners). This is twice the size of the equivalent ceiling for standard IS claims.

Rents are similarly affected by a number of factors. For instance, there are eligible rent ceilings, chiefly influenced by rent officers, who are empowered to set maximum ceilings for Housing Benefit, above which local authorities cannot reclaim Housing Benefit expenditure from central government. The rent officer sets a property-specific rent for the size of the property based on the local market, a higher rent being deemed 'unreasonable'. The Conservatives introduced the concept of the local reference rent, which is another form of ceiling on benefit expenditure, this time based on the median rent for a property type in a specific location – this is further discussed at the end of this chapter. Rents in the benefit calculation do not include fuel and service charges.

The basic level of the Income Support system is also important. Table 8.1 indicates the basic benefit levels that the Income Support system provides for different household circumstances. It also shows the relative weightings than different circumstances receive. The system has normally been up-rated by inflation rather than average earnings, which in the past meant that low-income benefit recipients become poorer over time if, as has been the case, average earnings tend to grow at a faster rate than inflation. There are also specific Housing Benefit rules on, for instance, the treatment of students, people in hospital, and so on, (discussion of the mechanics of the system can be found in McKenny *et al.*, 1996). Income Support with mortgage interest payments is discussed below.

A Worked Example

The system is formula-based, and can be readily explained with an example using 1995–6 allowances and tapers (following McKenny *et al.*, 1996). For each assessed household, net weekly income (from all sources, including assumed income derived from savings in excess of £3000, and with an earnings disregard to reflect working expenses) is set against the household's applicable amount (based on household composition, age and certain premia for disability and the like). Table 8.1 shows the 1998–9 applicable amounts, which can be thought of as reflecting the amount of resources that households in different circumstances should require to attain the minimum acceptable standard and quality of life. Thus, a single claimant aged between 18 and 24 receives £39.85 per week as an applicable amount, whereas a single parent over 18 receives £50.35

Table 8.1   Benefit levels: applicable amounts, 1998–9

Index numbers rounded to nearest whole number

Personal allowances	Index (couple = 100)	£ per week
Single claimant 16–17[a]	38	30.30
Single claimant 18–24	50	39.85
Single claimant 25 or older	64	50.35
Lone parent under 18[a]	38	30.30
Lone parent 18 or older	64	50.35
Couple both under 18	76	60.10
Couple, at least one 18 or older	100	79.00
Child/young person aged:		
less than 11	22	17.30
between 11 and 16	32	25.35
between 16 and 18	38	30.30
18 or over	50	39.85
Premia[b]		
Carer premium	17	13.65
Family premium	14	11.05
Pensioner premium (60–74):		
Single person	25	20.10
Couple	38	30.35
Enhanced pensioner premium (75–79):		
Single person	28	22.35
Couple	42	33.55
Higher pensioner premium:		
Single person	34	27.20
Couple	49	38.90
Severe disability premium:		
Single person	49	38.50
Couple – one qualifies	49	38.50
Couple – both qualify	97	77.00
Disabled child premium	27	21.45

Notes
[a] In some circumstances, a 16 to 17 year old may get the 18 to 24 rate.
[b] Lone parent premium was abolished in 1998–9.
Source: The Benefits Agency (1998).

plus a family premium of £11.05 (plus a dependant's allowance for each child varying from £17.30 to £39.85 depending on age).

In each assessment for Housing Benefit, there is essentially a six-stage process of calculation:

1. calculate assessable income for the household;
2. calculate the applicable amount;
3. the excess income is (1) − (2);
4. multiply excess income by 0.65 (the taper);
5. calculate eligible rent;
6. Housing Benefit is the eligible rent minus (4).

Scenario One

For our first example we will use a couple both over 18 (giving a basic allowance of £79.00) who have one child of 8 years (£17.30). Their weekly applicable amount A is therefore £79.00 plus £17.30 plus £11.05 which equals £107.35. If their gross unrebated rent R is equal to £35 per week and, in the first scenario, their net income Y from all sources is £85.00, then with the taper of withdrawal t is 65 per cent (20 per cent for council tax), we can calculate the net rent and Housing Benefit received by the family. In this example, there are no non-dependants in the household, so there need be no further deductions, and we assume that the contracted rent is 'reasonable' in terms of Housing Benefit determinations.

The basic formula for Housing Benefit HB can be expressed in the following way:

$$HB = R - t(Y - A)$$

If the household's income Y is above its applicable amount A, then Housing Benefit HB is reduced from the maximum level (100 per cent of gross rent R) by a fraction t (65 per cent) of the difference between income and applicable amount. Eventually, household income will be sufficiently greater than the particular applicable amount such that Housing Benefit will fall to zero. At the other extreme, if income is less than or equal to the applicable amount then Housing Benefit is equal to the gross rent (in other words, net rent is equal to zero for the household).

Thus, for our illustrative family, when their income, net of disregards, is at £85 (that is, below their applicable amount) their Housing Benefit is equal to their rent (£35 per week). This means that they qualify for income support (because their applicable amount is greater than their measured net income) and they receive the maximum eligible Housing Benefit.

Scenario One Summary
Net income $Y =$ £85.00 per week
Applicable amount $A =$ £107.35 per week
Rent $R =$ £35.00 per week
$HB =$ £35.00 per week because Y is less than A

Scenario Two

In our second scenario, the family's income is higher, at **£150.00**, and the HB calculation comes into play:

$$HB = 35 - 0.65(150.00 - 107.35)$$
$$HB = 35 - 0.65(42.65) = 35 - 27.72 = £7.28$$

The difference between the income figure and the applicable amount is now £42.65. We take 65 per cent of $Y - A$, that is, £27.72, and that figure is the reduction in Housing Benefit from the 100 per cent rent rebate. With an income of £42.65 more than their applicable amount, Housing Benefit falls to £7.28, in other words, the household must pay nearly 80 per cent of the gross weekly rent. Under the council tax rebate system, the calculation is exactly the same, except that $t = 0.20$.

Scenario Two Summary
Net income $Y =$ £150.00 per week
Applicable amount $A =$ £107.35 per week
Rent $R =$ £35.00 per week
$HB =$ £35.00 minus $0.65(150 - 107.35) = £7.28$

Council Tax Benefit

The formula for this is:

$$CTB = CT - 0.2(Y - A)$$

In the second scenario above, when the hypothetical household has $(Y - A)$ equal to £42.65 and a council tax of £15 per week (£720 per year on a 48 week financial year), then their weekly council tax benefit is equal to:

$$CTB = 15 - 0.2(42.65) = 15 - 8.53 = £6.47$$

In words, the maximum rebate of £15.00 per week is reduced by £8.53 per week as a result of their income rising above the $(Y - A)$ threshold. In net terms, of their additional £42.65 income in excess of the relevant IS threshold, our hypothetical family loses £27.72 in extra rent payments and £8.53 in council tax payments: 85 per cent *of the additional income is swallowed up in loss of benefits, an illustration of the disincentives associated with means-testing in the form of benefits withdrawal.* Also note that this hypothetical family will lose more of the marginal pound if it is eligible for and receives Family Credit. Family Credit is also means-tested (with a 70 per cent taper) but does possess the advantage of being time-limited, that is, receipt is guaranteed for six months on the same terms, even if the recipient's economic circumstances improve. However, Family Credit is being replaced with a tax allowance, the Working Family Tax credit, as a result of the 1998 Budget.

Housing Benefit Expenditure

Housing Benefit

Figure 8.1 gives an indication of the growth in Housing Benefit expenditure in recent years, in real terms, by 75 per cent between the introduction of the scheme and 1994. This has happened despite successive cuts to the generosity of the scheme and the stabilising of the caseload at around 4.5 million. Kemp (1994) argues that the growth in expenditure can be attributed to rising rents and the demographic changes ongoing in society, which together are producing an overall caseload made up of a disproportionate amount of benefit-expenditure-expensive households (pensioners and one parent families). Explicit policies toward all of the rental sectors have pushed up rents, and this has caused increases in Housing Benefit: producer subsidy has been replaced by personal subsidy.

Income Support for Mortgage Interest

Owner-occupiers with a mortgage may also receive help with their (current) housing costs. Income Support for Mortgage Interest provides mortgage payers with limited help with their interest payments when and if they qualify for Income Support (which may occur typically if a mortgagor becomes unemployed). In the context of the collapse of the housing market in the early 1990s, it is important to stress the quantitative significance of Income Support for eligible mortgagors. New policy introduced in 1996 delayed assistance for low-income mortgagors through the Income Support system with the basic intention to supplant social insurance with private insurance (discussed further later in this chapter). Housing Benefit and mortgage interest paid through Income Support now account for more than 12 per cent of all social security expenditure

Figure 8.1   Housing Benefit and Income Support for mortgages – expenditure Great Britain, 1980–1 to 1997–8

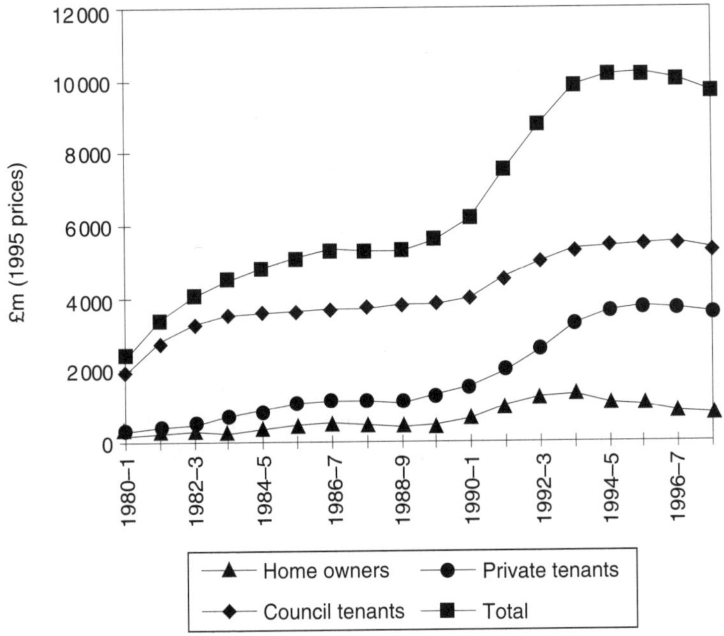

Source: Wilcox (1997a, table 116b).

(Kemp, 1994). This is expected to rise further and has been the chief motive for policy reform to restrict the growth of public spending in this area, including setting rent ceilings on social rents.

At the peak in 1993, more than 550 000 mortgagors received help with their interest payments (Wilcox, 1997a, table 104). This reflects mortgage repayments problems alongside inflationary increases in house prices and mortgages in the 1980s. The latter were associated with unemployment and family breakdown but also, increasingly, the uncertain and vulnerable nature of modern day working (Gibb, 1994) characterised by fewer permanent jobs. Figure 8.1 shows the increasing levels of expenditure in this field since 1979. In the period after 1990, there is a strong correlation between this uptake and the housing market recession. It is expected that the new provisions that encourage private insurance against mortgage non-payment will substantially reduce claims (although an improving housing market and economy help, too). The most striking trend in Figure 8.1 is the real-terms growth in rent allowances and income support mortgage interest payments in the early 1990s. This reflects, among other things, deregulation in the private rented sector, and has also been the subject of reforms aimed at slowing expenditure growth (see below).

The 1996 Housing Benefit and Income Support Reforms

Private Renting

The 1994 Budget introduced reforms to Housing Benefit for private tenants, and to the assistance mortgage payers get with their interest payments when qualifying for Income Support. These changes, introduced in January 1996 with subsequent amendments, were designed to bear down on the cost of Housing Benefit and have been the subject of much controversy. There have been some amendments as a result of the election of the Labour government in May 1997, but the main reforms remain in place.

For the private rented sector, rent determinations by rent officers were changed to limit 100 per cent benefit to any rent that is at or below the 'local reference rent for the area', rather than the previous measure (which is 100 per cent of the reasonable market price). That part of the rent between this 'average' and the 'market' rent receives a 50 per cent 'top-up'; the portion of rent twice as high or more than the local reference rent is ineligible for HB. In this way, the maximum eligible rent has a locally determined ceiling, which reduces the 100 per cent marginal subsidy above the local reference rent. The local reference rent is calculated by the rent officer using his or her own definition of the local market, and is based on the mid-point of rents in that locality, excluding extreme cases.

In 1997, the local reference rent principle was further extended. From October of that year, the local reference rent became a *de facto* ceiling for the eligible rent calculated for HB in the private rented sector (that is, there is no top-up beyond the local reference rent).

There are four wider changes alongside the local reference rent approach. This system also applied to housing association rents 'only where they [rent officers] consider the rent to be unreasonably high or the tenant to be over-accommodated' (SSAC, 1995, p. 9). The second point is that these new controls may damage the position of vulnerable groups, and the government therefore proposed that each local authority should have 'increased discretion' to fund higher amounts of HB in exceptional circumstances, funded by a cash-limited budget, alongside the local authority's own capacity to make payments itself. Third, a voluntary system of pre-tenancy determinations was introduced to provide prospective tenants with information about how much HB they are likely to get (although it is not mandatory to take part, those landlords that do are legally bound to keep proposed rent levels). Finally, eligible rents for single persons below the age of 25 have been set at the local reference rent for single rooms. This system obliges low-income single young people to move into shared housing and out of larger accommodation. This is a Treasury-driven approach, which is likely to force rents down to the ceiling, and to create the familiar rent control effects of a dwindling quantity and quality of stock in that portion of the private rented sector.

Income Support for Mortgage Interest Payments

In the owner-occupied sector, the 1994 changes were two-fold: reducing the mortgage ceiling to £100 000 and to lengthen the period for new and existing borrowers before they are eligible for limited and subsequently full Income Support. Under the new arrangements, existing borrowers who make a new claim for

Income Support assistance will receive no help with mortgage interest for 2 months before moving on to 16 weeks of 50 per cent help (and 100 per cent thereafter). New borrowers receive no help for 9 months before moving onto 50 per cent assistance (and 100 per cent only after a further 16 weeks). The presumption is that borrowers will seek private mortgage protection insurance to cover the gap.

Insurance is not equally available for all categories of need, and take-up has been low (estimates have variously placed take-up between 20 and 40 per cent of all mortgages). Companies can screen out bad risks for new borrowers on the margin, but lenders presently have a mortgage book in excess of 10 million borrowers, many of whom will possess insecure labour market characteristics. Some categories of workers will be ineligible or will not qualify for insurance (some modifications to the DSS position were made to ease the difficulties faced by disabled people who tend to find it difficult to obtain such insurance). There are also serious technical problems with private mortgage protection insurance. Will the insurer be able to assess and price a household's risk accurately before the household buys a home? (This is the problem of *adverse selection*: high-risk households will disproportionately seek out insurance relative to low-risk households.) Also, how will any household respond to labour market risk once it is insured and faces different incentives? (This problem is the one of *moral hazard*: once insured, a household will have less incentive to prevent unemployment occurring.) Because the introduction of mortgage protection insurance has occurred alongside the housing market and economic recovery, the impact of the scheme has not yet been seen. The next housing market recession will test its mettle. Increasing fears about the next downturn have prompted some housing commentators to contemplate a *compulsory* private insurance scheme.

PROBLEMS WITH THE HOUSING BENEFIT SYSTEM

Upmarketing

'Upmarketing' is a rather unhelpful term for a more general consequence for what some people believe to be the way Housing

Benefit is designed. The difficulty arises because of the way support is given to tenants. We saw above that benefit is given to tenants according to the calculation:

$$HB = R - 0.65(Y - A)$$

where HB is Housing Benefit, R is the eligible gross rent, Y is the appropriate measure of net income and A is the household's applicable amount for Income Support purposes. If income is less than or equal to the applicable amount then $R = HB$. The important point is that the system is designed to protect the recipient's post-housing level of income so that whenever rents rise, provided they qualify for Housing Benefit, then the recipient's net rent (the actual amount they must pay) remains unchanged. This also means that their income is preserved at the level designed to meet the costs of the minimal standards of life.

In the formula, HB meets the rise in R fully because it is only when the income-applicable amount relationship changes that eligibility to HB falls. Because of the *ex post* nature of the subsidy, the recipient tenant has their net rent completely insulated from changes in gross rents. The idea of 'upmarketing' therefore originates from the idea that any tenant receiving Housing Benefit has no incentive to economise on housing costs and will have an incentive to trade up and occupy housing larger than they require, since the marginal cost in rent terms is zero. It also implies more generally that households have less incentive to move in response to price signals. Lower consequent rates of mobility are likely to lead to greater misallocation of the housing stock to households, as a benefit-receiving household has little direct incentive to move to property of a better 'fit' for its present needs. This will be inefficient and will misallocate properties and households.

There is disagreement as to the extent of the problem of upmarketing. Economists argue that this inbuilt inefficiency will prevent market signals operating and distort the actual allocation of households to houses. Others would argue that there is no market mechanism for most rented housing (normally socially rented) existing in Britain, so there in turn is no logical case to be made for upmarketing. Kemp (1992) considers that the problem is specific to the privately rented sector and is an *empirical* question – it may exist in some market niches in particular locations for specific periods of time. It also often argued that other social security benefits (such as pensions and IS) are so low in Britain relative to elsewhere that Housing Benefit has to cover 100 per cent of housing costs at the margin, although this is to discount the long term housing policy consequences of such a rebate structure. It could also be pointed out that, for example, the council tax as a property tax dissuades households from over-consumption, but this would be a very simplistic perspective on a tax that has no general revaluations, is relatively flat in payment terms and, in any case, has a means-tested rebate.

Below we discuss the importance of moving away from flat and inconsistent rent structures to rent-setting based on (that is, pro-portionate to) capital values, for instance, target rents. Although the Conservatives introduced some safeguards to limit Housing Benefit upmarketing, such as locally varied ceilings on local authority rents and Housing Benefit rent limits, the advantages of such a shift (property rents reflecting current values, with advan-tages for enhancing choices, as well as intra-authority equity) would be wholly lost under the present system of Housing Benefit. In short, the fact that people's contribution to their rent is determined only by their income and not by the rent level negates the benefits of many reform strategies aimed at creating among other things more realistic and consistent rent structures. If the new rent regime was tied to higher average rents then this would probably increase the right to buy.

The extent of the problem is difficult to quantify because cross-sectional information will only clarify the whole picture if people are over- or under-consuming housing at the time of being asked – one needs to follow households over time to find out how they respond when household circumstances alter. The issue *is* an empirical one but in a broader, more longitudinal way than suggested elsewhere. Furthermore, the problem of zero marginal cost is an important constraint on wider reforms. Moving to a more coherent and market-influenced set of rent differentials may be seen as imposing considerable change on social housing. Again, it is important to stress that the personal impact of moving to such a system depends on average rents before and after the structural change – the objective is to improve the rational and efficient use of the housing stock which is compatible with a wide range of social housing 'roles'. Changes to the HB system as it applies to the private rented sector introduced in 1996 (discussed above) effectively place a ceiling on rents eligible for HB. This reduces the opportunities for upmarketing to the extent that those rents liable for HB are close to what rent officers deem to be the local median rent for a property type (known as the reference rent).

The Poverty Trap

The worked example illustrated that the Housing Benefit system is a major contributor to the very high marginal tax rates faced by a household as its gross earnings rise just above Income Support thresholds (that is, the change in net income arising from a small rise in gross income). The taper of benefit withdrawal has been 65 per cent of net income since 1988 (equivalent to 43 per cent of gross income and has been rising throughout the 1980s and 1990s – see Table 8.2). For a family on Family Credit, the marginal tax rate is as high as 97 per cent. Even with the end of Family Credit, the marginal rate of tax at these critical levels of income is in excess of 85 per cent. Gross earnings have to rise to more than double the IS threshold level of earnings for a family with one child before marginal tax rates fall to more normal levels of around 35 per cent. Housing Benefit contributes to this huge disincentive in order to target benefit and to save the Treasury money.

Table 8.2 Housing benefit means-tested income tapers, 1983 to 1995

Time period	Rent taper	Rates/council tax benefit taper	Community charge taper
Up to March 1983	17	6	
April 1983	21	7	
April 1984	26	9	
November 1984	29	9	
November 1985	29	13	
April 1987	33	13	
April 1988: gross	43	13	10
April 1988: net[a]	65	20	15
April 1995: net[a]	65	20	

Notes
[a] Income Support system based on net income rather than gross.
Source: Hills (1991, table 10.1, p. 168).

The government has set itself the objective of turning welfare into work. Labour market disincentives, partly the result of HB, are central to reform debates actively being encouraged in Whitehall and around the country. Countless schemes have been devised in the academic literature to address these disincentives, for instance, 'basic incomes', wherein all households are guaranteed a certain amount of money income, thus extending the personal allowance (but provided in cash). The major drawback of these schemes is that they would be highly expensive in increased taxation, as would any substantial increase in the personal tax allowance, and would inevitably draw more people into the welfare net.

The fact is that specific costed solutions such as the cutting of the taper to 50 per cent (Burrows *et al.*, 1993, estimate that this would cost £340 million per annum) do not mention that such a policy *widens* the poverty trap by significantly increasing the number of households in receipt of Housing Benefit and also increasing their marginal rate of tax (Hills, 1991). This may be an acceptable trade-off, but it must be made clear: a cost of reducing the depth of the poverty trap for those worst affected is to extend it to those on higher incomes than at present (see also, Wilcox, 1993). This is an inevitable consequence of means-testing through income levels.

How many people are actually affected by the poverty trap? Direct measures do exist (Hills, 1993, p. 24). Taking households with at least one earner, Hills estimates that for 1992–3 around 75 000 families face an implied marginal tax rate of between 90 and 99 per cent; some 175 000 face a tax rate of 80 to 89 per cent; 250 000 face a rate of 70–79 per cent and about 15 000 face a tax rate of 60 to 69 per cent (in 1985, another 230 000 faced a marginal tax rate of between 50 and 59 per cent). If we add in the numbers of households not on Family Credit plus the millions on Income Support (there were 2.3 million Housing Benefit cases in May 1991), then we can estimate the scale of the problem. In addition, as with the zero marginal cost problem, the problem not only refers to those in the trap but also it awaits households that face future loss of earnings or uncertain household income.

The key issue, one where there is little hard or compelling evidence, concerns how individuals actually respond to the labour market situation. Do they behave 'rationally' and actually change their behaviour in response to changing marginal tax rates, or do people value work for its own (non-pecuniary) sake and actually make labour market choices on that basis? While economists have produced many findings on the supply elasticity of employment with respect to wages, there is much less conclusive evidence on the elasticity of employment in relation to marginal tax rates (see Bowen *et al.*, 1990). In addition to the poverty trap there are wider barriers that many face which inhibit participation in the labour market and which government has to address – in particular, inadequate child care facilities, high transport costs and a lack of overall macroeconomic demand are barriers to participation in the labour market. In short, there are external as well as internal factors that contribute to labour market disincentives. This does not, however, in any way diminish the importance of reducing the negative impact of Housing Benefit.

The Unemployment Trap

Low-income mortgage payers receive help from the Income Support system to meet their interest payments. In practice, this means that those who are unemployed (for in other circumstances, where repayments become difficult such as relationship breakdown or one of two joint mortgagors losing work, income is often still too high to qualify for IS). Recipients are left with an all-or-nothing choice when a job offer arises: take the job and meet all your mortgage payments from your own resources or stay unemployed and receive help. The unemployment trap is created when the assistance provided by the social security system give no financial incentive for the unemployed person to take a job. It is, of course, a close parallel to the poverty trap. The disincentive effect in this case may prevent home owners returning to the labour market for even moderately well-paid jobs.

When Housing Benefit was reviewed in the mid-1980s, extending support to owner-occupation was rejected because of mortgage interest tax relief and because of understandable resistance to subsidise the ownership of an asset. This left only Income Support as a safety net for mortgagors who got into trouble. Of course, it was not expected in 1985–6 that 75 000 home owners could be repossessed in a single year (1992) or that more than 350 000 could be more than 6 months in arrears (1993). Government did not bargain for expenditure of more than a billion pounds in Income

Support payments spent in 12 months (1992–3). The extent of the unemployment trap is debatable (Wilcox 1993, pp. 16–17). The Department of Social Security estimates that only 5000 households were worse off working rather than being unemployed and receiving Income Support in 1992–3. Wilcox defends a figure closer to 100 000, mainly as a result of working home owners currently in mortgage arrears. As with the question of the poverty trap, one of the most heated controversies in the economics of the labour market is the effect on unemployment durations created by the replacement ratio, that is, the ratio between earnings in work and benefits out of work. Part of the 1980s deregulation of the labour market by the government targeted the replacement ratio, which those in office believed to be too high. Reducing benefits was supposed to make people accept lower wages and reduce unemployment, but this has to also take into account the large passported benefits associated with Income Support: that is, automatic eligibility for other benefits given receipt of Income Support not least help with housing costs, which is a large hidden constraint on getting people back to work, even in a deregulated labour market.

REFORM TO THE EXISTING SYSTEM

Kemp (in Hills *et al.*, 1989), compares the UK system with those of several European countries, and a number of conclusions emerge which serve as a useful starting point for this discussion of reform to income-related assistance with housing costs. First, housing costs of low-income owners who are slightly above Income Support thresholds are not catered for. And it is also true that very low-income, often pensioner, home owners without a mortgage receive no housing help. Second, the wide variations in average rents across Britain suggests that a maximum eligible rent would be practically impossible. However, a variant might in principle be based on individual property characteristics or on the basis of a property's assessed rental value, augmented by regional retail price indices to try to capture variations in purchasing power. Third, the requirement of paying 100 per cent of housing costs for those on Income Support should be maintained. Fourth, the taper of withdrawal of benefit is argued to be too steep in the UK. Finally, Kemp accepts that the emerging market context of British housing requires a movement away from the 100 per cent marginal benefit rate that applies to households in receipt of Housing Benefit (1989, pp. 67–8). The key point is that if tenants are to be able to exercise choice, then in the market-place these choices must be related to different levels of costs and prices. Breaking the 100 per cent marginal subsidy provides the basis for price signals about the state of demand to be sent to suppliers, thereby allowing resources to be allocated – at the least more efficiently than is the case at present.

In this chapter, we consider reforms to HB that fit into the present system of Income Support (with no more than minor alterations). Short-run reforms that have been proposed by the housing lobby and commentators can be categorised around two criteria:

(i) equity-based proposals;
(ii) efficiency-based proposals.

Equity-Based Proposals

There is a lengthy hit-list of reforms aimed at reducing disadvantage with inevitable public spending consequences (most of the alleged discrepancies were introduced as thinly disguised spending cuts in the 1980s). The most important 'problems' concern (in no particular order): students' ineligibility for Housing Benefit; the disadvantaged treatment of under-25-year-olds (and 16–17-year-olds) relative to older single people; the steep taper of benefits withdrawal which influences working incentives; uprating benefits by the retail price index and not average earnings; the case for increasing the earnings disregard, reversal of which would be a partial and temporary way of alleviating the poverty trap; and the rate at which savings are treated as net income.

The first-round annual costs of bringing students back into the system (£70 million), of increasing earnings disregards to £10 (single) and £25 (couple) (£100 million), of reducing the tariff income on savings from £1 to 50p for every £250 (£110 million) (thereby bringing more people into the system), and of restoring under-25s to full assistance (£25 million), would, if non-dependent deductions were ended for non-dependants on Income Support (£44 million), together total £349 million (all figures from Burrows *et al.*, 1993, p. 7) – and that would be before the costs of increased take-up. The present public spending context, however, makes this type of expansionary approach politically infeasible.

The higher costs are first-round effects only, however, and they assume no consequent change in household behaviour. Reducing the taper may encourage a greater take-up from those who experience reductions in their marginal tax rate. Whether this offsets the effect on other households who now face higher marginal tax rates is an empirical question. Reducing earnings disregards would, however, benefit low-income households. There would also be wider gains from mobile students moving to more preferred degree courses in the knowledge that they could rely on Housing Benefit to fund accommodation (with benefits to the privately rented sector). One may also expect to see wider benefits from the protection of 16- and 17-year-olds from homelessness that the reforms would allow. Reducing the savings tariff income rate may encourage more saving, especially among the elderly. In general, these reforms would bring about an increase in the general standards of living for the previously most poor sections of society. Thus, the wider net effects of these reforms should also be accounted for and, indeed, articulated, in the face of opposition on the grounds of public expenditure priorities.

Efficiency-based Proposals

Here, the focus is on two policy reforms: Hills's *Dual Taper* Scheme (Hills, 1991) and Webb and Wilcox's *Mortgage Benefit* Scheme (Webb and Wilcox, 1991). Both options would cost more money, at least on first-round estimates, but both have interesting behavioural implications.

Dual Taper Scheme

Hills set out to design a Housing Benefit reform with the minimum of administrative complexity that has favourable impacts on both the 'upmarketing' problem and the incentives problem. This is 'achieved' by inserting a second taper that is relevant to incomes above the household's Income Support threshold and which is only eligible to cover 60 per cent of housing costs (rather than 100 per cent at the margin, as at present). Furthermore, the taper is brought down below 65 per cent (Hills suggests 20 per cent), reducing the incentive problem associated with such a high marginal tax rate. The crossover point between the 65 per cent taper and the lower, second taper takes place 'where the excess of net income (less any disregards) over the appropriate Income Support rate exactly equals the rent' (1991, p. 177). In other words, tenants are on whatever taper leaves them better off. With tapers of 60 per cent and 20 per cent, Hills estimates that the net additional annual cost of the Dual Taper would be £239 million in 1992–3 prices Again, these are first-round effects: Hills argues that the 'upmarketing' problem will be restricted because of the impact of the second taper, and that incentives to work will be greatly enhanced for those worst affected by the poverty trap.

Mortgage Benefit

Webb and Wilcox (1991) present an argument in favour of means-tested support to low-income home owners. This reform would replace Income Support payments and add a new tier of assistance in the form of a tapered benefit for households with incomes just above the relevant Income Support threshold. Mortgage Benefit would operate in the same way as for tenants, except with a lower taper (on the general grounds that 65 per cent is too high for anyone) and with cumulatively less mortgage repayments becoming eligible for assistance as the total mortgage rises (to retain the principle of targeting). Webb and Wilcox estimate that the annual cost of the new benefit to be £453 million (re-calculated to 1993 prices), although they predict savings in the form of improved behavioural incentives in the form of more people choosing to work as a result of the tapered support at levels above Income Support thresholds.

The net cost (and behavioural effects) will turn on the controversy discussed above about how many households actually fall into this owner-occupied unemployment trap. One public expenditure issue that is not tackled in this proposed reform, however, is the possibility that interest rates might rise quite rapidly – with significant effects on the overall cost of the scheme; this may well force government to lower interest rate ceilings on mortgage benefit. And the device of putting a ceiling on mortgages eligible for support does not really tackle the 'upmarketing problem'. It would only really be effective at the upper end of the housing market. In other words, *where* the ceiling on eligible mortgage debt is set will be critical in determining the behavioural impact of Mortgage Benefit. Other criticisms are less valid: arguments used by the Social Security Review and others that home owners should not be subsidised in the purchase of an asset are not credible: helping poor households meet current interest payments is not actually subsidising the acquisition of an asset.

CONCLUSION

Housing Benefit is pivotal to housing finance in the UK. It is, unfortunately, caught between the differing objectives of social security and housing policy, and its structure is flawed in important ways. The 1988 reforms simplified the system's structure, but there remain serious weaknesses in the scheme that are due to the government's determination to cut public spending and the re-peated failure to act on their knowledge about the significance of the Housing Benefit system for housing finance and housing policy. The Housing Benefit system has failed to counter the poverty trap problem, or to provide assistance for low-income households while sending the correct signals to the housing system. The policy reform packages outlined by Hills and others represent potential ways to overcome or change the policy framework. The next chapter will argue that the labyrinth of housing finance and the maze of Housing Benefit and its consequences are inextricably bound up (for example, the relationship with rent-setting in the public sector, where three-quarters of tenants receive Housing Benefit). The efficiency and equity problems that are created by the interaction of these policy programmes are so great that the system must be simplified and reformed.

FURTHER READING

The annual publications by Ward and Zebedee (various) and McKenny *et al.* (various) are the standard works concerning the operation of the Housing Benefit and social security system in Britain. Kemp (1992) is a comprehensive discussion and appraisal of Housing Benefit. Glennerster (1997) provides a clear account of the arguments and development of the welfare state and the development of social security spending. In a very helpful report, Hills (1993) sets out the welfare state debate as it has developed in recent years. Housing finance discussion of the Housing Benefit system is rare, but can be found in Kemp (1992; 1994) and in Barr (1993). In terms of the interaction between Housing Benefit and reform of the overall system, the second report of the Inquiry into British Housing is well set out. Authors presenting alternatives to the present system include Hills (1991), Webb and Wilcox (1991) and Gibb (1994; 1995; 1996).

QUESTIONS FOR DISCUSSION

1. What are the main problems associated with the *structure* of Housing Benefit? To what extent does the Hills Dual Taper Scheme overcome these problems?
2. Imagine you are a civil servant charged to provide the Minister with briefing. Draw up a list of the effects on the housing system of a significant reduction in Housing Benefit eligibility. Which groups in which sectors would be most hit by an across-the-board reduction in benefits?
3. The wholly publicly funded system of Income Support for mortgage interest payments has now passed into history. Can an insurance-based system (or partly insurance-based system) provide stability and adequate coverage?

9 Key Issues in British Housing Finance

INTRODUCTION

The preceding chapters have defined and discussed the main structural elements of Britain's housing finance system. As well as conveying how these interact, the aim has been to show how the system has evolved, and to chart policy impacts, particularly over the last two decades. But what major issues are challenging the system now? And what impact might they have over the next two decades? In this chapter, four themes are considered:

- the refinancing of council housing;
- the pricing of social housing;
- the financial aspects of housing's role in urban regeneration;
- the financing of housing for community care policy.

FROM LSVTS TO LOCAL HOUSING COMPANIES AND THE PFI

Chapter 3 indicated that the possibilities for housing investment in the council sector have become increasingly constrained. Housing investment is currently (1998) running at less than 50 per cent of its *average* level of the 1980s. At the same time, the new financial regime has severely circumscribed discretion with respect to rent-setting and management and maintenance expenditure. With the convergence criteria for Economic and Monetary Union making it less likely that future governments could relax public spending definitions (even if they wanted to), it is increasingly unlikely that large, publicly funded capital programmes will be forthcoming to fund the modernisation and investment programmes required. It is not surprising, then, in such a hostile funding climate, that avenues have been examined to break out of the shackles imposed on council housing.

One way of thinking about the problem faced by council housing is that public sector housing is now a mature asset, outweighing outstanding (historic) debt such that it was recently estimated to be worth around £40 billion (Wilcox, 1994). Rental income derived from council housing makes a surplus, but this is being reclaimed by the Treasury through offsetting Housing Benefit, rather than being used to fund local capital investment.

In principle, housing stock can be transferred between landlords. A local authority could sell its stock to another social landlord (with the sitting tenants' consent) and the receipts raised could be used to pay off housing debt and any remaining receipts put to other uses.

Taylor (1996) has pointed out that there are several ways to transfer stock between landlords: the individual right to buy; neighbourhood strategies of transfer to community-based housing associations; or large-scale voluntary transfer (LSVT), primarily of local authority stock in England but also of Scottish Homes and New Town stock in Scotland. In this section, the focus is on large-scale transfers, although the principles equally apply to neighbourhood-scale transfers. Much of the focus of activity has been in England, where the first forty transfers raised £516 million in net receipts back to local authorities. There has been considerable change in Scotland too. Scottish Homes has transferred almost 36 000 of its houses (June 1998), and an indication of their value can be seen when we note that the 34 own-stock transfers between 1991–2 and 1995–6 transferred 13, 694 houses for nearly £89 million (Taylor, 1996).

LSVT requires a balloted tenant acceptance of transfer before the Secretary of State can approve the process, along with a range of consultancy and information-providing exercises. LSVT is wholly privately funded. Since 1989, some 70 councils had transferred their stock in England, all with stock valued well in excess of historic outstanding debt. This amounted to over 270 000 dwellings at a cost of over £2.5 billion. There are many issues associated with transfer: rent guarantees, tenancy guarantees (new tenants post-transfer must be given assured tenancies, while existing tenants may exercise the right to buy), debate over transfer of staff to the new organisation, conflict of interest, morale and so on. Our focus, however, is on the financial equation. How is the valuation of the stock worked out and how sensitive are the assumptions made?

Valuation

LSVTs are valued using a net present value discounted cash flow of net rents. In other words, the future flow of rents over thirty years is calculated for the likely effective stock (taking account of additions to the stock and RTB sales). Capital receipts from sales would also count as income. This income is then netted off against manage-ment and maintenance expenditure, plus the cost of 'catch-up' repairs. These are based on an assessment of required improvement expenditure prior to transfer (for the councils with particularly bad stock condition problems, the 'catch-up' requirement often makes LSVT non-viable). The net annual sum is then discounted by 8 per cent, to reflect the fact that a guarantee of money income in the future is worth less than possessing that money income now and that guarantees further in the future are worth cumulatively less the further forward the cash flow continues into the future. The net valuation is simply the sum of each year's calculations for the valuation period. Gardner and Hills (1992) among others have critically assessed the valuation methodology. Final valuations are sensitive to a number of key parameters:

• rent increases;
• flow of RTB sales, actual levels of discount and capital receipts;
• flow of assured tenancies after transfer;
• management and maintenance assumptions;
• the level of voids;
• the discount rate.

Basically, any valuation will vary with the assumptions made about each of these key items. Built into the transfer agreement is some form of rent guarantee that rents for transferring tenants will be held down in some form for an interim period of a number of years, after which rents will converge, in time, with those of assured tenants. Obviously, that rate of convergence and the implicit depth of the 'subsidy' to transferring tenants will have a major impact on the valuation. Transfers considered in 1988 would have had much more generous provision for future RTB sales than would transfers being considered in 1994 (given the collapse in the volume of RTB sales). Indeed, RTB sales are no longer a part of valuation calcula-tions in England and Wales. A similar unknown is the flow of new lettings (and voids) that will become assured tenancies on reletting. Assumptions about income will depend on all of these factors, and expenditure estimates will turn on the accuracy of assumptions made about allowances for management and maintenance.

A final point concerns the discount rate. The discount rate reduces the known value of income that will be achieved in the future, reflecting the fact that income is worth more to us now than in the future. A simple formula reduces income such that the further we go into the future the less income is worth to us relative to income received in the present. In the equation, Y is the annual flow of income received in year t which is divided by 1 plus the discount rate r to the power n, which represents the number of years into the future that the income is to be received:

$$Y_t/(1+r)^n$$

Higher values of r reduce the present value of income to be gained in the future, whereas relatively lower rates of r reduce the present value of future flows of income more slowly. It follows that a lower discount rate, *ceteris paribus*, applied to the total housing stock valuation will increase the size of an LSVT valuation (because the future value of money is worth more relative to the present as compared with a higher rate of discount). The DETR sets the discount rate for LSVTs at 2 per cent above the normal public sector discount rate of 6 per cent to 'reflect risk'. Many feel this is unsatisfactory and unnecessarily conservative, resulting in low valuations.

In the early years of LSVTs, there were many criticisms made that valuations had overestimated the value of the stock and that financial problems would arise. More recently, evidence reported by Wilcox suggests that some transferring associations will come into surplus up to ten to fifteen years ahead of schedule, earning potentially large surpluses from then on. In summary, the valuation debate shows the profound difficulties associated with valuing non-traded stock on the basis of an unknown future, as well as perhaps suggesting the need for alternative measures of valuation.

DoE Review of LSVT: 1992

In 1992 the Department of the Environment became increasingly concerned with the progress of LSVTS. Their concerns were fourfold. First, by moving into the association sector, rent rebates became rental allowances and the DoE lost control of them. Out-with subsidy control, the cost of Housing Benefit would clearly rise. Second, the government was concerned about creating new private monopolies out of previously council monopolies. Third, they were concerned about the number of transfers taking place each year, which threatened to swamp DoE administratively in time and cost terms. A fourth worry was the potential for LSVTs' private funding activities to crowd out mainstream HAG private finance (LSVT associations are already a quarter of all association stock and will be 50 per cent by the turn of the century). The little evidence that exists on the subject suggests that LSVT funding has not prevented private finance reaching mainstream association investment. How-ever, government responded to these concerns by introducing three reforms to the process: a 20 per cent levy on net capital receipts was imposed to make up the losses on the rent rebate part of HRA subsidy; individual transfers were limited to 5000 units (above which councils have to split the stock into different associations); and a general control was imposed over the number of transfers (set at an annual level of LSVT proposals, not at the level of half that number which would reflect the number of LSVTS that make it through the ballot).

Local Housing Companies and the Private Finance Initiative

The basic problem faced by local authorities is that, despite having a trading account for their own stock, any borrowing to finance investment will be treated as public expenditure and hence con-trolled as part of general government expenditure. In 1993, a joint study by the Joseph Rowntree Foundation and the Chartered Institute of Housing proposed a model based loosely on the arms-length municipal companies used to provide social housing (but in the private sector) across Europe. This would be funded essentially through an LSVT process (Wilcox *et al.*, 1993; Wilcox, 1994). The creation of a trading body wherein the council has only a minority stakeholding would unlock the ability to borrow as well as earning a capital receipt that could be spent either to redeem debt or, in part, on new investment. The most striking element of this proposal, apart from the fundamental point of demunicipalisation itself, is the argument that even those councils where debt on their stock exceeds any likely receipt (the type of authority that would not run a rental surplus on their HRA) would be rational candidates for transfer to a housing company. This is because it would save the Treasury money on catch-up repairs, improvements and so on, and would still allow net new investment that otherwise would not have taken place. Wilcox *et al.* (1993) contend that total net savings to the Treasury, discounted over thirty years, would be of the order of £16 billion.

The reasoning behind these results is not difficult to grasp. Wilcox (1994) assesses the financial impact of an LSVT on the Treasury. The Treasury gains in four ways:

(i)   VAT income is generated from repair and improvement work carried out by the new landlord but contracted to other bodies.
(ii) LSVT levy income of 20 per cent of the net capital receipt is earned.
(iii) Future credit approvals will be reduced because there may be no additional investment in 'council' stock (although there will be as company stock).
(iv) Local government debt is repaid by the transfer.

The additional cost to the Treasury arises in one main way, namely, increased expenditure on Housing Benefit.

In the study, 12 case-study local authorities were examined to judge the effects of a thirty year transfer calculation. For those where the receipt outweighed the existing debt, transfer was normally though not always viable (as with any normal LSVT transfer). In one case (Bristol), the LSVT levy of 20 per cent of net receipts would cancel out *local* gains, yet the Treasury would still have stood to gain nearly £200 million in savings over the 30 years. However, it was in the cases where debt exceeded the prospective receipt that the most interesting results were found. The study found that Derby, Newcastle and Edinburgh, all with no rental surplus and no hope of a net receipt, would all benefit locally in the form of improvements to the existing stock (through catch-up) as well as freeing future credit approvals for non-housing investment. Even if the receipt did not pay off all debt it would nonetheless reduce the PSBR, while the Treasury would still receive VAT income from the sale and would also not lose out in terms of Housing Benefit. The council, however, would be left with a residual debt with no means to fund it (hence requiring a subsidy or write-off from Treasury). The key issue therefore for such potential transfers is whether the cost of the catch-up repairs is viable. Wilcox (1994) argues that it is not the absolute cost of repairs that the Treasury should take into account, but their relative cost in terms of the cost of investment to the stock if transfer did not take place.

Proponents of local housing companies tend to support them as a way to lever in social housing investment, to make use of the asset base of council housing and to improve the stock's condition. This is a pragmatic response to macroeconomic spending realities. It is true that most other European countries have institutional arrangements that avoid these problems, but it is debatable whether the unique nature of council-owned social housing in Britain is a reason to dismantle it. It is also the case that the company option will not work where repair costs are too high, if the Housing Benefit levy is too great or the savings to Treasury do not meet additional Housing Benefit costs. Nonetheless, it remains an important opportunity for change and additional funding for social housing.

In 1996, the Conservative government announced that in future local authority housing could become involved in the Private Finance Initiative (PFI). PFI had been introduced in 1992 as a way of harnessing private funding and project management skills to deliver public services with noticeable impacts in transport, health and the prison service. The extension into housing relates potentially to three areas:

- armed forces' accommodation;
- local government non-HRA housing (special needs, hostels, care in the community);
- local authority housing.

In a recent report to the National Housing Federation, European Capital (1997) argued that under certain circumstances PFI could be used to fund local housing companies on the understanding that properties would be leased by the LHC from the local authority, who would therefore retain an ownership and strategic interest in the scheme. In such a model, European Capital suggests that the council in question would form a not-for-profit company jointly owned by the council, private partners (including construction interest and perhaps a local housing association) and local tenants. The council grants the LHC a lease and, in return, the LHC is obliged to enter into specific contractual obligations: capital works, management of the stock, rent policies, maintenance standards, and so on. In terms of funding, the LHC and its private partners would be required to raise funding in such a way that it fell outwith the capital control mechanism applied to local authorities and was off the balance sheet of the private sector partners. Normally, it would be private loan finance. European Capital concludes that such a PFI model of social housing would meet the objectives set out for LHCs but would in addition retain the strategic interest and ownership of the council in question.

The Labour government has now taken the debate one step further in Scotland by introducing the concept of 'New Housing Partnerships', which appear to be a form of local housing company. Again, it shows the widening role of housing in a more holistic set of arrangements to tackle social exclusion, which involves elements of both the public and private sector, as well as participation by the local community. It is too early to say whether this partially articulated model of social housing will succeed any more than its predecessors.

RENT STRUCTURES

A fundamental issue is the question of how social landlords set rents. In Chapters 4 and 5, rent levels were discussed in relation to the average charged by each landlord. It was shown that local authorities have limited discretion to set the overall, average rent. Housing associations similarly must decide rent levels themselves for assured tenancies, taking consideration of what is deemed to be an affordable rent (although, theoretically, high rents may be subject to Housing Benefit ceilings imposed by the new officer under the local reference rent regulations (see Chapter 8). Once the overall amount of rental income has been set, social housing landlords must make a different sort of decision, namely the structure of rents that should be set in place, which determines how the rent charged on individual houses is to vary.

When deciding on a rent structure, the housing organisation is likely to have in mind some considerations of *equity*. Although it would be possible simply to charge the same amount on each property, there appears to be a generally accepted principle that tenants should not be asked to pay the same amount for a very different sizes and qualities of accommodation. However, having decided that rents should in some way reflect the overall 'amenity' of the property, a further decision needs to be made on the differential that is to be set between different types of property.

A possible second consideration in deciding on a rent structure is levels of *demand* for different types of property. Many local authorities face a situation where they have apparent excess demand for their 'best' properties, witnessed in long waiting lists for these houses, and very little demand, or even none, for some parts of the stock that are 'difficult to let'. Many authorities have relatively flat rent schemes – that is, there is not a great difference between rents charged on the best and worst properties – and it has been argued that this has exacerbated the lack of demand in the difficult-to-let areas. If this is the case, then part of the solution to these discrepancies would be to allow rent structures to reflect demand more closely, by increasing the differential between the best and the worst stock.

The Conservative government accepted the principle of widening rent differentials in its guidelines for rent-setting (linked to capital values) introduced in the wake of the 1989 local authority housing finance regime (in England). A problem with this type of 'market-based' approach is the very high proportion of tenants who receive full Housing Benefit (see Chapter 8) and who therefore face no financial consequences in paying more rent for a better house (and equally gain no benefit from paying less in rent). Such households would be expected simply to choose the best and most expensive accommodation. This is a further discouragement for poorer households to seek work. Also, even where structured to reflect market differentials, and even were there a form of Housing Benefit that did not vary with rent levels, the fact remains that the allocation of low-income households to homes is still done bureaucratically according to locally defined measures of need, and there is little point trying to set up market signals to improve the allocation of the housing stock to households if the supply of households is effectively rationed by a non-market mechanism.

Another issue that militates against the 'market' solution of widened rent differentials is that increasing the rents of the most desirable property is likely to encourage sales in such areas, as the difference between mortgage and rent payments will also be reduced. Because of the limited value of receipts to local authorities, many councils may wish to avoid giving extra encouragement to sales in such areas.

In short, it is not practical for social landlords to operate exactly as private landlords would, that is, to charge what the market will bear for each property. Nor would such a policy be acceptable to the supporters of social rented housing, who see as one of its main advantages its capacity to cut across market allocations. However, the present patchwork of different rent structures within neighbourhoods, council areas and regions is a source of confusion and distortion. Ideally, one would have a national rent scheme, transparent, fair and differentiated according to a tenant's true perceptions of the rental value of a property. Of course, for the present, this is unrealistic (social landlords value their independence in rent-setting, even if it leads to incoherence between landlords). Rather, landlords of social rented housing must set a rent administratively that has some regard to notions of equity and appropriate differentials for different types of property. Local authorities are allowed to pool rents across schemes (that is, there is no requirement that each scheme should cover its own costs) and housing associations also have scope to pool rents across developments of different vintages.

Increasingly there is also a notion that rents should be maintained at a level that is 'affordable' to those tenants in (possibly low-paid) work. This is designed to reflect the nature of the social rented sector as a provider of housing outside the normal market forces, but is at present a poorly defined concept. In Scotland, for instance, housing associations use two measures of affordability: a net rent to net income ratio, and, a residual income method such that net income after housing costs should (at least) exceed 140 per cent of the relevant household threshold for income support. The latter criterion indicates that, by itself, a ratio of housing costs to income is an ambiguous and not always useful concept. Affordability is undoubtedly an important principle of setting non-market rents, but it is arguably an issue that should be dealt with directly by the social security system rather than by housing managers trying to set a structure of rent differentials.

Possible Rent Schemes

Most rent schemes seek to reflect 'amenity' or quality of the property. The quality of housing is a multifaceted concept, but it can be usefully summarised into two main elements: first, the house itself and, second, the area. Both are important elements of the perceived desirability of properties. Relevant house characteristics would include house type (for example, semi-detached compared with a flat), size, number of rooms, presence of features such as central heating, a garage, a garden and quality of construction and fixtures and fittings (for example, does it have a modern bathroom or kitchen?). The quality of the neighbourhood is similarly complex, and if anything harder to describe. It will include the visual appearance of the area and its upkeep; its location in relation to main shopping, employment and business areas; whether there are nearby environmental disamenities (railway yards, gas works and so on); and the quality of local schools. Neighbourhood quality may also include reputation as a 'good' or a 'bad' area, encompassing how potential tenants perceive the people already living within the area (for instance, whether there are problems with crime, vandalism or drugs).

There are four generic types of rent schemes that have been or could be employed, which have different methods of reflecting the variety in housing quality:

- gross annual value;
- capital value;
- points;
- *ad hoc* systems.

Apart from ability to reflect variety within the stock, other criteria can be used to judge rent schemes, including the administrative simplicity and cost of running the scheme, the comprehensibility of the calculation to tenants and others, and the degree of control that housing managers can exercise over the outcomes.

Gross Annual Value

This scheme relies on the district valuer's assessment of the amount of rent that each property would raise in a private rented market (that is, the rateable value). The total amount of gross annual value (GAV) available in the stock of housing is then divided into the total rental income required, to give a figure for the amount of rent that should be charged, per pound of gross annual value. The rent structure derived from this system depends entirely on the evaluation of the district valuer, whose decision-making process is not typically open to close scrutiny, either by tenants or by housing managers. It was a relatively simple scheme to administer, as the district valuer had to assess rateable values in any case. Because rates have now been abolished, this convenient basis for assessing the value of different properties will no longer be available to landlords (or at least, it will no longer be updated).

Capital Value

Under this system an assessment is made of each dwelling's value on the open market (again probably by the district valuer). Rents are then set by dividing the total rental income required by the total capital value in the stock to give the amount of rent per pound of capital value. Again, the differentials here would be determined by the valuations made and would therefore be related to factors similar to those used in GAV based schemes. Capital-value based schemes require a separate valuation from the district valuer, but such valuations have become increasingly available with the growth in the right to buy. Hills (1991) developed a variation on capital value rents known as target rents. This was designed as a nationally uniform rent-setting device for all social housing based on three elements: maintenance and management costs, an allowance for depreciation and a specific return to the capital value of the property. This final element would be explicitly subsidised by being set below the market rate of return.

A potential problem with value-based schemes (that is, both capital values and gross annual values) is that tenants may be penalised, through higher rents, for improvements they make to their house. However, this problem has been recognised and the Housing Act 1980 stipulated that tenants must not be penalised for such work, but rather that adjustments must be made to the rents charged to take account of the tenants' own improvements to their properties. A closely related problem is that tenants collectively may have considerable influence over the general amenity and quality of the neighbourhood (for example, tidiness, appearance of gardens, policing vandalism and damage) and, once again, tenants who work to maintain better-quality environments may be penalised by higher rents. It is virtually impossible to determine to what extent a good quality of neighbourhood can be regarded as due to the efforts of the people living there.

Points

Points schemes award points for different features of a dwelling (for instance, a number of points may be given per room, or bedroom, for having a garden, central heating, modernised fittings and so on, and a scale of points may be given to the different qualities and the desirability of area). The total amount of rent required divided by the total number of points for the local authority stock gives an amount of rent per point, which can then be applied to each dwelling to give the rent. In some senses, points schemes are simply a crude way of valuing differences in amenity, selecting a limited range of factors that add to value and giving a fixed weight to each. The main advantage of points schemes is that differentials (for example, between similar houses in the best and worst areas or between large and small houses) and the factors that are taken into account when setting rents are under the direct control of housing managers. Rent differentials are then explicitly determined as part of policy and are accountable to the local electorate. Such schemes are also relatively 'open', to the extent that the differences between the rents of different types of property can be relatively simply explained and understood.

Ad hoc *Systems*

Such systems would simply have a schedule of rents, perhaps by house type, size and area, probably adopted from previous years. A variation on this approach is the 'base rent' scheme where all properties have a basic amount of rent charged on them per annum and specific additions increase the annual rent charge on a consistent basis (£X per annum for an additional bedroom, £Y for a front and back garden; £Z for full central heating, and so on). Increases in rent required are likely to be implemented by a uniform percentage rise in rents in each class or on the base rent (or even a flat rate increase for each rent). Note that uniform increases tend to flatten the rent structure over time. The main advantages of such schemes are their simplicity and cheapness to administer.

The Conservative government encouraged moves towards capital-value-based rent differentials in England and Wales. Notional rents since 1990–1 (that is, those in the notional HRAs – see Chapter 4) reflect the differences between capital values in different local authorities. As this scheme was implemented, rents became increasingly subject to additional upward pressure in those areas that had high house prices. From the early 1990s onwards, however, it became apparent that the rising average level of rents was simply transferring rent increases into spiralling benefit expenditure. Apart from trying to tackle this at source through successive tightening of Housing Benefit, the Conservative government conceded that rents could not continue to rise, and Housing Act 1996 stated that non-market rents should not rise further towards market rents. This has not affected rent differentials, which remain at the discretion of local authorities. Registered housing associations have to put their rent schemes forward for regular monitoring by the appropriate regulator – The Housing Corporation, Scottish Homes or Tai Cymru/Welsh Housing Department).

All social landlords need to consider carefully their approach to rent differentials. At the same time, the effects of numerous conflicting and distorting schemes spread across the UK should be given consideration. While flat rent structures cannot be treated in isolation, they nonetheless form part of the solution of a more coherent and rational system of housing finance.

HOUSING AND URBAN REGENERATION

In Chapter 4, we noted that a high proportion of local authorities' housing capital investment in Britain has been devoted to repairing or renewing council housing, rather than to building homes anew. And in Chapter 5, we saw that the rehabilitation of older private housing, and of post-war council housing estates has been the focus of much housing association activity. Both of these forms of housing investment have clearly led to significant improvements in the quality of Britain's housing stock – dramatically reducing the numbers that fail to reach a tolerable standard (Scotland) or a standard fit for habitation (England and Wales). Public housing investments have also altered the physical shape of different neighbourhoods, and have levered in private housing and retail and other investments. It is for this last reason that housing investment has increasingly been seen as an essential catalyst to the physical renewal of poor neighbourhoods, and an important component of efforts to improve the life quality of the residents of these areas.

The main economic principle upon which regeneration policy has been built is *spillover*. There are two visible aspects of this:

- investments in upgrading housing can reinforce each other in small areas;
- a policy that concentrates investment in small areas may have clearer impacts than one that 'peppers' investment over a wide area.

Focusing housing renewal investment on an area basis has a long history in Britain, going back to the city improvement trusts of the nineteenth century. More recently, areas of poor-quality *private housing* (privately rented and owner-occupied) have been improved through individual grants (Chapter 6) and through housing associations' development programmes. Their success has led to housing associations and cooperatives also being charged with the leadership of renewal of run-down *council housing* areas.

The policy and legislative focus of 1960s and 1970s programmes and powers was generally on renewal, that is on physical housing and environmental improvements. Urban regeneration is a wider term, encompassing reducing unemployment, reducing crime, improving health and educational attainment, reducing isolation and helping resident integration into the mainstream of social and community activity. In these respects, urban regeneration is a vital component of strategies to counter 'social exclusion', the umbrella term drawn from European Union debate about social change and polarisation. Much policy change in the 1980s and 1990s has been about using housing investment alongside attempts to promote urban regeneration and mitigate the causes of decline. The clearest way this can be seen is that housing renewal is packaged with other social programmes, with very explicit government expectations of resource providers working in coordination to achieve specified goals. Thus, across Britain the current policy language (1998) is of holistic, multi-agency partnerships.

Different countries have, however, arrived at this point in different ways. In England, in the late 1970s, the Inner City Partnerships were devised on the principle of local government being a lead actor in regeneration. These partnerships set out to bring different government departments' programmes together, to agree a unified strategy. Implementation proved less easy than imagined, and the Inner City Partnerships dissolved.

As we saw in Chapter 3, the Conservative administration of the 1980s jettisoned bipartisanship between central and England's local governments. The response to political difference was centralisation, and privatisation seen in measures such as task forces, city action teams, urban regeneration grant and city grant. Most notably, the **Urban Development Corporations** (established in 1987) were set up and financed by central government to provide private sector, property-led regeneration. Their financial support grew, while support to municipal governments dwindled. And housing, education and welfare services suffered at the same time as government was, implicitly at least, trying to improve poorer parts of the country.

The housing-oriented parallel of the Urban Development Corporations were **Housing Action Trusts** (set up in the Housing Act 1988). Private-sector-led trusts could access central government funds to purchase and improve run-down council housing. Estate Action involved the direction of central funds to targeted estates of council housing. Local authorities were subordinate in the process.

Criticism of the entrepreneurial approach, its low impact and lack of co-ordination prompted government to change tack. In 1992 it introduced City Challenge, a five-year initiative designed to encourage cooperation and strategic planning. £37.5 million was allocated to each of 31 urban authorities via two competitions. Importantly, the competition also explicitly recognised the importance of local partners in determining priorities and tailoring appropriate plans. Centralisation was replaced by partnership. The principle of competitive allocation of resources for needy areas was received – not surprisingly – with some reservation or hostility. Yet, it seems likely that competition has encouraged higher-quality strategies than might otherwise have been possible.

In 1994, government created the **Single Regeneration Budget**, which was to be administered from its regional offices (see Chapter 1). The budget brought together a multiplicity of different programmes within a single fund for competitive allocation. It remains too early to judge its impact, though the Comprehensive Spending Review significantly increased provision for it (Treasury, 1998b), extending it to all of the most deprived local authority areas by 2002.

In Scotland, central government (that is, the Scottish Office) did not adopt an adversarial approach to local authorities. Instead, the 1980s were marked by general consensus, and a degree of policy continuity from the late 1970s. Scotland has no Urban Development Corporations, no City Challenge, and less centralisation than England. As we saw in Chapter 3, however, Scottish councils' budgets were squeezed just as hard as those of English ones.

Looking back at the history of British urban renewal policy, we can see that one of the most influential initiatives came from Scotland towards the end of the 1975–9 Labour administration. The Glasgow Eastern Area Renewal Project (GEAR) comprised the conjoining of different agencies' resources – including those of the local authority, councils, housing associations, local enterprise companies and health boards into the regeneration of a declining inner industrial area of Glasgow.

To a greater extent than south of the border, peripheral estates of council housing were identified earlier as the locus of many of the worst problems of urban deprivation. The political response to what analyses of the 1981 Census showed was the Conservative administration's *New Life for Urban Scotland* (Scottish Office, 1988). This transferred the GEAR model to four council housing estates. The Scottish Office chaired Partnership Boards, which developed and managed investment strategies between the various agencies and their responsibilities. These estates were selected for concentrations of funding over a ten-year horizon. One of the four estates moved out of Scottish-Office-chaired partnership within the decade.

In 1995, the Scottish Office reviewed the scope of urban policy. This resulted in *Programme for Partnership* (Scottish Office, 1995), which adopted the New Life approach to smaller areas of council and poorer private housing called Priority Partnership Areas.

For the whole of Great Britain, the Labour government elected in 1997 defined a strong policy focus on tackling Social Exclusion, and an Inter-Departmental Group, the Social Exclusion Unit was established to steer it. Two of its actions are particularly noteworthy:

- the New Deal for Communities – which operates across Britain, though to somewhat different mechanics in Scotland and in England and Wales, it aims at regenerating the 'poorest communities', on the basis of comprehensive strategies;
- Social Inclusion Partnerships – for Scotland only, evolving from the Priority Partnership Areas.

The net result of different policy initiatives, and of amendments to policy emphases, is that there are currently a series of financial mechanisms for promoting urban regeneration. The bases for action can be summarised as follows.

England and Wales

- *Renewal Areas*   in 1990, the Renewal Areas replaced the General Improvement and Housing Action Areas (which had designated as areas for investment since the late 1960s). Over half a million dwellings have been repaired or improved using the enhanced grant levels payable in these areas. They are similar in conception to Scotland's HAAs (see below).
- *City Challenge*   £37.5 million has been allocated to each of 31 authorities on a competitive basis.
- *Single Regeneration Budget (SRB)*   Funds are allocated to local authorities and their partners on a competitive basis, bids being made to the Department of Environment, Transport and the Regions. The SRB was set up in 1994, with government aiming to encourage holistic approaches to urban and economic regeneration by drawing together the funds from 20 separate programmes (representing £1.4bn in 1994–5). The evidence to date suggests that housing investment *per se* may not do as well under SRB as its predecessor initiatives (particularly the Estate Action programme). That negative conclusion may be offset by improved coordination between housing and other resource programmes.

Scotland

- *Housing Action Areas (HAAs)*   These are aimed at tackling poor conditions in private housing. The HAAs have existed since the late 1960s and have improved poor-quality city tenements, many of which were owned by private landlords or low-income owner-occupiers. Their mechanics include purchase by a housing association, and the housing association's committee choosing an appropriate redevelopment package. Resident participation on these committees has been an important aspect of the HAAs and therefore regarded highly for community involvement in regeneration.
- *Urban Partnerships*   Public capital expenditure in the partnerships has been of the order of £320m over the period 1988–97, and housing accounts for the vast majority of this (about 75 per cent).
- *Smaller Urban Renewal Initiatives*   These were set up by Scottish Homes in 1991 to apply a partnership approach to smaller areas of towns and cities in central Scotland. They have mainly tackled council housing areas and associated town centres, and housing capital investment has dominated activity to date.
- *Priority Partnership Areas (PPAs)*   The 12 were areas chosen by government in 1996 for dedication of Urban Programme funds. New government monies (£42m over the period 1996–7 to 1999–2000 period) were allocated on the basis of a balanced programme, showing partnership in the use of housing, Local Enterprise Company (LEC), health and other resources. The areas were selected on a competitive basis following bids from local authorities and their 'partner' agencies across Scotland. The expectation held by the government is that the PPAs should embrace a broad policy agenda and merit the new title of Social Inclusion Partnerships.
- *New Housing Partnerships*   These were established by Labour in the autumn of 1997. A capital fund of £35 million for 1998–9 was initially created then increased subsequently to £45 million. Funds were allocated on a competitive basis, for renewal and other projects demonstrating partnership in resource use. These were the main mechanism selected by government for spending additional resources under the Comprehensive Spending Review.

Great Britain

- New Deal for Communities - established by Labour in 1997, and allocated £800 million of funds for 1999–2002 under the Comprehensive Spending Review (Treasury, 1998b). Targeted at the poorest neighbourhoods, with separate administrations and mechanics for Britain's different countries.

Finally, it is important to note that the European Union has been an important source of urban renewal funding. There are two programmes of direct relevance:

- the European Social Fund;
- the European Regional Development Fund.

These were developed in the early 1990s, as European Union members embarked upon increasing economic integration. They were designed to support parts of the union experiencing low growth, suffering industrial decline, or suffering because of population scarcity. Grants are allocated on a competitive basis, with national or local governments, private and voluntary sources, being expected to match the EU award. Housing projects alone cannot be funded through the programmes, but housing has benefited from spillovers from training funds, and from workspace and community facility development.

PAYING FOR COMMUNITY CARE

Mainstream housing is not suitable and appropriate for everyone. There are three main types of reason why this can be so:

- the *physical* design of housing may not be suitable: for people with limited mobility, or wheelchair users, most mainstream housing is difficult to use (although this should gradually improve as standards of accessibility become incorporated into new build housing – in both the public and the private sector). There are well-established standards for 'barrier-free' and 'accessible' design which incorporate 'special' features (such as level access, wider doors, grab-rails and bathroom adaptions) that enable many people with physical disabilities to manage independently in their own homes.

- Additional *support* may be needed for some in managing a tenancy or running an independent household. People are not inevitably equipped with the organisational skills required to pay rent, to keep their property in good order or to manage living within a budget (people leaving care and those who have been homeless for some time often benefit from additional help of this type). This support can sometimes be needed only temporarily and then withdrawn as skills and confidence as required. Warden schemes for older people make available emergency help when it is needed.

- Additional *care* may be needed. Some people need more direct, personal care to manage independently. Such care can cover a wide range of needs. Some profoundly disabled people will need help with daily tasks of washing, dressing and feeding; some disabilities are such that fairly constant supervision may be needed (for example, for sufferers of dementia), and others are unlikely ever to be able to learn to manage tasks such as shopping, budgeting and cooking. These needs impinge on providers of social housing in a range of ways. Local housing authorities have had a long tradition in providing housing for those with 'special' needs, particularly older people for whom alarm systems, sheltered and amenity housing and dispersed warden schemes are increasingly common. Although provision often falls below recommended levels, local authorities also provide housing that is adapted for people with physical disabilities, including housing accessible to those in wheelchairs. In addition, many authorities have accommodation for those who have been homeless and have developed schemes that offer extra support to those requiring help to manage a tenancy. Housing associations provide many similar housing options independently, and some work more or less exclusively to provide accommodation for people with a particular type of need or condition. In addition, voluntary organisations co-operate with housing providers to produce schemes designed for particular groups, commonly with the voluntary organisation providing the care and support and the housing association providing the accommodation.

The impetus towards *community* care reflects a dissatisfaction with the care and living environments provided by many traditional, larger institutions. It also reflects a *positive* wish to enable all people to enjoy as near 'normal' a life as possible, within settings that are as much like 'normal' homes as possible, recognising that this is what most people want. A related benefit lies in people having contact with, and being supported by, the community at large. It has, however, proved difficult to translate these ideals into practice.

Despite its better intentions, the funding system of the 1980s operated in a direction contrary to these community care ideals. The system was biased towards the provision of residential care, even for those whose need was not such that it could only or even best be met in an institution. In addition, the policy was enormously expensive. These two problems prompted a review of the community care policy leading to two influential reports in 1988: the Griffiths Report, which focused largely on ways of improving the organisation and finding of community care, and the Wagner Report, which dealt with mechanisms to provide better quality and choice in community care. The suggestions made in these reports were largely adopted in the National Health Service and Community Care Act 1990, which has formed the basis for policy development since then.

The core groups identified as potential community care users cover an enormously wide range of individual capacities and disabilities (both within and between groups), comprising the following:

- physically disabled people;
- people with a learning disability;
- people suffering a mental illness;
- older people.

In addition, other groups are frequently considered as part of the planning and provision structures of community care, such as:

- young people leaving care;
- those recovering from drug or alcohol abuse;
- ex-offenders.

The changes implied in the 1990 legislation were wide-ranging. They emphasised the key role of social services in the co-ordination of community care, involving needs assessment and planning, and the promotion of joint work and networking among agencies, particularly health, social services and housing. In addition, there was a commitment to the closure of most long-stay institutions and their replacement by smaller, more individually tailored living arrangements in the community. The scope of the changes involved is too broad to be considered in detail here. A particular issue has been the role of housing in community care provision. It seems clear that the ideals imply a central role for the provision of good-quality, suitable housing to be coordinated with the provision of appropriate care. In principle, it seems clear that with appropriate housing and support packages people can be enabled to live more independent and satisfying lives, even with very profound disabilities, as much good practice in Britain and the rest of Europe has demonstrated. However, it is arguable that in practice housing has not been able to play this centrally important role, and problems with funding mechanisms are critical in this.

Providing Accommodation and Support for Community Care Users

The system for funding the care that people require in non-residential settings, whether in grouped or supported accommodation or in individual homes, is complex and is inevitably bound up with the system for funding housing more generally. The range of needs covered is enormous, and this inevitably adds to the complexity of available funding arrangements. It is difficult to envisage, let alone design, a unified system that responds fairly and flexibly to the competing demands from the very wide range of legitimate community care clients. For instance, funding can be given to providers of some occasional domestic help for an older person, to the provision of care and support for a profoundly mentally disabled adult living with elderly parents, and to those who are recovering from dependence on drugs. The need for the whole range of services is potentially very great and therefore very costly. So debates about *mechanisms* of provision inevitably become involved in ways of rationing services and prioritising access. It should never be forgotten that a great deal of community care is provided within households and by family members, neighbours and others on an entirely unfunded, more or less voluntary basis. Many people look to the statutory services only to cover the gaps in the support networks they are able to draw together themselves.

Housing agencies are involved with community care provision at many levels. Housing management is often the first contact point for people who suffer minor incapacities or difficulties in managing independently at home. The ability to offer intensive housing management may in some instances be sufficient to enable people to manage independently in their own home over the long term (the boundaries between what is legitimately 'housing management' and what is 'care' have been the subject of keen dispute, discussed in more detail below). Such additional demands may emerge through normal housing management activities (for example, in following up rent arrears, or dealing with neighbour complaints), or may be organised as separate, targeted schemes (such as support for young people in their first tenancy).

Housing agencies also play a central role in providing specific accommodation for community care groups. Very often specially designed accommodation is provided that, for example, allows groups of people with similar needs to share some parts of the accommodation and the support services provided, or that may allow for live-in support workers. Alternative models take the care and support required to individuals' own homes, perhaps specially adapted ones. This section will consider the way such options are accessed and funded.

Accessing Community Care: Assessment

Anyone who might have a need for community care services is entitled to be assessed by social services and to have an individual package of care developed. Although everyone is eligible for a preliminary assessment, this is used as a screening procedure for the allocation of care management services. The intention is that there should be a flexible and consultative process in which the potential user and their carers, along with an individual care manager, agree on the care and domiciliary support that is best suited to that individual, but it has been criticised as being a much less flexible process than this description would suggest – that is, one in which users can find it difficult to make their views count and where professionals may tend simply to allocate users into the 'best' available provision. Empowering and responding to users' wishes is an important but complex element of the intended reforms to community care. The great success of the independent living fund, for instance, which gives people money to make arrangements to meet their own needs, shows that many people are able and willing to take responsibility for managing even very complex care packages for themselves. There is an increasingly active lobby group asserting the full rights of disabled people – challenging conventional 'professional–client' relationships. These debates are rather beyond the scope of this chapter, though it is clear that funding mechanisms play a vital part in defining the overall flexibility for choice in the system and the balance of power in relation to decision-making about expenditure. The main outcome of the process for individuals is that they should have a preferred housing and care provision agreed, bringing with it the commitment of the statutory agencies to provide that for them.

Planning the Provision of Community Care

The cornerstone of providing accommodation and support for community care users is the community care planning system. This brings together all involved agencies (particularly health, social services and housing) to identify the major trends in demands for services (such as those arising from institutional closure programmes or an ageing population) and, where appropriate, to agree priorities for new provision.

Basically, the provision of all such services is limited by available capital and revenue budgets. And capital expenditure decisions have revenue implications, for example, the provision of a group home implies the future staffing of that housing.

Social services play a critical role in the day-to-day management of much provision as well as at the more strategic level of planning services. In order to foster an environment in which social services provision is treated equivalently to that of other providers, a split has been implemented in many social services departments between the provider and the purchasing function. Such a split was encouraged in the legislation, and, in principle, enables a distinction to be drawn between the strategic level decisions concerning the broad allocation of budgets and the operational level decisions made by providers concerning quality of care, value for money and so on.

Within the purchasing function, the intention is that expenditure should be organised by *contract*. The 'macro-contracting' at the strategic level can be organised either by *block* or by *spot* purchasing –

- *block purchasing* constitutes an agreement to buy a certain amount of provision, for a given period in the future (ten places in a home, or a thousand hours of home help for the next five years, for instance), while
- *spot purchasing* is where the service is bought only when a user has been identified through the assessment process, and provision is subsequently commissioned so that it just meets the needs of that user.

These alternative ways of organising activities can have major implications for housing providers who manage accommodation for community care users.

Block Purchasing

This clearly gives more security for providers, who are assured of longer-run financial underpinning for their provision. It is also argued to enable an authority to act *strategically* to encourage the development of a new type of provision or the growth of under-provided services. The major danger in block purchasing is that the very *existence* of provision encourages an allocation of users into what is available, instead of fostering a very individual approach to provision that is designed through the assessment process and arguably better implemented through spot purchasing.

Spot Purchasing

In principle, this allows the most flexible response to individuals' need's because care and support packages are designed and bought for each individual as they are agreed through the assessment process. However, such arrangements can cause concern to housing providers. They can be left facing considerable risks because there are no guarantees that their provision will be occupied at any one time, and so they will be forced to bear the cost of any unpredictable void levels. There is also, of course, no guarantee that it will always be possible simply to buy the desired provision as needed – providers may not be able to respond quickly and flexibly, particularly if they are faced with major changes in the demand for their services (for example, housing providers would find it very difficult to respond to a major switch in preferences for shared to individual accommodation, or *vice versa*).

Providing Joint Packages of Housing and Community Care

The main contribution that housing providers make to provision for community care users is the capital contribution of developing accommodation. For local authorities, most developments would be undertaken as part of social services capital expenditure (although accessible, barrier-free and sheltered housing are often part of the main capital programme). At the same time, housing associations can develop housing for community care users using HAG/SHG funding in the usual way (see Chapter 5). Projects for 'special needs' groups are not under the same obligation to raise private funding as other housing association developments and public capital funding may be provided for up to 100 per cent of costs. Even so, when developing a scheme for people who will need ongoing support, there will be significant continuing costs that need to be considered (especially for the staff required to provide that support).

The main source for meeting running costs is rental income. However, the additional care costs make this a more complex equation than usual. Rents to cover both running and care costs can often be very high. A significant area of debate between the government and housing providers was alluded to earlier: housing providers argued that a more intensive housing management function was a valid part of their activities and an important element of maintaining many people in their own homes in a cost-effective way, while the government has been very careful not to allow significant *care* costs to be incorporated into rents – and therefore borne by Housing Benefit. The providers' argument has been accepted to some degree, and limits have been agreed as to what types of activities can be considered to be 'enhanced' housing management. There is a special management allowance, SNMA (Special Needs Management Allowance) in England and Wales, and SNAP (Special Needs Allowance Package) in Scotland, which is available at varying levels to cover the costs of enhanced management in schemes.

In many cases, those in community care groups are dependant on benefits of various kinds. This makes the issue of 'affordability' less important than for others, but reframes the question of financial viability in terms of what costs the benefit system will cover. Housing Benefit can be claimed for rent, and SNMA or SNAP may be available for additional support. If this does not cover the whole costs of provision in the scheme then there are some additional sources of money. First, occupants can be asked to make a contribution. To the extent that this comes out of benefit income, it leaves them with less than the statutory minimum income, but this may be considered legitimate if some of the support provided in the scheme offsets the usual cost of living (if, for instance food, laundry and so on, are provided). Second, social services may pay for some elements of the care – this would be the case where social services had accepted the responsibility of funding care for particular people. Finally, charitable or other sources of grants may be sought.

The key problem with this system is that it is fragile and complex for housing providers contemplating undertaking a new development or faced with the ongoing task of managing an existing development. In a context of tight budget constraints, problems are exacerbated by the different organisations involved attempting to shift the financial burden between themselves. It can be very difficult, either at the development stage or even at each annual round of funding allocation, to be certain that a scheme remains financially viable, particularly as commitments to revenue or capital finance may be dictated by different administrative timescales. Revenue budgets can be subject to delays in agreement, leading to long periods of uncertainty when the future financial security of projects cannot be assured.

A core rationale for the changes implemented in the community care legislation has been to control overall public expenditure on community care more tightly. An important part of this agenda is reflected in attempts to keep Housing Benefit expenditure under control. Where housing and care are provided together, as in sheltered housing, hostels and so on, there is a clear potential for Housing Benefit to cross-subsidise the cost of care. If rents are set to cover the costs of both care and accommodation then the danger, from the government's point of view, is that the Housing Benefit system would provide an open-ended subsidy to support these costs. Of course, this was resisted and an important part of the debates that have existed around the financing of housing and community care has been around defining the costs that Housing Benefit can legitimately cover. The principle has been established that Housing Benefit should cover only the costs of providing accommodation, including the costs of managing it, and not the costs of care.

Residential Care

The 1990 legislation introduced radical changes to the system of providing funding support to those living in long-stay residential institutions. These changes particularly affected older people as the framework operating throughout the 1980s had been very generous in funding residential accommodation and there had been an enormous expansion of such provision. The new framework was intended:

- to redress the balance of advantage *towards* care solutions in the community and away from residential accommodation;
- to encourage a variety of providers rather than the social service departments of local authorities;
- to enable tighter control to be exerted on expenditure on long-term residential care.

It is beyond the scope of this book to analyse the system of funding residential care in detail. And, given the relatively long timescales involved in the provision of residential care, it is too early to evaluate fully the effectiveness of the funding framework. It is clear that the system does *not* produce the same incentives to place people in residential care, because the costs must now be met from a cash-limited budget. Other apparent consequences are as follows:

- More of those in residential care must now make a contribution to the costs of their care, both because of tight restrictions on the conditions in which people are able to get full state funding and because, even for those entitled to state help, funding rules mean that full costs are not necessarily covered.
- Controversy surrounds the means test for help with residential care costs. A person's *assets*, as well as their income, is considered, and in many instances these (including their own home) must be sold and much of the proceeds used to pay for care.

A central problem remains that there is still a greater degree of security – both physical and financial – available to those in residential care than to those seeking similar support in their own homes. There are many examples, particularly in Scandinavia, of innovative schemes that provide care equivalent to that available in residential homes, even to those with very demanding conditions such as severe dementia. Yet, in practical terms, the availability and flexibility of funding restricts the extent to which similar schemes can be developed in Britain. This is especially so because it is becoming clear across the board that there is no reason to suppose that community care will ever be a *cheap* option compared with large-scale institutions.

CARE IN THE COMMUNITY – CONCLUSIONS

The reforms to the funding of community care have been radical and wide-ranging. It will take a very long time for the full effect of some changes to become clear. There is no doubt that outcomes are shaped by the changing financial framework. Providers can and do have a range of organisational, professional and principled or altruistic aims, but can still be driven to follow the dictates of the funding system into producing what can most readily be funded.

Some major effects are evident at present. For the provider, revenue funding of support and care can comprise a poor and patched tapestry, made up of a variety of more or less fragile sources of income. Services can be forced to adapt or decline in response to changes in funding packages. For the user, the institutional and funding arrangements militate against a seamless service. Some aspects of the funding framework mean that the user's role as purchaser is increased in the quasi-market of community care. On the other hand, the security and freedom of choice of users may be undermined by resource constraints, funding insecurities and shifting priorities. There are serious difficulties in coordinating the joint action required between the various authorities, with some evidence of attempts to shunt responsibilities and costs among agencies where possible. In this context it is remarkable that the momentum to address more complex needs persists. There can be no doubt that the financial bias in favour of residential care is now dramatically reduced and the overall cost of community care is now much more effectively controlled. In making budget management more explicit, there is also clearly a more effective incentive for strategic management. Ironically, success in these objectives is making it *more* difficult to expand the mixed economy of care. Private residential homes are closing, and many voluntary agents are finding it very difficult to manage the more market-oriented and risky regime. In this broader context, the quasi-market nature of the reforms do not seem to be securely founded, particularly with respect to responding to users' needs and demands.

In the longer run, there are potentially serious issues of affordability for the country as a whole to be faced. Though expenditure may be better controlled with respect to residential care, it should not be assumed that care at home will always be cheaper. Indeed, there is growing evidence that the provision of effective care 'at home' can be *very* costly – consider, for instance, the costs of providing full-time support for an individual who is profoundly disabled, together with any required nursing care services. However, there is no doubt that increasingly imaginative and flexible solutions are becoming available that *do* achieve the ideal of responsive, individual care in 'normal' home settings, even for those with considerable support needs. There remains a danger that continuing emphasis on cost control will risk reducing the quality of service available to users and/or to burden further the great army of unpaid carers who already provide a considerable proportion of the total care.

FURTHER READING

Many of the issues raised in this chapter have been developed at rather greater length elsewhere. The key readings in relation to LSVTs are: European Capital (1997), Taylor (1996) and Wilcox (1993). In respect of urban regeneration, Leather and Morrison (1997) assemble considerable data on house condition and housing improvement policy for the different countries of Great Britain; for Northern Ireland, Nevin (1996) looks at England's Single Regeneration Budget, while Robertson and Bailey (1996) look at the development of Scottish HAAs. McGregor and Maclennan (1993) offer a critique of Scottish urban renewal policy and practice, and

Turok and Hopkins (1997) assess the evaluation of urban programme bids in a competitive environment. There has been a
tremendous amount written about community care, including a
lot of research examining the impact of the 1990 Act. There is
relatively little that focuses on the financial mechanisms, although
inevitably they impinge widely across more detailed evaluations.
Those interested in the goals of the original reform should consult
Griffiths (1988) and Wagner (1988). The Joseph Rowntree Foundation has sponsored a great deal of relevant research, including:
Clapham *et al.* (1994), Watson (1997), Griffiths (1995) and Morris
(1995). More theoretical discussion of the impact of quasi-markets
is in Means *et al.* (1994), and a more general assessment of the
community care reforms in Wistow *et al.* (1994).

QUESTIONS FOR DISCUSSION

1. Evaluate the economic arguments that can be made for and
   against transferring rented housing from councils to other
   landlord organisations.
2. How might market principles be operated to social housing
   landlords' rent structures? What problems might emerge and
   how might they be overcome?
3. Assess the mechanisms which could be used to promote urban
   regeneration. What are the costs and benefits of competition in
   programme allocation?
4. Imagine that you have been given the task of advising government on how it should reform housing's financial contribution
   to care in the community. What sorts of change would you
   advise, and why?

10 The Future of Housing Finance

INTRODUCTION

This chapter concludes the book with an overview of the current pressures on the housing finance system in Britain today. It considers possible directions for reform, as well as emerging challenges that a new or reformed system might have to meet in the future. The focus of the chapter is on the nature of how housing finance affects the housing system, rather than on the detail of the financial mechanisms.

The chapter:

- reviews recent trends in the housing system and the current context for financial decisions in relation to housing;
- evaluates the case for tenure-neutral reforms;
- considers the demands that are likely to be placed on the housing finance system in the foreseeable future.

In examining these themes, the chapter picks up and draws together many of the themes that have recurred throughout the book.

RECENT TRENDS AND CURRENT CONTEXT

Housing and Public Expenditure

The desire to contain the growth of public expenditure has emerged as a strong, over-arching theme of housing policy in recent years. Any consideration of the current context for housing finance reform must recognise:

- that the pressure to contain public spending is deep-rooted and there is no reason to think that this will fundamentally change;

234

- that there has been an increasing acceptance of the positive role that private organisations, private funding and market-like (quasi-market) incentives can play in service production and delivery.

These two factors have worked in tandem to change the housing system radically over the last twenty years and form the current starting position for any reform. We can summarise some of the main ways in which these factors have influenced housing policy:

- Direct public investment in new local authority housing has fallen dramatically. The balance of support for social rented housing has shifted away from general, bricks-and-mortar subsidy to means-tested, person-based subsidy.
- Local authorities are undergoing major change in respect of their housing role. In particular, they are moving towards an enabling role, with a diminishing function as a provider or a landlord. A major reason for this change is the requirement to invest more in social housing and to do so without it counting as public spending.
- Housing associations have been the main beneficiaries of the change in direction of social housing. Even here, however, recent growth has been curbed by declining capital programmes. Smaller programmes and lower grant per unit have led to a sharp decline in development activity in the association sector.
- Two other key areas of public spending are Housing Benefit and mortgage interest tax relief. Housing Benefit is a rapidly rising element of the social security, and there have been concerted efforts aimed at limiting growth. Further reforms of its structure are likely, and these will have a bearing on the wider housing system. Tax relief on mortgage interest is being phased out, though when it will finally disappear is a matter of speculation.

There remain major demands for spending on the social rented housing sector, both to rehabilitate and upgrade existing stock and to provide new homes for the future. It seems evident that the mechanisms that will be developed to enable such spending will involve private finance. The transfer of local authority rented housing to housing associations and arms-length companies will allow private money to be raised for improvement of existing stock. Other mechanisms, such as the PFI, or partnership arrangements, will no doubt become increasingly significant for other types of new investment.

The use of such mechanisms is at too early a stage to offer a full evaluation. However, it may be worth sounding a note of caution, which should be considered as part of a longer assessment. The long-term costs and benefits of the use of private finance have not been tested. While it may help ease the short-term constraints imposed by the system of accounting for public finance, it must be remembered that private enterprises seek to make a return on all capital invested. Ultimately, these returns must come from the consumers of the service (or public subsidy), unless efficiency savings are so great as to offset any additional costs.

Broader Impacts of the Housing System

A second major theme that emerges throughout the book is the extent to which the housing system is interconnected with many important dimensions of the macroeconomy. One key connection is forged through the central importance of interest rates to general macroeconomic health, as well as to the housing sector. Housing and mortgage markets have been seen to have major impacts on the wider economy:

- Rising house prices increase housing wealth and stimulate consumption. At the same time, rising interest rates can have a major negative impact through variable-rate borrowing.

Other important linkages have also been established:

- private renting plays an important role in the housing system, by adding flexibility to the owner-occupied sector and by housing households that are unable to access social housing. Despite a number of subsidy initiatives, deregulation and some short-term growth resulting from difficulties in the housing market, the sector has not grown substantially. The failure to close the yield gap, or even to accord the sector some priority means that a potential source of flexibility in the housing system is lost.
- The design of the Housing Benefit system makes a significant contribution to the barriers that face those trying to escape benefit dependency and take up work (particularly the poverty

and unemployment traps). These problems remain significant for the development of effective 'welfare to work' policies.

Many of these problems are well established and have become widely recognised. There are many suggested reforms designed to deal with specific aspects of the problems created by the housing finance system. It is clear, though, that reform should focus not just on the housing system in isolation, as there may be important spillover effects to consider.

TENURE-NEUTRAL REFORM?

This book has traced the development of the housing finance system over recent decades to explain how the system came to have the particular construction that it does. A central point that has emerged is that the housing system is fundamentally *not* fair, to the extent that all aspects of the housing finance system are strongly differentiated by tenure. Tenure is the crucial determinant of the subsidy arrangements that can be accessed. Thus the benefits received from the housing system by individuals are dependent on their tenure rather than on other more salient characteristics such as income or housing need.

The debates about reform of the housing finance system that were conducted in the 1980s look less relevant to the conditions of the 1990s and beyond. A decade ago, the Duke of Edinburgh's First and Second Inquiries into the housing finance system raised awareness of the distributional and wider consequences of the housing finance system. In particular, the Inquiries highlighted the *regressive* nature of the system of housing finance by which more affluent people, because they were predominantly owners, gained markedly more from the housing finance regime than those on lower incomes (and tenants of local authorities in particular).

Many commentators of the time proposed tenure-neutral reform, with the following objectives:

- to remove the relatively favourable tax treatment of owner-occupiers;
- to devise a much more rational and nationally coherent system of setting rents in the public sector – particularly, to allow differ-

entials to widen to reflect differences in quality across the housing stock more closely;

- to reform Housing Benefit so that it is equally available to those in all tenures and to remove the inefficiencies and potentially distorting effects of allowing 100 per cent of rents, and rent increases, to be covered for most people.

When looking to the future, would we expect demands for a tenure-neutral subsidy system to emerge more strongly? The *underlying* pressures on the housing finance system over the next few years are likely to remain *broadly* the same as in the 1980s and 1990s. The desire to present low tax rates to voters and to maximise the efficiency of public expenditure leads to continuing downward pressure on housing subsidies. However, in the light of the significant erosion of the major tax-benefit to owner-occupiers (MITR), and the recognition that the tenure now encompasses a very much broader cross-section of British society, there appears to be little appetite for making further inroads into the benefits that remain in the tenure.

The suggestions for fundamental and rational reviews of subsidies and rent-setting in the social rented sector, which were also an important element in the search for tenure-neutral subsidy systems, arguably never really reached political agendas. There are certainly few signs that such ideas might have influenced the more recent changes in the funding regimes. There are strong arguments in favour of providing a more rational and consistent basis for subsidising rented housing, particularly in relation to the fair treatment of tenants of different landlords and those in different parts of the UK and different qualities of housing. But it may be that such considerations have been sacrificed to the project of creating a more diverse rented sector, where inevitably different landlords are given a range of subsidies (for instance for the improvement of the housing stock) and some autonomy in managing their affairs as part of the overall incentive for taking on the landlord role. The move towards more 'business-like' social rented landlords, as seen variously in housing associations, the 'new public management' in local authorities and the development of housing companies contributes to a perception of rents as an organisational, operational decision rather than something for the public policy sphere. The debate may not have disappeared completely, however.

If private investors are to be persuaded to play a greater role in providing housing for rent then their potential to compete on an equal footing with the social rented sector inevitably remains an issue. This would probably need to be allied to measures of the sorts discussed in Chapter 7, which would be required to make the private rented sector a more attractive proposition for the potential tenant too.

The final element of tenure-neutral reform proposals – that of dealing with Housing Benefit inefficiencies – has arguably also been somewhat overtaken by events. As discussed, Housing Benefit reform is clearly on the agenda because of its cost and its unhelpful interaction with the welfare system. However, there is little apparent impetus behind equity-based reforms of Housing Benefit (for example, to treat owner-occupiers more generously). Nor is there much point in implementing a full 'in principle' tenure-neutral reform of Housing Benefit, unless all other elements of the housing finance system are also to be brought into line. At present, therefore, a move to a fully tenure-neural finance system appears to be unlikely.

CHALLENGES FOR TWENTY-FIRST CENTURY HOUSING FINANCE

This book has shown how the housing system has become increasingly privatised. The great majority of households are owner-occupiers, and by all accounts preferences to remain or become owners also remain high. The greater part by far of housing is also produced by the private sector. The direct role of government in providing accommodation has been greatly reduced. The role of central government in influencing outcomes in the housing sector has accordingly diminished.

What are likely to be the issues that will face the housing finance system in the future? Inevitably this must be speculation, but this book has shown that the 'classical' housing problems of ensuring access to (affordable) housing and ensuring that households are not forced to live in very poor housing conditions have not been solved. In addition, new agendas of sustainability are likely to become more and more important. And the role of housing in relieving poverty and disadvantage – social exclusion – continues to have a justifiably high political profile. We will finish this book with a brief consideration of how these factors might impact on debates and developments in the housing finance system.

Meeting Future Needs

A major issue facing the housing system is the anticipated growth in the demand for housing. Average household size continues to fall, driven by increased divorce rates, increased longevity and declining fertility rates. Recent projections have estimated that there will be an additional 4.5 million households in England alone by 2016 (that is, increasing by almost a fifth in two decades). The housing and planning system faces a great challenge in providing these homes, *where* they are needed and of a quality that will reflect the demands of the next century. Real resistance to new developments is emerging in communities that want to protect their open, green land. Increasingly, housing developments must face issues of *sustainability* in two senses:

- *Green homes* Are we identifying the energy used in housing production and finding ways of reducing it? Are we taking account of the ongoing housing-related energy consumption (particularly for heating) that can be dramatically reduced with better initial design and thermal efficiency?
- *Green neighbourhoods* Are we building houses that require occupiers to have cars? Are we creating living neighbourhoods and cities where people feel safe, can walk to work, the schools and the shops? Or is what we currently see in parts of the United States and Australia, housing estates separate from shoppping malls, what we will increasingly see in the UK?

There is no indication that new developments are taking environmental costs and benefits seriously into account, because although energy efficiency ratings are higher than in older houses they are far from the best that can be achieved. Further, there is no systematic attempt to address the broader agenda of environmental issues involving attempts to use materials that create the least adverse environmental impact as evaluated over the whole life cycle of the house. There are some policy initiatives responding to these concerns – such as the Agenda 21 planning frameworks – but they are not yet part of mainstream policy development (Raemaekers, 1999). Future policy responses to these issues could well involve financial incentives, and will inevitably have financial consequences. Implementing green housing policy is problematic to the extent that the costs and benefits of environmentally friendly housing policies may not easily mesh together. So, for example, there may be higher initial costs to gain lifetime savings in energy usage, but the first owner may not benefit greatly from these longer-term savings. The increased use of cars demanded by greenfield development will increase the greenhouse effect for the whole planet, not just the affluent British commuter choosing to live the rural idyll.

Mechanisms to improve the performance of British housing against such criteria will surely become more central to policy agendas. Yet at present there seems little evidence that the private sector is able or willing to take the lead in improving the quality of the new build stock. It may currently be a problem of consumer ignorance; if at present there is no effective demand for high energy efficiency in domestic appliances and houses, it should not be forgotten that re-cycled paper and ozone-friendly sprays are relatively recent arrivals on the supermarket shelves. While better consumer education may eventually create a climate of demand for environmentally friendly housing, the legacy of the existing housing stock may mean that improvements are difficult and costly to implement.

The Future Sustainability of Owner-Occupation

It seems clear that more houses will be required to meet the demands of the growing number of households. However, *access* to affordable housing is likely to remain an issue. The production of housing for social rented housing is likely to be limited for the reasons discussed above – particularly the continuing demand to control public expenditure. It is very clear that the majority of people are owner-occupiers, and that many others wish to be. Is it possible to expand owner-occupation still further?

Access to the *owner-occupied* sector is essentially mediated through the ability to pay. Access to insurance cover (both for life and for periods of unemployment) will also determine the ability of people to become owners, or at least the level of risk that they face when doing so. Initial evidence suggests that private insurance is *not* well able to cover owners' risks of unemployment, and low levels of take-up expose many to the potential risks of job loss. Recent changes that have reduced the availability of income support for owners in financial difficulty also increase the risk that owners face. On the other hand, the mortgage market may ultimately be sufficiently flexible to respond. As discussed in Chapter 6, the deregulation of the mortgage industry has led to a dramatic increase in the variety of mortgage products that are available, to the extent that consumers are perhaps more likely to be overwhelmed with the choice and find it difficult to understand all the subtleties of the choices on offer than to feel that there is not a mortgage that suits their particular circumstances. Already there are mortgage products available that allow for some 'holidays' in the repayment schedule, but at present it is not clear whether the industry will be able to respond to the new patterns of working.

Perhaps the most pressing issue will be how (and indeed whether) people are to be maintained in owner-occupation if they become unable to pay their mortgages over a longer period. A low-inflation environment reduces some of the risks of entering owner-occupation (particularly as the future pattern of repayments are more stable) and decreases the extent to which random patterns of gains and losses occur following relatively more and less rapid house price inflation. However, it also means that real levels of debt are not eroded so quickly, and this can make it harder for people to cope with a period of reduced income, whether this has been anticipated (such when one partner – usually the woman – leaves the labour force for some time while children are young) or is unexpected (such as during a spell of unemployment). Marital breakdown and separation can also leave one partner in a house that had been bought reflecting joint financial circumstances. However, even if the state helps people to maintain occupancy of their house through the benefit system, the question may well arise as to whether this is an acceptable solution in the longer term. If interest payments are made only by the public purse, then the occupant is not likely *ever* to own the house outright. Indeed, it is arguably fair that the taxpayer should not contribute to the purchase of an asset for owners that they can profit from later. Maintaining people in owner-occupation may prove a relatively expensive way of providing a household that is relying on benefits over the longer term with satisfactory accommodation. Longer-term problems of inadequate maintenance of the property may also arise if low-income people are being supported in owner-occupation for long periods.

A further major challenge for the future sustainability of the owner-occupied sector lies in the changes that are occurring in the labour market and the impact that they might have. These changes are described as 'labour market flexibility' and have created less security for individual workers. No longer are people to expect 'jobs for life', but a series of contracts, periods of self-employment, portfolio and part-time work. This poses at least two major challenges for housing policy:

- How can labour market insecurity be reconciled with high levels of owner-occupation, which requires stable income over a long period (particularly when inflation is low)?
- Is the housing stock sufficiently flexible to accommodate demands to work from home, allowing home office space in 'electronic cottages'?

As indicated above, it may be that the competitiveness of the mortgage industry will enable some solutions to be developed, but there is no doubt that the basis of the mortgage system is a long-term stable income from which to make steady repayments of what is a very large debt.

In summary, it is not evident that there is substantial scope for growth in the owner-occupied sector. If, in Hutton's terminology, we are turning into a 40–30–30 society, where only the 'top' 40 per cent have secure jobs and career paths and the 'middle' 30 per cent face uncertainty, then owner-occupation has probably already captured most of its potential market, assuming that the socially excluded 'bottom' 30 per cent are unlikely ever to be able to buy.

Reshaping State Housing

So what about the 'bottom' 30 per cent? If the private market cannot provide the whole solution to the growing demands for housing, then the question returns to whether a new model of social housing might fill that gap. The dominant ideology of the 1980s emphasised the benefits of allowing markets to operate, with the intention of capturing the benefits of diversity, choice and cost-effectiveness available from ideal 'free markets' (see Chapter 2). The dynamic nature of markets was contrasted with the constraining, bureaucratic, paternalistic hand of state provision. This led to a dramatic change across all areas of social welfare, most notably in the development of so-called 'quasi-markets'. These are mechanisms that are intended to reproduce some of the main advantages of pricing, profit and competition, within the state sector. These ideas led to very significant reforms in the operation of the National Health Service for instance, where internal markets, purchaser/provider splits and fund-holding GPs were intended to introduce competition between providers of health care. Similar changes were implemented in the education sector, with the introduction of provision for parental choice and grant-maintained schools opting out of local authority control. These changes were intended to foster more consumer control and market responsiveness. While much housing provision has simply been privatised directly, there is a wide range of parallel changes designed to reduce the direct role of the state in the housing sector. Involvement of non-public sector bodies has become established as conventional 'good practice' in much housing activity.

Across housing policy (as in other policy areas), there have been moves to increase public sector–private sector partnerships. These are intended to increase the level of private investment as well as to capture the benefits of cooperation across agencies. There have also been new institutions developed that may receive subsidy from central government to provide housing but are very different in structure, accountability and governance than the traditional model of council housing provided by local authorities (local housing companies and registered social landlords, for instance – see Chapter 9). The central question has become the most appropriate way for central and local government, along with these other providers, to produce the desired housing policy outcomes. The potential difficulties that may arise in trying to pursue policy goals at 'arms length' rather than through direct provision will become increasingly salient issues for housing analysis. However, the context of continuing public expenditure constraint is bound to remain, and there can be no doubt that there will continue to be a search for imaginative and flexible mechanisms that make the best use of available public sector money.

FURTHER READING

Housing systems, housing policy and housing finance are dynamic not static concerns. This means that there is constant change in mechanisms and budgets to be kept up with. This book has aimed to give readers keys as to how to interpret day-to-day change. A lot of policy changes, and their financial repercussions, can be accessed through the web: we recommend that you start by looking at the organisations via *http//:www.open.gov.uk*, and it is well worthwhile referring to Wilcox (1997a and updates). You should certainly also keep browsing the trade press – *Inside Housing, Housing Today* and *Social Housing*. Commentary on what policy changes signify in broader terms is the concern of journals such as *Housing Studies, Urban Studies, Policy and Politics* and *Environment and Planning*. A good reader on many of the topics we have reviewed is Williams (1997).

QUESTIONS FOR DISCUSSION

1. What are the main reasons why housing finance should be pertinent to questions of social exclusion? How should the UK's system be reformed in the search for greater social justice?
2. How well does Britain's housing finance system tackle issues of environmental sustainability? What steps, if any, should be taken to change that position?

Bibliography

Aughton, H. and Malpass, P. (1994) *Housing Finance* (London: Shelter).

Bailey, N. (1996) *The Deregulated Private Rented Sector in Four Scottish Cities, 1987–1994*, Scottish Homes' Research Report no. 50 (Edinburgh: Scottish Homes).

Bain, A. (1992?) *The Economics of the Financial System*, 2nd edn (Oxford: Pergamon).

Balchin, P. (1996) *Housing Policy: An Introduction*, 3rd edn (London: Routledge).

Balchin, P. and Rhoden, M. (eds) (1998) *Housing: The Essential Foundations* (London: Routledge).

Ball, M. (1988) *Rebuilding Construction: Economic Change in the British Construction Industry* (London: Routledge).

Barlow, J. and Duncan, S. (1994) *Success and Failure in Housing Provision: European Systems Compared* (Oxford: Pergamon).

Barr, N. (1993) *The Economics of the Welfare State* (Oxford University Press).

Begg, D., Fischer, S. and Dornbusch, R. (1997) *Economics*, 5th edn (London: McGraw Hill).

Benefits Agency, The (1998) *Social Security Benefit Rates, 1998* (London).

Black, J. and Stafford, D. (1988) *Housing Finance and Policy* (London: Routledge).

Bovaird, A. (1985) 'Private Rented Housing: Its Current Role', *Journal of Social Policy*, vol. 14, no. 1, pp. 1–23.

Buckle, M. and Thompson, J. (1992) *The United Kingdom Financial Systems in Transition* (Manchester University Press).

Burnett, J. (1986) *A Social History of Housing, 1815–1985*, 2nd edn (London: Routledge).

Chaplin, R., Jones, M., Martin, S., Pryke, M., Royce, C., Whitehead, C. M. and Yang, J. H. (1996) *Rents and Risks: Investing in Housing Associations* (York: Joseph Rowntree Foundation).

Chartered Institute of Public Finance and Accountancy with National Federation of Housing Associations (1994) *An Introductory Guide to the Financial Management of Housing Associations* (London: CIPFA).

Clapham, D., Kemp, P. and Smith, S. (1990) *Housing and Social Policy* (Basingstoke: Macmillan).

Clapham, D., Munro, M. and Kay, H. (1994) *A Wider Choice: Revenue Funding Mechanisms for Housing and Community Care* (York: Joseph Rowntree Foundation).

Cole, I. and Furbey, R. (1994) *The Eclipse of Council Housing* (London: Routledge).

246

Cope, H. (1990) *Housing Associations: Policy and Practice* (London: Macmillan).

Council for Mortgage Lenders (various) *Housing Finance* (London: CML).

Crook, A. D. H. and Kemp, P. (1993) 'Reviving the Private Rented Sector?', in Maclennan and Gibb (1993) pp. 67–86.

Crook, A. D. H., Hughes, J. E. Tand Kemp, P. A. (1995) *The Supply of Privately Rented Homes: Today and Tomorrow* (York: Joseph Rowntree Foundation).

Crook, A. D. H. and Kemp, P. (1996) 'The Revival of Private Rented Housing in Britain', *Housing Studies*, vol. 11, no. 1, pp. 51–68.

Crook, A. D. H., Kemp, P., Anderson, I. and Bowman, S. (1991) *Tax Incentives and the Revival of Private Renting* (York: Cloister Press).

Currie, H. and Murie, A. (eds) (1996) *Housing in Scotland* (Coventry: Chartered Institute of Housing/Longmans).

Department of the Environment (1986) *Paying for Local Government*, Cmnd. 9714 (London: HMSO).

Department of the Environment, Transport and the Regions, Scottish Office Environment Department, Welsh Office (1998) *Housing and Construction Statistics, 1986–1996*.

Department of the Environment, Transport and the Regions (1998) *The English House Condition Survey: 1996* (London: HMSO).

Department of the Environment, Transport and the Regions (various dates) *Survey of English Housing* (London: HMSO).

Ermisch, J. (ed.) (1990) *Housing and the National Economy* (Avebury: Gower).

European Capital (1997) *Private Finance Initiatives in Social Housing* (London: National Housing Federation).

Fallis, G. (1985) *Housing Economics* (Toronto: Butterworth).

Forrest, R., Murie, A. and Williams, P. (1990) *Home Ownership: Differentiation and Fragmentation* (London: Hyman).

Gibb, K. (1990) *The Problem of Private Renting*, CHR Discussion Paper no. 20 (University of Glasgow Centre for Housing Research and Urban Studies).

Gibb, K. (1994a) 'Before and After Deregulation: Market Renting in Glasgow and Edinburgh', *Urban Studies*, vol. 31, no. 9, pp. 1481–95.

Gibb, K. (1994b) *Oppositives not attracting: Labour market flexibility and housing in Britain* (Glasgow: Centre for Housing Research and Urban Studies, University of Glasgow).

Gibb, K. (1994c) *Not Enough Benefit: The Housing System and the Need for Debate* (Edinburgh: Scottish Homes).

Gibb, K. (1995a) *Housing Benefit: The Future* (London: National Federation of Housing Associations).

Gibb, K. (1995b) 'An Housing Allowance for the UK: Preconditions for a Tenure-Neutral Income-Related Housing Allowance', *Housing Studies*, vol. 10, pp. 517–32.

Gibb, K., Munro, M. and MacGregor, A. (1995) *The Scottish Housebuilding Industry: Opportunity or Constraint?*, Scottish Homes' Research Report no. 44 (Edinburgh: Scottish Homes).

248 *Bibliography*

Glennerster, H. (1997) *Paying for Welfare: Towards 2000* (Oxford: Prentice-Hall).

Glennerster, H. and Hills, J. (eds) (1998) *The State of Welfare* (Oxford University Press).

Goodlad, R. (1997) *Housing and the Scottish Parliament*, CHRUS Occasional Paper no. 30, (Glasgow: Centre for Housing Research and Urban Studies, University of Glasgow).

Grant, C. (ed.) (1997) *Built to Last? Reflections on British Housing Policy*, 2nd edn (London: Roof/Shelter).

Griffiths, R. (1988) *Community Care: An Agenda for Action* (London: HMSO).

Griffiths, S. (1995) *How Housing Benefit Can Work for Community Care* (York: Joseph Rowntree Foundation).

Hamnett, C. and Randolph, B. (1988) *Cities, Housing and Profits: Flat Break-Up and the Decline of Private Renting* (London: Hutchinson).

Harloe, M. (1995) *The People's Home? Social Rented Housing in Europe and America* (Oxford: Blackwell).

Hills, J. (1991) *Unravelling Housing Finance: Subsidies, Benefits and Taxation* (Oxford University Press).

Hills, J. (1993) *The Future of Welfare: A Guide to the Debate* (York: Joseph Rowntree Foundation).

Hills, J., Berthoud, R. and Kemp, P. (1989) *The Future of Housing Allowances* (London: Policy Studies Institute).

Holmans, A. (1987) *Housing Policy in Britain* (Beckenham: Croom Helm).

Housing Corporation (various dates) ADP *Bulletins, 1990–91 to 1997–8.* (London).

Housing Corporation in Scotland (1989) *Circular 3/89* (Edinburgh: HCiS (Scottish Homes)).

Jowell, R. *et al.* (eds) (1997) *British Social Attitudes: The 13th Report, 1996* (London: Dartmouth Publishing).

Karn, V. and Sheridan, L. (1994) *New Homes in the 1990s: A Study of Design, Space and Amenity in the Housing Association and Private Sector* (York: Joseph Rowntree Foundation).

Kemeny, J. (1982) *Housing and Social Theory* (London: Routledge).

Kemp, P. (1990) 'Shifting the Balance between State and Market: The Reprivatisation of Rental Housing Provision in Britain', *Environment and Planning*, vol. 22, pp. 793–810.

Kemp, P. (1992) *Housing Benefit: An Appraisal* (London: HMSO).

Kemp, P. (1997) 'Ideology, Public Policy and Private Rental Housing Since the War', in Williams, P. (ed.) *Directions in Housing Policy* (London: Paul Chapman).

Kemp, P. (ed.) (1988) *The Private Provision of Rented Housing: Current Trends and Future Prospects* (Aldershot: Gower).

Kemp, P. and Rhodes, D (1994) *Private Landlords in Scotland*, Scottish Homes' Research Report no. 39 (Edinburgh: Scottish Homes).

Leather, P. and Mackintosh, S. (1994) *The Future of Housing Renewal Policy* (Bristol: University of Bristol, School for Advanced Urban Studies).

Leather, P. and Morrison, T. (1997) *The State of UK Housing: A Factfile on Dwelling Conditions* (York: Joseph Rowntree Foundation/The Policy Press).

LeGrand, J., Propper, C. and Robinson, R. (1993) *The Economics of Social Problems*, 3rd edn (London: Macmillan).

Likierman, A. (1988) *Public Expenditure* (London: Pelican).

Lipsey, R. G. and Harbury, C. (1992) *First Principles of Economics* (London: Weidenfeld & Nicolson).

McCrone, G. and Stephens, M. (1995) *Housing Policy in Britain and Europe* (London: University College).

McGregor, A. and Maclennan, D. (1993) *A Review and Critical Evaluation of Strategic Approaches to Urban Regeneration*, Scottish Homes' Research Report no. 22 (Edinburgh: Scottish Homes).

McKenny, J., Simmons, D., Tait, G., Webster, L., Knights, E. (various) *National Welfare Benefits Handbook* (London: CPAG).

Maclennan, D., Meen, G., Stephens, M. and Gibb, K. (1997) *Fixed Commitments, Changing Incomes: Sustainable Home Ownership and the Economy* (York: Joseph Rowntree Foundation).

Maclennan, D. (1982) *Housing Economics* (Harlow: Longman).

Maclennan, D. (1994) *Housing Policy for A Competitive Economy* (York: Joseph Rowntree Foundation).

Maclennan, D. and Gibb, K. (eds) (1993) *Housing Finance and Subsidies in Britain* (Aldershot: Avebury).

Maclennan, D., Gibb, K. and More, E. A. (1991) *Paying for Britain's Housing* (York: Joseph Rowntree Foundation).

Malpass, P. (1990) *Re-shaping Housing Policy* (London: Routledge).

Malpass, P. (ed.) (1997) *Ownership, Control and Accountability* (Coventry: Chartered Institute of Housing).

Malpass, P. and Murie, A. (1999) *Housing Policy*, 5th edn (Basingstoke: Macmillan).

Malpass, P. and Warburton, M. (1993) 'The New Financial Regime for Local Authority Housing', in Malpass, P. and Means, R. (eds) (1993) *Implementing Housing Policy* (Buckingham: Open University Press).

Means, R., Hoyes, L., Hart, R. and Taylor, M. (1994) 'Quasi-Markets and Community Care: Towards User Empowerment?', in Bartlett, W., Propper, C., Wilson, D. and Le Grand, J. (eds), *Quasi-Markets in the Welfare State* (Bristol: Policy Press) pp. 158–83.

Meen, G. (1996) 'Spatial Aggregation, Spatial Dependence and Predictability in the UK Housing Market', *Housing Studies* vol. 11, no. 3, pp. 345–72.

Merrett, S. (1979) *State Housing in Britain* (London: Routledge & Kegan Paul).

Miles, D. (1994) *Housing, Financial Markets and the Wider Economy* (Chichester: Wiley).

Morris, J. (1995) *Housing and Floating Support: a Review* (York: Joseph Rowntree Foundation).

Mullard, M. (1993). *The Politics of Public Expenditure*, 2nd edn (London: Routledge).

National Federation of Housing Associations (1989 *CORE Quarterly Bulletin no. 1* (London).

National Federation of Housing Associations (1991) *Report of the Second Inquiry Into British Housing* (London).

National Federation of Housing Associations (1994) *CORE Lettings Bulletin no. 17* (London).

National Federation of Housing Associations and Chartered Institute of Public Finance and Accountancy (1995) *Manual of Housing Association Finance* (London).

National Housing Federation (1997) *CORE Lettings Bulletin no. 30* (London)

National Housing Federation (1998) Unpublished (CORE data).

Nevin, B. (1996) 'Estate Regeneration: From Estate Action to the Single Regeneration Budget', in Wilcox, S. (1996) *Housing Finance Review, 1996–'97* (York: Joseph Rowntree Foundation) pp. 23–30.

Newton, J. (1994) *All in One Place* (London: Catholic Housing Aid Society).

Northern Ireland Housing Executive (1998) *The Northern Ireland House Condition Survey: 1996* (Belfast).

Page, D. (1993) *Building for New Communities: A Study of New Housing Association Estates* (York: Joseph Rowntree Foundation).

Pawson, H. and Kearns, A. (1998) 'Difficult to Let Housing Association Stock in England: Property, Management and Context', *Housing Studies*, vol. 13, no. 3, pp. 391–414.

Raemaekers, J., 'Planning for Sustainable Development', in Allmendinger, P., Prior, A. and Raemaekers, J. (eds) (1999) *An Introduction to Planning Practice* (Chichester: John Wiley) ch. 3.

Ravetz, A. with Turkington, R. (1995) *The Place of Home* (London: Spon).

Robertson, D. and Bailey, N. with Gilbert, J. and Beaton, J. (1996) *Review of the Impact of Housing Action Areas*, Scottish Homes' Research Report no. 47 (Edinburgh).

Robinson, R. (1981) *Housing Economics and Public Policy* (London: Macmillan).

Saw, P., Pryke, M., Royce, C. and Whitehead, C. M. (1996) *Private Finance for Social Housing: What Lenders Require and Associations Provide* (Department of Land Economy, University of Cambridge).

Scottish Federation of Housing Associations (1993) *Affordability*, Briefing Note no. 11 (Edinburgh).

Scottish Federation of Housing Associations (1997) *New Housing Association Tenants in Scotland, The SCORE Annual Digest 1996–'97* (Edinburgh).

Scottish Homes (1997a) *The Scottish House Condition Survey: 1996* (Edinburgh).

Scottish Homes (1997b) *Investment Bulletin, 1997–'98* (Edinburgh).

Scottish Homes (various dates) *Investment Bulletins, 1990–'91 to 1996–'97* (Edinburgh).

Scottish Office (1988) *New Life for Urban Scotland* (Edinburgh).

Scottish Office (1995) *Programme for Partnership* (Edinburgh).

Scottish Office (1998) *Statistical Bulletin*, Housing Series no. HSG/1998/2 (Edinburgh).

Social Security Advisory Committee (1995) *Memorandum to the Social Security Advisory Committee: Housing Benefit Changes for Private Sector Tenants* (London: HMSO).

Spencer, P. (1990) 'The Credit Monster Leaves Home', *Roof*.

Stephens, M. (1993a) 'Housing Finance Deregulation: Britain's Experience', *Netherlands Journal of Housing and the Built Environment*, vol. 8, pp. 159–75.

Stephens, M. (1993b) 'Finance for Owner Occupation in the UK: The Sick Man of Europe', *Policy and Politics*, vol. 33, pp. 337–51.

Stewart, J. and Stoker, G. (1995) *Local Government in the 1990s* (Basingstoke: Macmillan).

Stiglitz, J. (1993) *Economics* (New York: Norton).

Taylor, M. (1996) *Transferring Housing Stock: Issues, Purposes and Prospects*, Occasional Paper on Housing no. 10 (University of Stirling Housing Policy and Practice Unit).

Thain, C. and Wright, M. (1990) 'Coping with Difficulty: The Treasury and Public Expenditure, 1976–'89', *Policy and Politics*, vol. 18, pp. 1–15.

Todd, J. E. (1986) *Recent Private Lettings, 1982–1984* (London: HMSO).

Todd, J. E., Bone, M., and Noble, I. (1982) *The Privately Rented Sector in 1978* (London: HMSO).

Treasury, Her Majesty's (1998a) *Stability and Investment for the Long Term: Economic and Fiscal Strategy*, Report 1998, Cm. 3978 (London: The Stationery Office).

Treasury, Her Majesty's (1998b) *Modern Public Services for Britain: Investing in Reform, Comprehensive Spending Review: New Public Spending Plans 1999–2002*, Cm. 4011 (London: The Stationery Office).

Turok, I. and Hopkins, N. (1997) *Picking the Winners or Passing the Buck? Competition and Area Selection in Scotland's New Urban Policy*, CHRUS Discussion Paper (University of Glasgow Centre for Housing Research and Urban Studies).

Wagner, G. (1988) *Residential Care: A Positive Choice* (London: HMSO).

Walshe, G. (1987) *Planning Public Spending in the UK* (London: Macmillan).

Watson L (1997) *High Hopes: Making Housing and Community Care Work* (York: Joseph Rowntree Foundation).

Webb, S. and Wilcox, S. (1991) *Mortgage Benefit* (York: Joseph Rowntree Foundation).

Whitehead, C. M. E. and Kleinman, M. P. (1986) *Private Rented Housing in the 1980s and 1990s* (University of Cambridge Department of Land Economy).

Whitehead, C. M. E. and Kleinman, M. P. (1988) 'The Prospects for Private Rented Housing in the 1990s', in Kemp (1988).

Whitehead, C. M. E. and Kleinman, M. P. (1990) The Viability of Private Rented Housing, in Ermisch (1990).

Wilcox, S. (1993) 'Making the Most of Council Housing', *Fiscal Studies*.

Wilcox, S. (1997a) *Housing Finance Review 1997–'98* (York: Joseph Rowntree Foundation).

Wilcox, S. (1997b) 'Incoherent Rents', in Wilcox (1997a) pp. 9–15.

Wilcox, S. with Bramley, G., Ferguson, A., Perry, J. and Woods, C. (1993)
Local Housing Companies: New Opportunties for Council Housing (York:
Joseph Rowntree Foundation).

Wilson, D. and Game, C. (1994) *Local Government in the United Kingdom*,
2nd edn (London: Macmillan).

Wistow, G., Knapp, B., Hardy and Allen, C., (1994) *Social Care in a Mixed
Economy* (Buckingham: Open University Press).

Wood, M. and Zebedee, J. (various) *Guide to Housing Benefit* (London:
CIH/SHAC).

Index